University of Strathclyde
SCHOOL OF ARCHITECTURE
INFORMATION ROOM

DEVELOPING PATTERNS OF URBANISATION

CENTRE FOR ENVIRONMENTAL STUDIES

Members of the Study Group on Developing
Patterns of Urbanisation

Peter Cowan, Chairman of Study Group,
       Joint Unit for Planning Research, London

David Bayliss, Centre for Environmental Studies, London.

Nicholas Deakin, Institute of Race Relations, London.

David Donnison, London School of Economics and Political Science.

Peter Hall, University of Reading.

Emrys Jones, London School of Economics and Political Science.

Cedric Price, Architectural Consultant, London.

Brian Rodgers, University of Keele.

Peter Stone, Greater London Council.

Mel Webber, University of California, Berkeley.

Peter Willmott, Institute of Community Studies, London.

Alan Wilson, Centre for Environmental Studies, London.

DEVELOPING PATTERNS
OF
URBANISATION

Edited by
PETER COWAN

Director, Joint Unit for Planning Research
London

1970

OLIVER & BOYD
EDINBURGH

OLIVER AND BOYD

Tweeddale Court, 14 High St.
Edinburgh

A Division of Longman Group Ltd

These papers are the first published results of the
Centre for Environmental Studies Working Group.
With the exception of those by Bayliss and Price the
papers appeared in *Urban Studies*, Vol. 6 No. 3 Novem-
ber 1969 and are here reprinted under the title
Developing Patterns of Urbanisation.

SBN   05   002289 X

Printed in Great Britain
by Robert Cunningham and Sons, Ltd., Alva

FOREWORD

During the past few years the notion of trying to forecast the various aspects of future society has become increasingly important, both to research workers and to policy makers in government and in private industry. The first steps towards formal forecasting were taken by several large corporations in America and in this country with a view to assessing technical developments which might be pursued as part of the general research and development programme in various sectors of the economy. These efforts of technological forecasting showed that it was possible to make some reasonably precise forecasts which would be useful to those concerned with investing in various lines of development and innovation.

Such technological forecasting was by definition somewhat limited, and it quickly became apparent that broader based social forecasts were needed to study the possible technological futures in a proper context. Perhaps the most sophisticated attempt at social forecasting so far is that prepared by Herman Kahn and Anthony Wiener of the Hudson Institute, under the general title of *The Year 2000*. This book takes a very broad view of possible futures at a world scale and was centred around a long term multi-fold trend which is described in some detail and upon which various alternative senarios are played out. More recently it is becoming apparent that urbanisation, defined in a very broad sense, subsumes and is intermeshed with both social and technological forecasts. The future pattern of society and of technology result in changes in our urban life and structure and these in turn condition the possible social and technological futures which are open to us. As a result of this various groups began work directed specifically towards forecasting patterns of urbanisation as they might develop during the next thirty years. Again a number of these groups were set up in the United States and in this country the Centre for Environmental Studies established a working group on Developing Patterns of Urbanisation in Britain. The task of making such forecasts is difficult but not impossible.

The most essential point to bear in mind is that this kind of forecasting exercise is not aimed to predict particular futures but rather to suggest alternative futures which might develop out of current trends. In this country it is possible to identify those parts of future life which are susceptible to control and direction according to various policy decisions. Thus both research and policy can be associated by forecasting methods and techniques and the future can at least be sketched in with more clarity.

There is perhaps a broader need for a more unifying attempt at forecasting in the social sciences, in technology, and in regional and urban studies. Planners are by definition forecasters but so far all our efforts have been piecemeal and ad hoc. The development of formal forecasting techniques is moving quickly ahead and the next few years could see the establishment of institutes for forecasting studies, both in this country and in Europe. This volume marks a first step rather than a finished programme.

RICHARD LLEWELYN-DAVIES

CONTENTS

INTRODUCTION

PETER COWAN

In 1967 the Centre for Environmental Studies established a working group
to consider developing patterns of urbanisation in Britain. This issue of
Urban Studies presents the first fruits of this work. More remains to be
done, and we expect the work will continue in the years to come.

Recent years have seen a major expansion of forecasting studies, both
here and abroad. The work of Herman Kahn and his colleagues at the
Hudson Institute; the Futuribles group in Paris; and the Committee on
the Next 30 Years of the Social Science Research Council in London are
only a few of the many groups now forecasting various aspects of life
during the near, and not so near, future.

Aspects of urbanisation enter into many of these forecasts, for it seems
that more and more of the world's population will live in a culture dominated by urban values even if they remain on a remote farm. But not many
groups have taken the notion of urbanisation as their main focus. Of course
everyone concerned with urban studies, in the broadest sense, has his own
view of the future, and quite specific forecasts have been made for particular
cities or regions—Peter Hall's *London 2000* is an outstanding example. But
such forecasts are by definition partial and limited. Our object is to provide
an overview of Britain's urban future, within which other plans and forecasts may fit.

This first set of papers is largely exploratory. They present current
trends and trace out the future consequences of evolving patterns. The
papers raise policy issues and questions for research, but do not set goals.
Our next step may be to delineate some normative goals, and thereafter to
trace out the consequences for urban development in Britain of achieving
these different goals. We shall then be in a position to write various
'scenarios' for Britain, making clear the effects of policy decisions and
choices as they interact through the years to come. The present collection
of papers thus provides a framework of exploratory forecasts for the next
stages of our work.

We have not adopted a very strict or rigorous method for our work.
Sophisticated techniques, such as the 'Delphi' method, were beyond our
scope or resources. We simply hope that by meeting very frequently over a
considerable period of time we have become sufficiently aware of each
other's work so as to inform our separate papers. The amount of cross-

Peter Cowan is Director, Joint Unit for Planning Research, London

referencing contained in the papers shows this approach has been quite successful.

Of course there are some aspects of urbanisation which we have not covered. Waste and pollution are obvious subjects and we lack an overall economic framework. We are aware of these gaps, and shall try to fill them in the next stages of our work. In the meantime we have managed to cover a fairly wide spectrum of subjects, and our forecasts give a fairly comprehensive picture of the future.

The Problems of Forecasting

In the course of our work we have come across a number of problems and issues which will affect any group trying to forecast the future of urbanisation and it may be worth reviewing them. Some of these problems have to do with definitions and methods of work, others are concerned with the subject matter of our studies. No doubt there are other problems which we may have missed or been unaware of.

 Our first problem concerned the choice of a suitable horizon. Clearly the further ahead we look the more uncertain the future will be, but on the other hand if horizons are too close our work will lose much of its value. (The most obvious thing is to choose a date, preferably a dramatic one 'Towards 2000', or the 'Daedalus' group on 1976—the 200th anniversary of the American Revolution, are examples. Even 1984 might be a choice with a certain cachet.) But such dates seem rather fictitious—one year is very like another, and not much will separate 2000 from 1999 or 1976 from 1975. Another problem is that these 'dramatic years' (especially the millennium) are likely to become over-subscribed with titles in the next few years.

A more useful horizon might be couched in terms of generations. For instance, there may have been a genuine 'change of outlook' among he current generation of young people, and we might suggest the kind of futures which the next generation will encounter. Thinking in terms of a generation allows us to trace the consequences of current or just-emerging patterns more easily—it suggests a horizon of 30 years or so from now, which brings us neatly to the end of the century and to the charismatic date—2000!

Another problem is raised by the kind of 'models' we take for the future. How far can the United States, and especially West Coast development, be taken as a model for the future pattern of urbanisation in Britain?

The level of car ownership in Britain today is similar to that of the U.S. in the mid-forties, and our standard of mobility has been lagging some 20 to 30 years behind the U.S. since the early decades of the century. Why, then, does Britain not look like the United States in the 1940's, and why has urbanisation in Britain not followed the American pattern? And if the two patterns are different now is there any reason to suppose that they will become more similar in the future? Indeed *have* patterns of urbanisation in Britain become more like those of the United States during the past few decades? These questions are very important to our work, for it is easy to fall back on the U.S. as a model of the future, assuming some kind of

'affluential determinism' which holds that surplus wealth can or will only be
used to buy increasing mobility, and that this in turn must lead to a certain
kind of settlement pattern.

Of course there are geographical and historical reasons for the differences
between British and American patterns of urbanisation. The cities of
Britain grew earlier than those of the United States, and Britain has a
massive existing stock of urban investment and development which imposes
a very large constraint on the rate of physical change. But there may be
deeper-rooted *cultural* factors which affect each nation's attitude towards
the use of land, and which must be taken into account in any study of the
future.

For example, the British have a very special attitude towards their
countryside and landscape. They like their landscape tamed but romantic,
and they care greatly that the countryside should be *designed*. The town-
planning movement in Britain had its roots in a reaction *against* urban
growth, as represented by the nineteenth-century industrial city. Interest in
the preservation of the countryside has been part of British planning policy,
and the numerous official or quasi-government institutions which have
preservation of the countryside as their aim, point to a strong and continuing attitude of the British towards their land. Above all the British have
felt that the city must be *contained*—it cannot be allowed to spread across
the face of the nation, eating up land unchecked.

The position in the United States is entirely different, both historically
and geographically, and can be traced to a different cultural attitude
towards the use of the land. The vastness of the North American continent
makes the idea of open land as a scarce resource unfamiliar to most
Americans. The pioneer tradition, the need to tame and overcome nature
and the knowledge that there is always something better farther west, has
become a firm part of the American outlook. It has often been noted that
Americans are always 'moving on'—if one place does not prove good one
can always travel to somewhere better. Partly because of this, the American
attitude towards places has been characterised by successive exploitation
and abandonment. If an area becomes obsolete for immediate practical
purposes it is left behind, and no attempt is made to rescue it from the
waste products of the former occupants. The scene which Peter Blake has
described as 'God's Own Junkyard' may typify the American attitude to
land—a resource that can be used, even squandered, with little thought for
the future.

Might it not be that these cultural differences are at least partially
responsible for the differences between the British of today and the United
States of 20 years ago? And if there are deep-seated differences between
the two cultures in their attitudes towards urbanisation are we right in
taking the Western United States as a model for the future of this country?
It has often been observed that the urban areas of the post-industrial era
are becoming more alike, but the process may not go on for ever, and there
may come a time when cultural differences over-ride other forces. Certainly
the examples quoted above may lead us to suspect that a straight super-

imposition of trends in thc United States will provide a misleading portrait
of the future of Britain.

In this connection it is interesting to note that Sweden is also a wealthy
country, with a high car-ownership rate, but that it has developed very
differently from the United States so far as patterns of urbanisation are
concerned. The small size of the country and the relative homogeneity of
the population are obvious reasons for some of the differences between
Sweden and the United States. Thus, it is worth remembering that there
may be other models for the future of developing patterns of urbanisation
in Britain than the United States. Forecasting urbanisation carries some
particular dangers, not the least of which is the trap of orthodoxy. There
exists a 'standard modern future' concerning future patterns of urbanisation. A few years ago, anyone in Britain seeking to forecast urbanisation
would have thought mainly in physical terms. He might have suggested
that, if left to itself, the pattern of urbanisation would result in larger
concentrations of population in the larger cities, and that 'ribbon development' would spread around the edges of urban areas. The agency of
metropolitan growth would have been the factory. The motor car, although
making some impact on the urban scene, would not have occupied a central
position on the stage of the future. The policies recommended to deal with
the coming situation were the same as had been recommended at the turn of
the century by Howard, Geddes, Parker and Unwin—new towns of moderate size located at sufficient distance from major cities to reduce commuting
journeys. These new towns would house people from the large cities,
whose growth was restricted by green belts. Thus, both the problems of
the future and their solution were stated in physical terms.

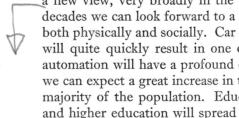

About five years ago a different set of views began to appear. These
questioned past orthodoxies on the future of urbanisation, and suggested
a new view, very broadly in the following terms. During the next few
decades we can look forward to a population which is increasingly mobile,
both physically and socially. Car ownership will increase dramatically and
will quite quickly result in one car for every family. At the same time
automation will have a profound effect upon the utilisation of labour, and
we can expect a great increase in the amount of spare time available to the
majority of the population. Educational opportunities will be increased,
and higher education will spread very widely, leading to a more sophisticated populace. All these events will combine to bring about a pattern of
urbanisation which is more diffuse and less centred upon 'place' than in the
past. People will travel more, both for business and pleasure, and their local
community may assume a less important rôle. The city will be less
centrally-orientated and many different nuclei will be linked together in an
'urban area'. Hierarchical systems of cities will give way to a pattern at
once more complex and dynamic. Finally, urban areas will merge to
produce super-cities or megalopoles stretching for hundreds of miles
across the face of different parts of the nation—in Britain such an area may
stretch from London to Manchester—'Megalopolis England'. The problem
posed by these developments will be both physical and social. The physical

problems will relate to achieving effective linkages between the variety of locations which each individual will use in his new way of life. Social problems will arise as the population is confronted with the need to change from a work-orientated to a leisure-orientated society.

I have sketched in this future—albeit as a caricature of certain current views—for two reasons. First, it is a current orthodoxy, just as the previous views of the future were orthodoxies based upon different premises. Thus our orthodoxies have just as much chance of being wrong as others in the past. True, the current orthodoxy is more sophisticated than in the past— especially in recognising that the pattern of urbanisation means more than the changing physical facts of land uses and buildings. But we must recognise that what was revolutionary thought yesterday has become today's accepted dogma. We would be wise to examine very carefully whether we really do believe all the package or whether there might be other ways of looking at the future. The second reason for sketching in the modern orthodox future is to point out that, even if we accept its predictions as generally the most probable, we still have a long way to go in tracing out all the consequences of such a series of events. The consequences of increasing mobility and spare time could take many different directions, and the interactions of all the forecast variables could lead to a variety of futures. We do not want to repeat old mistakes in new dress. There are many different interpretations of the meaning of the 'standard modern future', and we must deal with at least a few of the most likely ones.

One of the most pressing issues of the future will be the relationship between the citizen and the planners. We can already see signs of such issues around us. It is no longer 1945 people are more sophisticated about the Welfare State and what it can and cannot do—they know their rights, and planners cannot, any longer, continue to impose their ideas upon a naïve and inarticulate population. Education, welfare, health, and town planning are coming increasingly under the scrutiny of the people. And this pattern must inevitably continue. As people become better educated by staying at school longer and by increasing higher education; as they become more sophisticated and informed by television; as they read more in newspapers and information brochures; as the younger generation becomes more articulate and demanding; so they must demand a greater say in the planners' actions. It will not in future be possible for planners to behave as they have in the past.

This may have all sorts of other effects—especially on the political front. If we assume that planners will have to accommodate more and more to the wishes of the planned, the consequences for traditional party alignments are most significant. Suspicion of planners is a common view, and the seeming failure of economic planning may turn to a more general malaise with planning in general. The consequences for the future of urban planning may be severe indeed.

And to all this we must add the possible effects of the 'new planning'. If it becomes possible, within the next decade or two, to tie together all kinds of planning issues in some kind of computer system the whole nature of the process will be changed. Not only will the consequences of a particular planning decision be displayed almost instantaneously to the planners, but one can imagine some kind of 'push-button democracy' in which the electorate could demand a say in all decisions—government by referendum would be possible. Of course the effect of a new sophistication in planning techniques might be to make them even more inaccessible to the population at large, and discontent might increase considerably if people saw their ability to control their own lives being eroded by planning machines. Such changes would be profound, and I have a feeling that the issue of 'the planners and the planned' could become one of the most crucial and decisive questions facing the nation during the next few decades.

Imponderables

Any forecast might be affected by a number of imponderables, which will divert the future from our 'surprise free' projections. Such imponderables are by definition, difficult to foresee, but it is worth considering the general headings under which they might fall.

First of all there are economic imponderables. If a world-wide recession set in during the next few decades we should perhaps consider the effects of a massive reduction in growth patterns of urbanisation. We know that the construction industry is particularly susceptible to fluctuations in the economy and clearly the physical side of urbanisation could be altered radically by a really bad slump. The effects of such a recession upon the social side of urbanisation would be more difficult to trace, but I am sure they would be most significant.

The second set of imponderables which might affect developing patterns of urbanisation, are those which are loosely collected under the title of 'life-style'. Here we are dealing with issues of taste and fashion and people's behaviour in general. For example, we do not know how far middle-class attitudes towards size of family will filter through to working-class behaviour. We do not know how far attitudes towards work and leisure will really evolve and change in a particular direction. We might, for example, pose a future in which present life-styles hardly change at all, and in which old class and social divisions remain right up until the year 2000. We would thus paint a portrait of a static society. In such circumstances, the patterns of urbanisation in Britain by the end of the century would be very different from the dynamic future which we now accept.

A third group of imponderables concerns policies, and especially the evolution of the planning process. I have suggested that a new kind of planning activity, closely geared to the use of computers and large-scale data banks, could come about within the next two decades. But, on the other hand, there is a tremendous 'planning establishment', and a great deal of planning machinery already in existence. It is difficult to judge exactly how fast the 'new planning' will overtake the existing framework. This raises many serious problems concerning the nature of planning in the future and things might evolve very differently if the present system continued almost unaltered, for another thirty years.

Finally, there are imponderables connected with actual physical events which may or may not happen, for example, suppose green belt restrictions were done away with? Or suppose the Channel Tunnel were completed within the next fifteen years? Suppose both the Thames and Wash barrages were put in? All these events would have a considerable effect upon the physical pattern of urbanisation in the country and might also alter the economic growth pattern.

Policies

After all this is said, what kind of benefits might evolve from our activities? Very broadly these could fall into two main classes. First of all, our findings might be of benefit to policy makers in central and local government. If we are successful in sketching a future or futures for urbanisation in Britain, we should be of some help in deciding what issues are important, and in what order problems are likely to arise over the next thirty years.

The second group of policy makers to whom our work might be of benefit are those concerned with the direction of research. We have already begun to indicate some areas in which more study is needed, and if we can identify problems which will be presented to society in the not too distant future, we shall assist greatly in the planning of research investment.

I do not think that we are yet in a position to say anything more definite about either of these two sets of policy issues, but there is one area in which I think we can be fairly sure of our ground. This concerns the impact of the 'new planning' upon society. The issue of the planners and the planned seems to me of absolutely crucial importance for the next few decades. I have suggested that it might become an issue which divides the country, and I am sure that it will cause major upheavals, both in the limited context of the 'town planning' profession as it exists today and in the more general framework of the broad rôle and method of national planning. I think our work as a group has already shown some of the consequences of this, and that we can say very clearly to policy makers in central and local government, and to those directing research policy, that their attention must very soon be turned towards ways and means of accommodating this new issue and the problems it will create. That is the first lesson from our study of developing patterns of urbanisation in Britain; others will follow.

SOME SOCIAL TRENDS[1]

PETER WILLMOTT

The purpose of this paper is to discuss some of the ways in which the social structure of Britain and the patterns of social life are likely to develop during the next two or three decades. What has been happening in the past is obviously one guide to what is likely to happen in the future and the paper, taking this as its starting-point, begins by discussing past and present trends in the occupational structure and in social class. It then examines in particular the suggestion that the social class structure is fundamentally changing—that 'we are all middle class now' and likely to become even more so in the future. This is followed by a discussion of some trends in social relationships and behaviour, first in family life and secondly in social life outside the family. Finally, some of the major questions are posed and some suggestions offered on research priorities.

If one looks to the past for guidance and asks how British society has changed since, say, 1900, one comes face to face with a paradox. Put simply, it is that the social structure seems both to have changed radically and not to have changed very much.[2] This is particularly true of the occupational structure and social class.

Occupations and mobility

The stereotype of what has happened to the British occupational structure since about 1900 is something like this: it has altered dramatically, particularly since 1945, the main changes being major shifts from unskilled to skilled occupations and from manual to clerical, with a large increase also in the professions and management.

In fact, as Routh shows in his *Occupation and Pay in Great Britain 1906-1960*[3], the trends are much less dramatic than they are commonly thought. The proportion of clerical workers among working men, for instance, was 5% in 1911 and 6% in 1951. The proportion of professional men was 3% in 1911, 6% in 1951. The comparable figures for unskilled male manual workers were 12% in 1911, 14% in 1951. In 1961 workers in 'manual' occupations, both men and women, still accounted for two-thirds of all the employed people in the United Kingdom.

Of course, there have been important changes in the economy. One is the entry of women into the labour force and the extent of the shift among them, much more marked than among men, from manual to clerical work. There have also been major changes, among men as well as women,

Peter Willmott is Director of the Institute of Community Studies, London

between industries—notably the movement from agriculture, mining and textiles to new light industries, and the switch from manufacturing to services.

There is also some evidence that, despite the relatively slow rate of change until recently, the process may have speeded up quite sharply between 1951 and 1961.[4] In particular, the proportion of scientists, engineers and technologists in the United Kingdom increased by 56% over that decade, and that of industrial technicians by 67%. Between them, however, they still amounted to less than 3% of the total labour force in 1961.

To the occupational changes already mentioned, others could be added. Manual work has, on the whole, become lighter, hours shorter, working conditions better and the structure of authority at work less oppressive. But in many respects the fundamental occupational structure seems relatively unchanged, especially for men. We may, as is sometimes suggested, be on the brink of major changes in technology that will radically transform that structure. All one can say is that the experience of the past 50 years or so should encourage caution.[5]

Another common assumption is that there is now much more movement across occupational strata from one generation to the next—that more sons of carpenters and dockers than in the past become managers and surgeons. The latest figures on this are not very up to date; they come from the study in 1949 by Glass and his colleagues at the London School of Economics, whose findings were published in 1954.[6] This study showed virtually no change, as compared with the end of the last century, in the extent of inter-generational mobility in Britain. As Glass put it, the general picture was of 'rather high stability over time'.[7] A review by Lipset and Bendix, drawing on historical data from a number of other industrial countries, also found little change over a period of about 40 years.[8] A more recent study of American society, by Blau and Duncan, came to the same general conclusion.[9] With occupational mobility, as with the broad occupational structure, the main impression is therefore that society has changed less than is commonly supposed.

Education and wealth

At first sight, education presents a different picture. For one thing, there is clearly more of it. The proportion of 14 year olds at school in England and Wales was 9% in 1902 and 30% in 1938. By 1954, 32% of 15 year olds were at school and ten years later 59%. The proportion aged 15 to 19 in grant-aided schools went up from 10% in 1956 to 19% in 1967.[10] The numbers in full-time education in England and Wales have more than trebled in the past 20 years and nearly doubled in the last ten alone.

All this does not of course necessarily mean that working-class children are now getting a larger *share* of university places. What has apparently happened is that working and middle classes alike are benefiting from university expansion; their relative shares are, or at any rate were at the beginning of the 1960s, similar to what they used to be in earlier periods. The Robbins Report showed that, of 18 year olds from non-manual homes, 8·9% entered university in 1928 to 1947 and 16·8% in 1960; from manual homes, 1·4% of the 18 year olds entered in 1928 to 1947 and 2·6% in 1960.[11] While later figures would show higher proportions for both, there is no reason to think that the relative shares have changed.

In other words, despite the changes, the divisions of social class are still formidable. It is, as far as one can judge, much the same with wealth and income. Meade has shown that there has been little change in the distribution of wealth in Britain: the proportion of total personal wealth owned by the richest 5% was 79% in 1936-38 and 75% in 1960.[12] On incomes, the changes are more difficult to trace. But Routh shows that there was little change between 1911-12 and 1958-59 in the share of incomes, both before and after tax, by the different occupational strata.[13] Nicholson's study suggests little radical change in the distribution of income over recent years.[14] Furthermore, Titmuss has pointed out that 'fringe' benefits— firm's cars, housing, school fees, pensions, etc.—ought to be taken into account, and that if they were the better off would undoubtedly be shown to benefit most from them.[15]

These facts point to two general impressions about the last half century. The first is that, despite some changes, the social structure has in some of the essentials remained extraordinarily constant. The second is that this is particularly true in terms of social class.

The other side

That is only part of the story. If one looks at it the other way round and asks how people's day-to-day lives have changed, the impression is utterly different. As is well known, living standards have risen. Mass production has put into the hands of the many what were formerly the privileges of the few. Social policy has plainly helped as well; the 'price' of primary and secondary education and that of health services have been fixed at zero, and social security has aided the poorest.

As a result of all this there has undoubtedly been some 'convergence' in tastes, consumption and behaviour within British society. There has also been an improvement in the social status of manual workers and their families.[16] And there is a ring of truth in Marshall's suggestion that social inequality has been reduced over the past three centuries by the spread of 'citizenship' among the social classes, characteristically through 'civil rights' in the eighteenth century, 'political rights' in the nineteenth and 'social rights' in the twentieth.[17]

This then is the paradox—the mixture of change and 'unchange' in the British social structure, particularly in terms of social class. How is one to reconcile these apparently contradictory trends and not only make sense of what has happened but, more relevant, make sound judgements about what may happen over the next two or three decades?

Clearly both sets of trends are likely to continue. First, despite the current economic setbacks, we are likely to get richer and, compound growth being what it is, at an accelerating rate. As Abrams has put it, in stating the first of his 'assumptions' about consumption in the year 2000:

> . . . it is assumed that the average standard of living in Britain will be substantially higher in the year 2000 than it is in 1967; reasonably, it may be double; and, very optimistically it may have trebled. Within these limits the precise measure of growth, however, is not important; whatever the rate of increase, the broad mass of the population at the end of the century will have incomes that today are enjoyed by only a minority of richer households.[18]

That is an assumption that this paper makes also. Yet the relative shares of wealth and income by different sections of the population are unlikely to change fundamentally. In other words, though all will be richer, 'inequality' will not be reduced; indeed it may well increase. Meade demonstrates convincingly that there is a fundamental conflict between economic efficiency and what he calls 'distributional justice'[19]: the greater the emphasis on economic growth therefore—and it is likely to dominate national policy in the decades ahead as much as in the recent past—the greater the pressures towards economic inequality. For this reason, another of Abrams's 'assumptions' seems more questionable than the one already quoted. This second 'assumption' is that in the year 2000 'the distribution of net personal total incomes will be more equal than it is today'.[20]

Enough has been said to show that it would be a mistake to assume this. The example brings into sharp focus the two contradictory elements—the trend towards some sort of social equality and cultural homogeneity, and the tendency for many of the essentials of the British social structure to stay as they are. With this theme in mind, the paper now looks in more detail at some emerging social patterns.

Economic growth and standards of living

First, a closer look at what has happened to standards of living. As is well known, Britain's Gross National Product has been increasing, with some short-term ups and downs, since the 1880's. Real incomes have risen at the same time. Consumer spending has been increasing at least since 1900/05 and particularly since 1945; it rose by over a fifth between 1950 and 1960.[21]

The biggest proportionate increases in consumer spending since 1900 have been in 'transport' and 'entertainment'. Spending on most other things has increased too. More and more working-class families have bought, as well as cars, household equipment like washing machines, refrigerators and television sets. This is especially noticeable with housing. More working-class people live in modern homes; a quarter of our housing stock has been built since 1945. More own their homes: Donnison, using data from surveys in 1958 and 1962, has shown how much home-ownership increased over those four years alone. The proportion of skilled manual workers owning or buying their own houses went up from 33% to 39%, and of unskilled and semi-skilled from 20% to 26%.[22]

It seems reasonable to assume that this process will continue—that the Gross National Product will rise and, with it, household incomes and living standards. As a broad guide one can accept Abrams's suggestion, referred to earlier, that the average standard of living is likely to rise by the year 2000 to somewhere between double and treble what it is now.

Past experience seems a fairly good pointer to the main ways in which the extra consumers' income will be spent. The 130-year-old dictum described by Bell as 'Tocqueville's Law'—'What the few have today, the many will demand tomorrow'[23]—seems to have been largely borne out by events. Though of course an over-simplification, it has proved not at all a bad general indication of likely future trends in consumption and patterns of life.

Thus many features of what is now middle-class life are likely to spread. More cars, more household equipment, more suburban-style homes and communities would not surprise anyone. Modern societies (perhaps to some extent all societies) seem to be characterised by a continuing process of 'diffusion', by which some values and patterns of behaviour percolate 'downwards' through the social strata. Some examples of change in food consumption in the nineteenth century have been recently cited:

> The growth of town-living encouraged competition and social
> imitation among all classes, leading ultimately to far more
> sophisticated tastes and eating habits. The outstanding
> examples of this are white bread and tea, both of which were, in
> the eighteenth century, the luxuries of the well-to-do.[24]

Of course some diffusion is 'upwards'—one example is the dining-kitchen, originally a peasant and then an urban working-class pattern which is now fashionable, with the decline in domestic help, among the colour-supplement middle class. Some diffusion, and probably an increasing proportion, is not so much across social strata as across age-groups —fashions in men's clothes, for instance, often move not from 'top' class to 'bottom' but from young to old. Perhaps in general the greater degree of homogeneity over a certain span of the standard of living means that 'fashion' will in certain spheres increasingly take the place of the steady 'downward' drift from rich to poor. Yet over large areas of life, the latter kind of diffusion clearly still sets the style and will continue to do so.

It seems that diffusion is a cumulative process; that acquiring, for example, a car or a house of one's own can lead to changes in behaviour. Thus a working-class man living with his family in a 'semi' in the suburbs is more likely to live like his middle-class neighbour than like a man who is his neighbour only at work and still lives in an Islington slum. A Stevenage capstan operator with a Cortina is likely to use his car for shopping, for holidays, for family visits and Sunday 'drives into the country', and from the side of the road at any rate is indistinguishable from his white-collar counterpart in Hertford or Hitchin. As more manual workers own homes and cars, people's patterns of life will merge further.

The process is surely encouraged by TV and the other mass media which, whatever one's final judgement about their influence for good or evil, help to make for cultural homogeneity, by bringing the same models of behaviour into the homes of people in all strata. We increasingly share in a broad national, in some respects international, culture—the 'global village'. It is a matter for speculation how far regional, local and class sub-cultures can continue to survive in such a setting, and how far we can preserve 'pluralism', the 'diversity within unity' that seems so desirable. It is possible that the recent upsurge of Celtic nationalism represents some sort of reaction against the growth of cultural uniformity, and in that sense testifies to the extent to which cultural homogeneity has already taken hold. There are, of course, still important variations in behaviour, in values and in tastes, not only as between different occupational or economic strata and different kinds of people within them but also as between the different regions of Britain (some of them striking).[25] In some respects, too, contemporary British society encompasses more 'deviance' and more variety than in the past. At the same time the general trend is clearly towards a broad homogeneity, over the great majority of the population, in consumption patterns and in social behaviour.

Social class and life-styles

How can these suggestions be reconciled with the warning earlier— that in many fundamental ways the social structure remains unchanged? The key seems to lie in a distinction, first made by Weber, between people's situation in the economic structure and their 'style of life', reflecting their consumption standards and social patterns outside work.[26]

The difference between the work situations of manual workers and others is marked, and this difference affects values and behaviour. A study in Luton by Lockwood and his colleagues found, for instance, that most manual workers recognised that their prospects of personal advancement in their work (i.e. of promotion) were negligible.[27] Manual workers know that almost their only hope of economic advance is in the company of their fellows. Since they are paid by the week or hour, their security is limited. The middle-class man can with more justification see his job as a career-ladder up which, if all goes well, he will climb as he gets older, and he usually gets more 'satisfaction' from his work. The working-class man, may or may not like work; either way he sees it mainly as a means of earning a living. To the middle-class man work, or advancement in work, is more often the 'central life interest', to borrow Dubin's phrase.[28]

There are a number of other related differences. Working-class people, for obvious reasons deriving from their work situation, are disposed to collective rather than individual action to achieve economic advance.[29]

Similarly, the attitude of most working-class men to politics seems relatively 'traditional', tied to class attitudes.[30]

There is some evidence, too, that the working-class view of leisure is rather different from the middle-class. Here it seems that the gap between the classes may in some respect be widening. Reisman has suggested that some members of the middle class, particularly professional people, increasingly see their leisure as 'instrumental'; for example, they use their social life to promote contacts with colleagues and professional clients, or they read the newspapers with an eye to their work interests. Manual workers, by contrast, are said increasingly to separate work and leisure.[31] Nevertheless, as is shown later, what people actually *do* in their leisure seems to vary less, and many middle-class patterns of leisure behaviour are likely to spread.

In some other aspects of social life there are still sharp class differences. In the old districts the familiar working-class attachments to kinship and neighbourhood die hard,[32] and even in the new areas substantial elements of the old life survive or are re-established.[33] As the Luton study shows, working-class people also remain unlike middle-class for instance in belonging less often to formal organisations. In particular they certainly do not 'become middle-class' in the sense of mixing with white-collar workers.[34] Our own study in Woodford even suggested that in a suburb where there was a growing homogeneity of life-styles, the middle-class residents were increasingly inclined to lay emphasis on the small social differences that distinguished them from their working-class neighbours.[35]

Merging of social classes

To sum up so far, it is clear that in some respects the classes are 'merging' but also that there are limits to the process. In general, life outside work has changed more than life inside it. Diffusion, it seems, is more likely to occur with consumption patterns than with basic values linked to political attitudes or class loyalties.

Something more can be said about the influences upon such values. The Luton study suggests that though 'traditional' class and political loyalties may be somewhat influenced by 'affluence'—that is, that higher-paid workers are somewhat more inclined to vote Conservative—there is a much closer correlation with family affiliations. The manual workers whose fathers or fathers-in-law have non-manual backgrounds, whose wives work in white-collar jobs or who themselves have had such jobs in the past— these are markedly more likely to support the Conservatives than others without such links.[36] There is ample evidence that the type of community has an influence too, that in a homogeneous working-class community the 'traditional' loyalties and values hold more sway than they do, for example, in a mixed-class suburb.[37]

In discussing what is likely to happen, these various influences have to be reckoned with. The first suggestion is the familiar one: that, in patterns of consumption and in associated behaviour, middle-class styles are likely to spread. The second is that changes in behaviour—and to some extent in values—will also be influenced by the extent of geographical mobility and even more by changes in the occupational structure (which are likely gradually to reduce the proportion of manual occupations and increase the proportion of families having some links with white-collar milieux).

The limits to the process of class 'merging' have been noted and are obviously substantial. It would clearly be wrong to talk as if the working class was near to extinction. Even more important, increasing affluence and 'bourgeoisification' will not in themselves eradicate poverty. First, there is the point made earlier that national emphasis on economic growth will if anything lead to a less equitable distribution of income and wealth. Secondly, even if the distribution of national income does not become less equitable, there will, as long as there are any variations in incomes, continue to be a distribution 'curve' and therefore a poorest 10% or 25%; in this sense, 'poverty' is obviously common to all industrial societies. Thirdly, even in the richest societies, some of the poorer strata remain so locked in a vicious circle of economic and social deprivation that they combine together in a 'culture' or, more correctly, 'sub-culture of poverty'; they thus remain in important senses excluded from the national society. It seems that in certain conditions economic expansion, far from reducing this sense of exclusion, may actually sharpen it and thus deepen social divisions.

We do not know whether the sense of 'relative deprivation' will grow. It certainly does not seem strong in British society at present. Reporting his 1962 survey, Runciman said: 'On the evidence of this question, relative deprivation is low in both magnitude and scope even among those who are close to the bottom of the hierarchy of economic class.'[38] But this may change with increasing cultural homogeneity and with increasing emphasis upon economic prosperity, national and personal, as the key index of achievement.

There are minorities of colour as well as of income. Again nobody can predict with any confidence whether the coloured minorities will, as they improve their lot, actually become more embittered about what they lack because of their skin colour—as has happened in the United States. Nor whether the same improvements may not sharpen the sense of 'relative deprivation' on the part of poor whites. What does seem likely is that the two linked problems of poverty and colour will continue and questions of income distribution and differential opportunity grow in importance at the same time as living standards rise generally.

Family and home

The paper now looks more closely at some particularly important changes in patterns of behaviour. First, the family. The kind of diffusion mentioned earlier affects the family as it does other social institutions. Despite the continuing rôle of kinship, there is increasing stress upon the immediate family and particularly the husband-wife relationship. The shift is from the 'consanguine' family, emphasising ties of kinship, to the 'conjugal', emphasising the husband-wife bond. It is clear that this pattern is becoming increasingly dominant, spreading 'downwards' from the middle class inside each country and from the richer to the poorer countries, as part of the growing 'Westernisation' of the world.[39]

One of the most striking trends in Britain, as in much of the rest of the world, is the growing popularity of family life. In the 1920's about 80% of women could expect eventually to marry;[40] now the proportion is 95%.[41] Marriages also now start at an earlier age: among women aged 20 to 24, in 1921 27% were married; in 1961 58%.[42] Because of the longer expectation of life, marriages end later as well.

The change in the 'life-cycle' of marriage is shown in Table I (this is based upon assessments of the available demographic data, which are not all that one would like).[43]

TABLE I

FAMILY LIFE-CYCLE 'PROFILE' FOR WOMEN
ENGLAND AND WALES, 1911, 1951 and 1967

	1911	1951	1967
Women's mean age at first marriage	26	25	23
Women's mean age when last child born	34	28	27
Women's mean age at husband's death	54	63	65
Women's mean age at death as a widow	73	78	80

These figures show a transformation in marriage. Marriages start earlier, as noted above, and last longer. The 'average' marriage, if wives outlived their husbands, lasted 28 years in 1911 and 42 years in 1967. If one assumes that children cease to be fully dependent at 15, then the period when the couple are largely alone has changed even more—from five years in 1911 to 23 years in 1967. The figures indicate that, in contrast with the earlier period, about as much of a couple's family life is now spent without dependent children[44] as with.

Some years ago Titmuss, using rather different calculations, pointed out the implications of this change for the status of women,[45] and the effect is shown in the change in the employment of married women, which has been touched on earlier. The proportions of wives working has gone up in Britain from 9% in 1921[46] to 27% in 1951 and again to 40% in 1966.[47] The biggest increase has been among wives aged 35 to 44.

This means, for an increasing proportion, a different sort of marriage and a different sort of family life. Instead of the husband going away for long hours at work, leaving the wife at home with the children, more of marriage involves their both going out of the home (the wife for at least some of the time), working together in the home and sharing their leisure time together.[48] The demographic change is an expression of the growth of partnership in marriage and has also helped to encourage it.

The partnership takes three main forms. First, it is a partnership in power, with major decisions being discussed and made jointly. Secondly, it is a partnership in the division of labour within the home, as the old distinctions between men's and women's jobs (though still made) become increasingly blurred. More wives go out to work and help paint the kitchen; more husbands take the children out in the pram and help wash the nappies. Thirdly, it is a partnership in social life, with couples spending more of their free time together and with their children. One could sum up by saying that, despite the inequalities that remain between the sexes, women now have higher status, and that there is greater equality in society and in the family. Children, too, have a higher status.[49]

The changes in social rôles inside marriage reflect a more general tendency. As a recent article on American society points out, in dress and hair styles the sexes are more alike than they have usually been in the past; men now spend more than women on perfumed preparations; boys and girls are increasingly given 'ambisexual' names.[50] In all sorts of ways, in Britain and in the United States, the sexes are becoming more alike and sex rôles less 'polarised'.

Associated with the changes in family relationships is a trend towards what has been called the 'home-centred' society.[51] For most families, homes are more spacious and better equipped. More time is spent in the home and a number of trends support and encourage this. Television, for instance, means that the family can be entertained—or bored—together in the home, instead of separately in the cinema.

In studies of three contrasted communities in East London, three stages of this process were noted. In Bethnal Green, the established working-class community in the East End, there was a change compared with earlier decades—a shift towards the home and towards marriage partnership. In the new housing estate of 'Greenleigh', to which ex-Bethnal Greeners had moved, the process had gone a stage further.[52] The middle-class couples of suburban Woodford were further still along the same path.[53] This comparison suggests two generalisations. First, this is another example of class transmission, with the working-class following the middle. (There is, however, no neat correlation between class and marriage partnership; it seems that among the most 'successful' professional and managerial people many spend less time at home, help less around the house and are in some respects as far from 'partnership' as are unskilled workers.) Secondly, the example illustrates how the change can be accelerated: in working-class families the move to the new community and the break with the old helps to hasten the process of diffusion.

One general question has to be posed about this process: will the changes to family and home in fact continue along the present lines, or will the next few decades see instead a reaction against the family, as Leach has suggested?[54] Certainly there are likely to be some modifications. The 'Dual-Career Family', described by the Rapoports,[55] is likely to become more common, and at the same time the demand will grow for domestic arrangements that help it, including perhaps family 'service houses' like those appearing in Denmark and Sweden. Also, as living standards rise, children are likely to withdraw from the family circle at an earlier age and in particular more young people are going to demand the residential independence that their better-off fellows already enjoy. Even inside the home, there is likely to be greater emphasis on personal privacy and individuation, which involves more space, better internal sound-proofing, personal record players, television sets and telephones.

It is possible that the family may change more dramatically, that, as Leach suggests, some variant of the Israeli kibbutz or the Chinese commune may take the place of the present form of family.[56]

However, the present trends seem so powerful, so world-wide, that it is hard to believe that Leach is right. What seems much more likely is that, with some modification, the shift to home centredness and family-centredness will continue. The two sets of changes reinforce each other; the changes in family relationships and the shift to home-centredness increase the demand for a suitable home, and the 'home-and-garden' life further encourages home and family-centredness. More and more people will choose to take part of their higher real incomes in the form of a home of their own. More and more families will have their own swimming pools and tennis courts, garages and workshops. All in all, the next 30 years or so are likely to see an ever-growing demand from an increasing number of families for separate spacious homes with gardens and for the lives that go with them. The suburban way of life may be expected to spread to more sections of the population.

Yet there may be a counter-trend to urban spread. The long period that couples now have and will have without children and the increase in wives working may between them somewhat check the rush to the suburbs. For one thing, since the average married couple are spending as much of their lifetime without dependent children as with them, many may be willing as they get older to exchange their three- or four-bedroomed house with garden for a smaller dwelling. Secondly, wives who work may prefer to give up suburban life for the greater accessibility to work they can find in inner areas.

Family size and population size

A question mark hangs over another aspect of family structure—family size. This is important for the future of urban life. The pressures on space, described earlier, will intensify even more, particularly in the most crowded regions, if the population grows rapidly. Of the population increase from 1961 to 1981 forecast in *The South East Study*, more than two-thirds was due to the growth in the Region's existing population, less than one-third to migration from other parts of the country.[57] But population projections for the end of the century (vital as they evidently are) could well be out by many millions either way—representing an immense variation in the demand for new housing, new road systems, new amenities.

This is because population size is so difficult to predict. Mortality and even migration are relatively easy to forecast; the big unknown is the birth-rate. The post-war 'Baby Boom', at first thought to be temporary, seemed to have ended in about 1952. But the birth-rate started to rise again in 1956 and through to the early 1960's. Time and again over those years, as the latest figures for births came in, the Government Actuary had to raise his sights. Over the past two or three years, however, the birth-rate has fallen; the estimates have been revised again, this time downwards.

What nobody knows is what lies behind these variations in birth-rate, yet this is just what we need to know to improve our guesses about the future. The increase in the marriage rate and the lower marriage age, referred to earlier, are apparently part of the explanation, but only part: the Registrar General has estimated that, of the increase in legitimate births between 1955 and 1962, the increase in the number of married women accounted for 12% and earlier marriage for 21%, leaving 67% due to more births per family.[58] Thus the crucial two questions remain: why have couples had more children and what is likely to happen over the coming decades? To answer the first may go some way to answering the second.

One key to the answer lies in the change in the relationship between social class and family size. In the second half of the nineteenth century, the upper and middle classes led the way in controlling conception, and for about 70 or 80 years there was a clear-cut negative correlation between social class and family size. The lower the class, the larger the family. The correlation held throughout the century because family size fell more or less proportionately in all classes.

After 1940, as the birth-rate in general showed its first real rise, a new pattern began to emerge. In Britain and in the United States, the very sections of the population who had in earlier generations limited family size most effectively now started having more children. The 1951 Census confirmed the trend and the 1961 Census suggested that certain professional groups in particular were drawing still further ahead. Thus the larger-than-average families are now to be found among the professional classes and the unskilled, among some of the richest as well as some of the poorest sections of the population. There is a similar correlation with education: the most educated and the least have families larger than the average. Though the Pill may cause some check in the birth-rate (and may partly explain the recent fall) it does not follow that it will lead to a long-term decline in family size; many of the professionals having large families are apparently doing so not because they cannot control conception but because they want to have children.

Why this is so is a matter for speculation. One hypothesis is that at some level of material prosperity (absolute or relative) the 'value', or what might be called the marginal utility, of an extra child is greater (i.e. gives more satisfaction) than alternative ways of spending one's money.[59] Having relatively large numbers of children (which means, nowadays, having four instead of two) seems also to be associated with a sense of economic security and of confidence about one's future. Two points are worth noting. First, professional people, above all others in our society, have reasonable expectations that as they get older their income will rise fairly steeply; not so the manual worker, who apart from general advances can expect no more at 55 than at 25, or the clerk, who can expect only modest increments. Secondly, it has been plausibly suggested that since the war the national birth-rate has fluctuated with levels of economic growth and employment (with people postponing births until the hoped-for better times return) and that the recent falling-off in births may be a reflection of Britain's economic difficulties in the past year or two.[60]

The central issue is whether family size will prove another example of class diffusion. As the unskilled follow the skilled manual workers in becoming skilled, at any rate about contraception, will a second and contrary wave spread 'downwards' through society? Will greater prosperity lead the clerks, then the skilled workers, and eventually the unskilled to turn back towards larger families as the professional people have already done? One would guess not, unless the occupational structure changes so radically that the lathe operator has as much security and can expect, as he gets older, as 'progressive' a climb in income as the architect or university teacher. In other words, it seems that family size is one aspect of life-style which depends more on work-situation and career prospects than on living-standards. But we cannot be sure. On this issue so central to future urbanisation, since we do not know the reasons for what is happening now, we cannot be at all confident in guessing what may happen in the future.

Leisure time

From the general discussion of family and home, it might appear that people's interests are becoming narrowed down. More time is spent in the home; with television, telephones, deep freezers and the like, more activities can take place there—entertainment, education, even work. All this might seem to point to a future in which there is relatively little mobility. As is well known, however, there is also a contrary trend. As well as the concentration inside the home, there is also the tendency to go longer distances when outside it. This is likely to continue.

These changes are associated with the increase in leisure time. People have—and will have—more time to spend in the home, but also more to spend outside it. The 'standard working week' has fallen from the 60 hours that became general when the 'ten-hour' day was secured in the 1840's to 48 after the First World War, 44 after the Second, 42 in 1960 and 40 today. The fall in the actual hours worked has, because of overtime, been much less marked. Indeed, the average has remained fairly stable over the past 30 years.[61] There are some suggestions that professional people may work longer hours than in the past.[62]

Another *caveat* is about second jobs—'moonlighting'. It seems that some people, faced with the prospect of more leisure, prefer to fill this time with extra work (and earn extra money) instead. The rubber workers in the American town of Akron have enjoyed a six-hour day since the 1930's; Swados, studying them, found that the extra leisure was not always welcomed and that moonlighting was common.[63] Wilensky, in another American study, found that one in ten of middle-class employees currently had a second job and one in three had been a 'moonlighter' at some time in the past.[64]

Thus there are likely in the future to be some people who choose to fill their time with second jobs and others, mainly senior professionals and managers, who continue to find long hours essential to a successful career. These apart, the general long-term trend is unmistakable—for most people, the proportion of total time spent at work can be expected to continue to fall over the coming decades.

So far the discussion of free time has been solely in terms of hours worked per week. The balance of work and non-work time can be discussed in a number of other ways. One perspective is that of the life-cycle: if less time in total needs to be spent at work, then people could start work later in life and finish earlier—they might stay longer in full-time education or they might retire earlier. Both trends are already evident, and it is reasonable to predict that they will continue. In particular, more young people are likely to stay longer in further education. In addition, the expected changes in technology and in the occupational structure will mean that more and more adults will later in life need (and want) to re-enter the educational process in one way or another, often including some full-time study.

The division of work and non-work time can also be looked at on an annual basis. If less time is needed at work, there are broadly these choices:

        a) Shorter hours each day;
        b) Less days at work each week;
        c) Longer annual holidays.

What seems to have happened in the last 20 years or so is that the emphasis has been on the last two rather than the first. In 1945 the five-day week was the exception; now it is almost universal. Annual paid holidays increased in most industries from one to two weeks in the 1950's; now nearly half of all manual workers have a paid holiday of more than two weeks.[65]

It seems probable that leisure time will continue to extend in these forms. Thus for example the 30-hour week, when it comes, is more likely to take the form of a four-day week than a six-hour day. Annual holidays are in general already longer for non-manual workers, especially professional and managerial,[66] than manual, and the expected long-term changes in the occupational structure will encourage the existing trend to longer paid holidays.

It is worth noting that these trends in the division of leisure time fit in with the home-centred life described earlier. If the husband in particular has a lengthy journey to work, it is better for him and for the family if he can concentrate his work-life into a limited number of days each week and keep whole days free for home and family. It is at the weekend, above all, that family life comes into its own. And large slices of holiday, away from work and with the family instead, are also well suited to a society that values family life so highly.

Second homes, holidays and travel

Much of the leisure outside the home is—and will continue to be—still in a family setting. With many activities the impression is that the strongest wish is to create another miniature 'home' elsewhere. The family car can be seen as a sort of home on wheels even without a caravan and, when the children are young, very much one for the whole family. Many recreational activities now increasing in popularity—for example, caravanning, cruising and sailing—are things that families usually do together. The impression is also that there is an increase in 'independent' family holidays—families renting chalets, country cottages, seaside flats, Mediterranean villas.

'Second homes' are an even more obvious means of combining family life with frequent 'holidays', and though firm evidence is sparse, these are surely on the increase. In a recent small survey in London in which 100 people were interviewed, we found a marked difference according to social class in the ownership of country cottages and other second homes. In a middle-class area of Kensington, a quarter of households had a second home, compared with none in a working-class area of Hackney. But among the latter, two-thirds expressed the desire for one as did over half the Kensington people without one. This and more substantial evidence[67] suggest that with rising living standards, a growing proportion of town-dwellers will acquire second homes, and a growing proportion of leisure time, mainly weekends and annual holidays, will be spent in them, either in Britain or abroad.

In addition, as more families get cars and higher real incomes, there will be an increase in travel and holidays generally. In 1967, according to the Family Expenditure Survey,[68] households whose 'head' was middle-class in occupation, as compared with those whose 'head' was a manual worker, spent 76% more on 'private motoring' and nearly three times as much on 'holidays, hotels, etc.'. These are clear pointers to future growths in demand. So as well as the growing importance of home and family in leisure, there will also be an increase in mobility, including family mobility. More time and money will go into travel for social and recreational purposes, into holidays in hotels and the like, into rented holiday homes of various kinds, and into second family homes.

Leisure and geographical dispersal

The likely developments in leisure patterns are discussed in the paper by H. B. Rodgers. The main point here is that much of the growth is expected to be in recreations that need large quantities of space. With the expected increase in population, space is in any case likely to become more precious, particularly in the heavily-populated areas like the South East. Thus the result will be that more people will have to travel much longer distances for their golf, dinghy sailing, riding or countryside walking. The value of open country and seclusion is likely to increase, along with the price that people have to pay, in travel time, to reach it. This will further encourage the trends noted earlier—more time at home (whether first or second home), and longer distance travel when outside it.

The development of mass education and the influence of television and other mass media have also helped to awaken appetites for new and more specialised interests, ones that depend on a larger population to draw from and on a large catchment area. Increasingly people, as individuals this time rather than as family members, travel longer distances to engage in specialised interests. All this represents a greater variety and more choice. As was noted earlier, changes like these represent a qualification to the general picture of growing social homogeneity; it seems that we are moving both towards a greater homogeneity in certain areas of life and towards an increasing diversity in others. In any case, because of improved communications, the trend is indisputably away from the 'place community' and towards what Webber has called the 'interest community'.[69]

Of course, it does not follow that the 'place community', i.e. the local community, is going to be rubbed out by the ease of communications. It continues to figure importantly in most people's lives. Its significance varies among other things by age, sex, social class, income and car ownership: on the whole women's social contacts, being more tied to the home, are less dispersed than men's; those of young children, of their parents and of old people are less dispersed than those of other people and those of unmarried adolescents and young adults most dispersed of all; those of car owners more than of people without cars; those of middle-class and richer people more than working-class and poorer. These variations showed up in the small pilot study in London already mentioned, when people were asked what was the longest journey they had made during the previous month. For example, among working-class people one in seven had made a journey of 100 miles or more; among middle-class people the proportion was over a third; in particular, among middle-class people earning £3,000 or more a year it was well over half. Such local ties as there are differ too: for instance, they may be mainly with relatives (as in working-class areas) or with friends (as in middle-class). Furthermore, the proportion of a person's total social contacts that are local as against those that are dispersed varies along similar sex, age and class lines.

This suggests a continuing rôle for local community, even among many for whom local relationships account for only a relatively small part of their social life as a whole. But it does also suggest that a whole series of pressures —higher living standards, more cars, more education—are likely once again to cause middle-class styles of life to spread, mobility to increase and dispersed 'interest communities' to flourish still more.

* * *

This paper has suggested that, although the social structure of Britain seems relatively unchanging, especially in terms of the shares and opportunities of different social classes, there is a long-term general trend for middle-class tastes and consumption patterns to spread, for patterns of life and culture to become in some important respects more homogeneous.

In particular, as one example of this homogeneity, the growth of partnership marriage and home-centredness has been noted. It has also been
suggested, as another example, that travel will increase and with it the
importance of geographically dispersed 'interest communities', which means
that the greater homogeneity in one respect (dispersal becoming more
common) will mean greater heterogeneity in another (more variety of
interests). The paper ends by discussing the relevance to patterns of
urbanisation of these two trends in turn and raising some major questions
that remain.

Homes and suburbs

The shift towards home and family suggests that the spread of the city
(if it can still be called that) will accelerate. The trends are already clearly
evident—in what has happened around London and other large British
cities and in the experience of the United States—and it seems as if nothing
can stop the process of further dispersal as living standards rise, even more
so if at the same time the population increases substantially. It seems that
something like Los Angeles is bound to be the urban model for Britain's
future.

But there are some doubts. People want—or think they want—large
houses and gardens in suburbs, exurbs or new towns. When they get them
they have still not arrived in Paradise. The evidence on this is somewhat
contradictory. Gans seems to have found in his study of *The Levittowners*,[70]
a high degree of satisfaction with suburbia, though some of his interpretations might be regarded as tendentious. Other studies, mainly in Britain,
show general 'contentment', particularly with the new house, but also
strong criticism, particularly by wives, of loneliness, of the absence of shops,
entertainment and other amenities, and of public transport.[71]

On the journey to work in particular there is again some apparent conflict.
Gans states that most of the Levittowners he studied did not mind a long
journey to work, though he did find that nearly two-thirds had a journey of
over 40 minutes and that 30% of those taking 40 to 59 minutes 'disliked' it,
as did 44% of those taking an hour or more.[72] Our own study in Ipswich
showed that, of the people whose journey to work took over 20 minutes,
a third considered the journey 'inconvenient'. And in our recent pilot
interviews in the London area, again a third of those living in suburban
areas said they 'disliked' the journey to work. Certainly on the face of it
one would assume that, although some people might actually enjoy a long
journey to work, many commuters resent the loss of leisure time. They have
to surrender a larger proportion of the very 'family life' for which they have
moved.

The issue is whether an acceptable environment could be provided for
family life, something with the essential elements of the 'home-and-garden'
but without a continuing geographical spread. The question is pointed up
by the other demands for space in and around cities. The growth in car
ownership means more space will be needed for parking and for roads.

Higher standards mean larger school sites and playing fields. Changing tastes in recreation generate extra 'needs'. Golf courses and marinas may soon be 'essentials'.

These pressures mean that we must at least question whether suburban-isation is inevitable, or whether it would be possible to strike a balance that would more successfully meet people's needs. Two trends that have been noted earlier might encourage the alternative to Los Angeles: the changing family structure which might create a growing demand for smaller, garden-less dwellings, and the increase in wives working which might make more attractive the greater accessibility of inner urban areas.

There is also the predicted growth in second homes: it is possible that, particularly with a longer weekend, more and more families might choose high-density urban living close to their work, if this were combined with a second home in more rural surroundings.[73] These are all questions that deserve further research.

Local and dispersed communities

Now to the implications of the geographical dispersal of leisure activities and social networks. For most people, these no longer bear any relation-ship to local authority boundaries. Some of the activities and networks spread across the nation and the world. But for most of the population, most of the time, the urban region is the meaningful setting.

The conclusion is surely that we need to order and plan the environment and the pattern of communications on a regional basis, the central idea being that the region could satisfy most of the day-to-day or week-to-week needs of its residents, and that public and private transport should be planned and organised so as to facilitate this. The regional transport networks should include not only links from peripheral communities into the centre but across the region as well.

Examples of the facilities with a regional catchment are further education, theatres, art cinemas, concert halls, exotic restaurants, top-level football grounds and competition swimming pools. There will, of course, be needs that people living in a region could meet only by going further afield—to London for the Covent Garden Opera or Scotland for a ski-ing holiday in the Highlands, to New York for a conference or the Riviera for sun. And there will naturally be inter-regional lines of communication—national motorways, railways and air routes, linking up with international routes.

Within the regional communication networks, however, there will still be a function for local community. Local social relationships are important to many people,[74] as suggested earlier, and people do after all depend on local shops, schools, etc. The planning task is to create a neighbourhood structure to meet these functional and psychological needs without such a marked separation of different localities as characterised the first new towns.

Outstanding questions

This paper suggested at the outset that what had happened in the past could help in looking ahead to the future. In trying to make some forecasts about changes in the social framework, this is the main approach that has been used—existing trends have been extrapolated, with modification where this seemed appropriate. The method has of course its limitations and a good many questions remain obscure.

It is not just that technology may surprise us all, that some innovations may change social life much more radically than has been suggested here. It is also that, though in a general way 'Tocqueville's Law' has proved reasonably useful, we do not really understand much about it. We do not know how diffusion works, what aspects of the lives of the 'few' will in fact prove attractive to the 'many' or which 'few' (i.e. the 'top' minorities in income, education or occupation) will provide the models for which sorts of taste or behaviour. Nor do we know in what conditions diffusion may operate 'upwards' instead of 'downwards' or 'vertically' (e.g. in terms of age) instead of 'horizontally'. We can make guesses, as this paper has done, but they may prove wrong.

The bigger underlying question is the one raised in the first paragraphs of the paper. This is the paradox about the class structure—how far can the process of 'merging', of increasing cultural homogeneity, go while the fundamental differences remain apparently unchanging? Above all, to echo the questions posed earlier, what will happen to poverty, colour and 'relative deprivation' in the emerging society? Again, further research is needed.

In particular, the older and poorer urban areas certainly pose planning problems. The environment of the future must provide not only for the affluent car-owning suburbanites but also for the minorities of income and colour, who at present live mainly in the older areas. What happens in these older areas clearly affects the city as a whole. As the rush to the suburbs continues, a social 'polarisation' seems to be taking place inside the cities, though we do not have clear evidence about what is happening to the social composition of different types of residential areas. The inner urban areas seem to contain the poor and the very rich, while the rest live outside.[75] The process has gone even further in the United States, where divisions by colour and geography are all-important.[76] It could obviously happen in Britain too.

At present the impression is that some of the older central areas are deteriorating, physically and socially, much faster than they are being renewed. A co-ordinated attack, combining physical renewal and rehabilitation with the kind of 'positive discrimination' envisaged in the Plowden Report and in the Government's 'Urban Programme', is needed in the Brixtons and Notting Hills and in a different form in the Bethnal Greens and Bermondseys.

It would be tempting, in looking to the future, to concentrate resources upon new transport networks, better-planned new settlements, regional parks and the like. The older areas, particularly the poorest, plainly need attention as well. To strike the right balance between preparing for tomorrow and dealing with the inheritance from yesterday will not be easy, but it must be done. Thus, as well as social research on such topics as differences in the class structure, 'relative deprivation', life-styles, diffusion and suburbanisation, there needs to be detailed investigation of the poorer urban areas, so as to suggest the appropriate combination of social and planning policies.

NOTES AND REFERENCES

[1] Apart from the help of fellow members of the DPU Group and its advisors, I am also indebted to my colleagues at the Institute of Community Studies, particularly Richard Mills, Michael Young and Sheila Yeatman. Useful comments on earlier drafts of the paper were made by Herbert Gans, David Grove and Phyllis Willmott.

[2] In *Britain Revisited* (Gollancz, 1961) Tom Harrisson describes his impression, in comparing the Bolton of 1960 with that of 1936, of how much 'unchange' was mixed with 'change', pp. 25-45.

[3] Guy Routh, *Occupation and Pay in Great Britain 1906-1960*, Cambridge University Press, 1965; see especially Table 1, pp. 4-5.

[4] *Occupational Changes 1951-1961*, Manpower Studies No. 6, H.M.S.O., 1967.

[5] The American experience so far seems to suggest that the likely effects of automation have been exaggerated. See Daniel Bell in 'Towards the Year 2000: Work in Progress', *Daedalus*, Summer, 1967, p. 676, particularly the reference to the President's Commission on Technology, Automation and Economic Progress.

[6] D. V. Glass (Editor), *Social Mobility in Britain*, Routledge, 1954.

[7] *Ibid.*, p. 188.

[8] S. M. Lipset and R. Bendix, *Social Mobility in Industrial Society*, Heinemann, 1959, pp. 33-38.

[9] P. M. Blau and O. D. Duncan, *The American Occupational Structure*, John Wiley, 1967, p. 424.

[10] P. R. Kaim-Caudle, 'Selectivity and the Social Services', *Lloyds Bank Review*, April 1969, pp. 28-29.

[11] *Higher Education*, H.M.S.O., 1963, Appendix I, p. 54.

[12] J. E. Meade, *Efficiency, Equality and the Ownership of Property*, Allen and Unwin, 1964, p. 27.

[13] Guy Routh, *op. cit.*, Chapter II.

[14] J. L. Nicholson, *Redistribution of Income in the United Kingdom in 1959, 1957 and 1963*, Bowes and Bowes, 1964. See also John Hughes, 'The Increase in Inequality', *New Statesman*, 8 November 1968.

[15] Richard M. Titmuss, *Income Distribution and Social Change*, Allen and Unwin, 1962, Chapter 8.

[16] W. G. Runciman, reviewing changes in class, status and power in Britain from 1918 to 1962 concluded that 'inequality of status (i.e. prestige) was diminishing'. *Relative Deprivation and Social Justice*, Routledge, 1966, p. 118.

[17] T. H. Marshall, *Citizenship and Social Class*, Cambridge University Press, 1950, Chapter I.

[18] Mark Abrams, 'Consumption in the Year 2000', in Michael Young (Editor), *Forecasting and the Social Sciences*, Heinemann, 1968, p. 37.

[19] Meade, *op. cit.*; see also Hughes, *op. cit.*

[20] Abrams, *op. cit.*, p. 38.

[21] D. C. Rowe, 'Private Consumption', in W. Beckerman, *et al.*, *The British Economy in 1975*, Cambridge University Press, 1965, p. 180.

[22] David Donnison, *The Government of Housing*, Penguin, 1967, p. 194.

23 Quoted from Alexis de Tocqueville, *Democracy in America*, by Daniel Bell in 'Towards the Year 2000: Work in Progress', p. 643 and p. 937.

24 John Burnett, *Plenty and Want*, A social History of Diet in England from 1815 to the Present Day, Penguin, 1968, p. 16.

25 See D. Elliston Allen, *British Tastes*, Hutchinson, 1968.

26 See e.g. H. H. Gerth and C. Wright Mills (Editors) *From Max Weber : Essays in Sociology*, Routledge, 1948, p. 187.

27 John H. Goldthorpe, David Lockwood, Frank Bechhover, and Jennifer Platt, 'The Affluent Worker and the Thesis of Embourgeoisement: some preliminary research findings', *Sociology*, Vol. 1 No. 1, January 1967. See also their *The Affluent Worker : Industrial Attitudes and Behaviour*; Cambridge University Press, 1968; *The Affluent Worker : Political Attitudes and Behaviour*, Cambridge University Press, 1968.

28 R. Dubin, 'Industrial Workers' Worlds', *Social Problems*, Vol. 3, No. 3, January 1956, pp. 131-42.

29 See Goldthorpe *et al.*, 'The Affluent Worker and the Thesis of Embourgeoisement', pp. 19-20.

30 Goldthorpe *et al.*, *The Affluent Worker : Political Attitudes and Behaviour*, pp. 11-19.

31 See e.g. David Reisman 'Leisure and Work in Post-Industrial Society', in Eric Larrabee and Rolf Meyersohn (Editors), *Mass Leisure*, Free Press, 1958.

32 Among recent British studies, see Hilda Jennings, *Societies in the Making* (Bristol), Routledge, 1962; C. Rosser and C. Harris, *The Family and Social Change* (Swansea), Routledge, 1965; Goldthorpe *et al.*, *op. cit.* See also, among American studies showing the rôle of kin and neighbours, Herbert J. Gans, *The Urban Villagers*, Free Press, 1962; M. B. Sussman, 'The Isolated Nuclear Family—Fact or Fiction?', in *Selected Studies in Marriage & the Family*, R. F. Winch, R. McGinnis and H. R. Barringer (Editors), Holt, Rinehart & Winston, 1962; M. Axelrod 'Urban Structure and Social Participation', in *Cities & Society*, P. K. Hatt and A. J. Reiss (Editors), Free Press, 1963.

33 Bennett M. Berger, *Working Class Suburb*, University of California, 1960; Peter Willmott, *The Evolution of a Community* (Dagenham), Routledge 1963; Herbert J. Gans, *The Levittowners*, Allen Lane The Penguin Press 1967.

34 Goldthorpe *et al.*, 'The Affluent Worker and the Thesis of Embourgeoisement' pp. 22-23.

35 Peter Willmott and Michael Young, *Family and Class in a London Suburb*, Routledge, 1960, p. 122.

36 Goldthorpe *et al.*, *The Affluent Worker : Political Attitudes and Behaviour*, pp. 49-62.

37 *Ibid.*, pp. 74-75. Also *Family and Class in a London Suburb, op. cit.*, p. 115.

38 Runciman, *op. cit.*, p. 192.

39 See William J. Goode, *World Revolution and Family Patterns*, Free Press, 1963; Dorothy R. Blisten, *The World of the Family*, Random House, 1963.

40 P. R. Cox, 'Marriage and Fertility Data of England and Wales', *Population Studies*, Vol. 5, November 1951, p. 140.

41 *Registrar General's Statistical Review for 1964, Part III, Commentary*, H.M.S.O., 1967, p. 31.

42 *Ibid.*, p. 17.

43 These calculations were kindly made by P. R. Cox.

44 This term itself could be criticised. Since, as noted earlier, more young people stay in education until a higher age, in one sense there is a contrary trend— children are economically dependent on their parents for longer than in the past. Even so, most are socially independent, or largely so, after about

15, and, as I argue later, this is likely to continue and to extend to residential independence.

[45] Richard Titmuss, 'The Position of Women' in *Essays on the 'Welfare State'*, Allen and Unwin, 1958.

[46] Quoted in S. R. Parker, *et al.*, *The Sociology of Industry*, Allen and Unwin, 1967, p. 50.

[47] Colin M. Stewart, 'The Employment of Married Women in Great Britain', Paper to International Union for the Scientific Study of Population, London, 1969.

[48] This pattern is described and discussed by Rhona Rapoport and Robert N. Rapoport 'The Dual-Career Family: A Variant Pattern and Social Change', *Human Relations*, Vol. 22, No. 1, February 1969, pp. 3-30.

[49] Michael Young and Peter Willmott, *Family and Kinship in East London*, Routledge, 1957, pp. 6-15; F. Zweig, *The Worker in an Affluent Society*, Heinemann, 1961, pp. 30-32 and pp. 207-8; John and Elizabeth Newson, *Four Years Old in an Urban Community*, Allen and Unwin, 1968, pp. 522-4.

[50] Charles Winick, 'The Beige Epoch: Depolarisation of Sex Roles in America', *The Annals of the American Academy of Political and Social Sciences*, Vol. 376, March 1968, pp. 18-24.

[51] Mark Abrams, 'The home-centred society', *The Listener*, 26.11.59; Young and Willmott, *Family and Kinship in East London*, op. cit., p. 119 and pp. 127-36; Zweig, op. cit., pp. 206-9; Josephine Klein, *Samples from English Culture*, Routledge, 1965, Vol. 1, pp. 283-8.

[52] Young and Willmott, *Family and Kinship in East London*, op. cit., Chapters I and X.

[53] Willmott and Young, *Family and Class in a London Suburb*, op. cit., pp. 21-27.

[54] Edmund Leach, *A Runaway World?*, BBC, 1968, pp. 42-46.

[55] Rhona Rapoport and Robert N. Rapoport, op. cit.

[56] Leach, op. cit., p. 45.

[57] *The South East Study*, H.M.S.O., 1964, p. 24.

[58] *Registrar General's Statistical Review for 1962, Part III, Commentary*, H.M.S.O., 1964, p. 50.

[59] This kind of interpretation has been challenged in a recent article—Judith Blake, 'Are Babies Consumer Durables?', *Population Studies*, March 1968. See also a thorough discussion of the reasons for differential fertility, including hypotheses of this sort—Geoffrey Hawthorne and Joan Busfield, 'A Sociological Approach to British Fertility', in Julius Gould (Editor), *Penguin Social Science Survey 1968*.

[60] *New Society*, 14 December 1967, p. 847.

[61] B. C. Roberts and J. L. Hirsch, 'Factors Influencing Hours of Work', in B. C. Roberts and J. H. Smith (Editors), *Manpower Policy and Employment Trends*, London School of Economics and Political Science, 1966, pp. 111-13.

[62] H. L. Wilensky, 'The Uneven Distribution of Leisure', *Social Problems*, Summer, 1961, p. 39; this shows that half his (middle-class) sample worked 45 hours or more a week and one in five worked an average of eight hours or more at weekends.

[63] H. Swados, 'Less Work: Less Leisure', in Larrabee and Meyershon (Editors), *Mass Leisure*, op. cit.

[64] H. L. Wilensky, op. cit.

[65] *Statistics on Incomes, Prices, Employment and Production*, September 1968, H.M.S.O., p. 65.

[66] Many of the senior civil servants, top managers, architects and doctors who work a 50- or 60-hour week have a complete break of a month or more each summer.

[67] At present about 5% of households in Britain own second homes or caravans, according to the BTA/Keele survey of leisure (British Travel Association/

University of Keele, *Pilot National Recreation Survey, Report No 1*, 1967, pp. 21-22). But rapid increases are reported in particular areas and in some villages (Blackeney, Norfolk is one example) the second homes account for as many as a third of all dwellings.

[68] Quoted in Mark Abrams, 'Britain: The Next 15 Years', *New Society* 7 November 1968.

[69] Melvin M. Webber, 'The Urban Place and the Non-Place Urban Realm' in Melvin M. Webber *et al.*, *Explorations into Urban Structure*, University of Pennsylvania, 1963, and Melvin M. Webber 'Order in Diversity: Community without Propinquity', in Lowdon Wingo Jnr. (Editor), *Cities and Space*, Johns Hopkins, 1964.

[70] Herbert J. Gans, *The Levittowners, op. cit.*

[71] Peter Willmott, 'East Kilbride and Stevenage', *Town Planning Review*, January, 1964, pp. 310-11; Hilda Jennings, *op. cit.*, pp. 145-6; London County Council, *Survey into Design Aspects of Expanding Town at Huntingdon, Haverhill and Thetford*, LCC, 10 January, 1964, p. 2.

[72] Herbert J. Gans, *The Levittowners, op. cit.*, p. 222 and p. 246.

[73] This possiblity has been suggested by David Grove: 'Physical Planning and Social Change', *Forecasting and the Social Sciences, op. cit.*, pp. 93-94.

[74] See Peter Willmott, 'Social Research and New Communities', *AIP Journal*, November 1967.

[75] See Ruth Glass's discussion of the process of 'gentrification', by which middle-class owner-occupiers are displacing working-class residents: Ruth Glass, 'Introduction', in Centre for Urban Studies, *London: Aspects of Change*, MacGibbon and Kee, 1964, pp. xviii-xix.

[76] See Ruth Glass, *op. cit.*: '... the impression remains—and often it is the dominant one—that there is increasing segmentation' (p. xxii).

RESOURCES AND THE ECONOMIC FRAMEWORK

P. A. STONE

Introduction

One of the more important restraints on the developing pattern of urban-isation is the availability of resources, both real and financial. The de-velopment, renewal and maintenance of the built environment requires a large proportion of national output, currently about an eighth. Increases in the output of construction work can be obtained through increases in the productivity of construction, by reductions in the resources available for the provision of other goods and services, or from increases in national output. The built environment is not alone in being inadequate in quantity and quality. There are many claims on the national output; more resources are required for improving industrial capital, for developing education, and the health and social services, and for increasing the availability of consumer goods and services. Urban development involves a large use of land, the supply of which is largely fixed. Moreover, the community is concerned not only with material standards but also with the quality of life and with leisure, the demand for which tends to compete with the demand for higher material standards. On the other hand, the built environment is not by any means just a form of consumption goods; part of it consists of productive goods which help in increasing national output and hence with the resources for improving the built environment. Thus, some aspects of urban development have greater priority than others.

Of course, not all aspects of urbanisation have a significant effect on the use of resources. Environmental quality depends on the way in which the resources are used as well as on the amount used. A change in the geo-graphical patterns of location may not affect the national resources re-quired, although it would require a change in their regional distribution. Again, new patterns of urbanisation resulting from changes in social patterns might have little effect on the use of resources, although it might result in changes in the directions of their use.

Programmes of development need to satisfy three economic tests. First, does the development provide good value for money? Secondly, are the resources required to carry out the programmes of development available, or can they be made available by the time they will be required? Thirdly, is the finance available to ensure that the resources are moved in the re-quired directions and are people prepared individually and collectively to

Until the early part of this year Dr Stone was at the National Institute of Economic and Social Research where he was directing studies in the field of urban economics

transfer the money into the sectors of the economy appropriate to the achievement of the programmes of development? Such tests need to be applied nationally, regionally and locally.

The tests themselves raise all the difficulties of communication in planning, some aspects of which have been considered in other papers in this series. Over much of the economy the consumer can indicate his wishes through the price mechanism; he can set his own innate sense of value against the price asked by the market. This is not possible over a large section of the built environment. This is because either the facilities and amenities are provided free (that is collectively), or because the prices which are paid are shielded from the market forces by various types of controls, subsidies, grants and other indirect forms of payment. Hence the decisions on the supply of facilities are, to a large extent, administrative and political. This does not solve the problem of value. The decision-taker cannot apply the test of value for money unless he can measure the comparative values of the alternatives to the final consumers. Moreover, where facilities and amenities are provided free or partly free by the public sector, the required finance can only be obtained by taxation and this provides no indication of the way the user values the service obtained.

In the last few years methods have been developed for bringing market forces into the supply of built facilities. These are aimed as much at rationing scarce facilities, for example, urban roads and rural recreational space, and obtaining some measure of the consumers' sense of value, as at raising finance, However, while the use of the market provides a measure of value and relates demand and supply, unless there is a considerable degree of equality of income, a substantial part of the community may in practise be excluded from the facilities provided by the market. This difficulty can be overcome in a number of ways, for example, by providing grants to members of the community with inadequate incomes and by providing all members of the community with a ration of points which can be used as the means of gaining admittance to a range of facilities in short supply.

However, the use of marketing and quasi-marketing devices would not solve all the problems of value. Many of the external economies of facilities, for example, the amenity provided by a view and the nuisance of traffic noise and pollution, would not be adequately reflected in market prices. The development of reliable techniques for measuring value would still appear to be necessary. With the development of better methods of simulating the consequences of patterns of urbanisation and with more efficient computers and computer techniques, it will tend to become easier to evaluate urban choices. In the meantime, it is possible and useful to apply tests of economic feasibility to the alternative patterns of urbanisation which are available for consideration.

Population, Human Activities and National Resources

The supply and demand for resources depends basically on population and human activities, and on their interactions with natural resources. Population increases result in more consumers as well as more producers. The movement in output and demand per head depends, other things being equal, on the demographic structure of the population.

The size and demographic structure of the population is the result of four separate types of change, births, deaths, and inward and outward migration. The difficulty in projecting future population for Great Britain tends to lie mainly in projecting the rate of birth. Birth rates have varied considerably in the past (Fig. 1). Live births per 1000 of population exhibit a cyclical pattern rather than a trend. The patterns of crude live birth rates depend partly on the age and sex structure of the population, partly on the age at which women marry and partly on their fertility, the probability of a married or unmarried woman of a given age having a child. Birth rates have been rising in the case of married women of all ages, a greater proportion of women have been marrying, they have been marrying younger

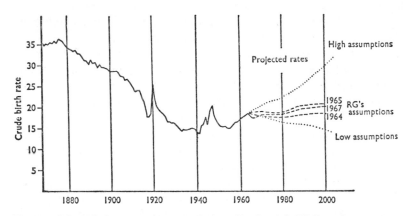

FIG. 1. Live births per 1000 population, England & Wales, 1870-2004.

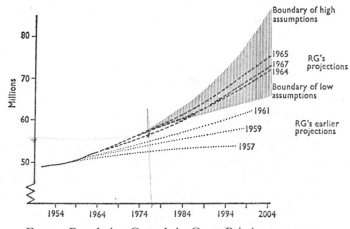

FIG. 2. Population Growth in Great Britain, 1951-2004.

and the proportion of births outside marriage have been increasing. While these factors explain the recent rise in birth rates they do not indicate whether the rise can be expected to continue in the long term. This depends on whether it is the timing of families which has changed or their ultimate size. The statistical data available only indicates what has happened in the case of cohorts of women who have completed their families and whose experience may not be relevant to women now of child-bearing age. In contrast changes in death rates, assuming no catastrophes, are reasonably predictable. In the past the scale of net migration has generally not been large enough to have much effect on population but changes in national policy for migration or changes in rates of emigration could result in their being more important in the future.

Thus the difficulty in projecting population is largely because of the volatile fertility and marriage rates and the unpredictability of the scale of migration. The official statisticians, the Registrars General, have made considerable modifications to their projections in the last few years (Fig. 2). The range of possible variation in future population could be very considerable. The shaded area (Fig. 2) indicates the limits of some projections made with 1964 data. While on the official basis of projection 53 million in 1964 would have increased to 72 million by 2004; boundary figures are 85 million and 56 million. The boundaries indicate what the levels would be, on the one hand, were marriage rates to continue to rise in accordance with the 1931-61 trend and if fertility rates were to rise by no more than two-thirds of the recent rate, and on the other hand, if marriage and fertility rates were to decline gradually to the levels of 1940. Both assumptions produced birth rates within the margin of experience of the last 80 years. Over a period of 40 years, projections on such assumptions would increase the official projections by 18% or reduce them by 9%.[1]

However, not only could the total future population be very different from the total which appears probable today but its demographic structure could also be very different. While the number of persons over 40 at the end of the period cannot be affected by changes in births, the number of young people, under 15, could be 50% greater in the one case and 27% less in the other.[1] The number of working age, 15-69, could be 9% greater against a population 18% greater, in the one case and 3% less as against a population 9% less in the other case.[1] Thus the faster population increased as a result of natural increase, the more young people there would be to support and the smaller the proportion of population of working age to produce the national output. Of course, if the official projection is correct, the proportion of working age would still fall in the future; over a period of 40 years it would fall from about 70% to about 66%.[1]

The working population, that is the total number of people actually available for work, is likely to increase more slowly than the number of people of working age. This is because it is expected that the increase in young people remaining longer in full-time education[2,3] and a slight tendency to earlier retirement will more than offset expected gains from increases in the proportion of married women in employment.[4] Over the period of 40 years the reduction in the overall activity rate might be nearly 2%. The combined effect of a smaller proportion of people of working age with lower activity rates would reduce the proportion of workers by about 8%.

National output depends not only on the size of the population actually available for work but also on the rates of productivity, on the activities on which they are employed, on the number actually employed and on their hours of work. Clearly any projection of these factors over a long period must be very hazardous. The general expectation has been that it should be possible to achieve an annual growth rate in gross domestic product per person employed of 3% to 4%; the figure given in the National Plan[5] was 3·4% a year over the period 1964-70 while Beckerman[6] suggested a figure of 3·1% over the period 1960-1975. It has not been possible to achieve rates as high as these over the last few years because of balance of payment difficulties and other short-term problems.

The average annual rate of productivity per man employed depends both on the rate of productivity in each industry and on the industrial structure of the economy. Productivity generally increases faster in manufacturing industries than in service industries and faster in new industries and in industries producing new products than in other industries. The higher the rate of productivity in an industry, the less labour tends to be necessary for that industry and the lower the contribution it makes to the average rate of productivity. Moreover, the demand for the products of some industries is expected to fall, while for others demand may only increase in proportion to the rise in population. The generally expected disproportional rise in the demand for services would tend to reduce the rate at which average productivity rose. Moreover, in the long run productivity increases can generally only be achieved by using additional capital and the greater the rate of increase in productivity the greater the required rate of capital formation generally required. Thus net output will tend to rise more slowly than gross output.

The hours of work might fall in the long run because as a result of a desire for increased leisure the working week was shortened and more time was taken in annual holidays. For example, if, today, no statutory overtime was worked the working week would fall by nearly 20%. An additional week's holiday would reduce the hours of work by about 2%. Thus, even if high rates of productivity per manhour were obtained in future the result might be only a small increase in net output per man.

Since the war national output per head in Great Britain has increased rapidly, though not as fast as in some other countries. Since 1951, the average rate of increase has been about 3%, although it was substantially higher in the earlier part of the period.[7] Output per head has not always risen as fast as this, or even risen at all. In the early part of the century, certainly the first 20 years, output per head was falling.[8] The level at the beginning of the century was probably not bettered for about 30 years. Over the first half of the century output per head probably only rose by just over 10%.

There can be no certainty that output per head will rise at current rates over the rest of the century. The higher the level of productivity reached, the more difficult it may be to sustain such rates of increase. The achievement of high rates of increase tends to require a high rate of capital formation and an adaptable and hard working labour force. The exchange of higher levels of goods and services for more leisure and a more comfortable industrial life might be preferred.

It can be argued that the current methods of measuring national output are unsatisfactory, especially in a period when services and leisure are likely to be of increasing importance. National output is currently measured through the cash transactions of the economy. The output from voluntary services is thus not measured. Even if other things remained equal, output as measured would fall if hours of work fell and the extra time was devoted to providing voluntary services formerly provided by paid labour, and would rise if housewives and other voluntary workers increasingly took paid employment and paid others to carry out their household duties. Services provided without a direct charge are usually measured through the costs of their supply; the services might, however, be valued more or less than this cost. Clearly, an attempt to measure output so as to make an allowance for the quality of life would be difficult. It would be necessary to decide which activities added to national output and which were purely recreational. For example, voluntary work in a hospital which reduced paid labour for other work would appear to add to the real national output, while playing a game without spectators would be recreational; the presence of spectators might result in the activity becoming an addition to real output. Thus while there is some force in the objections to current methods of measuring output, it is difficult to measure output in a qualitative way. An increase in leisure and a more comfortable industrial life might not reduce the real value of national output as much as would be indicated by current statistical measures.

Despite the difficulties in projecting output, the projection of requirements is possibly even more difficult. This is because, basically, output depends on the size of the labour force, which, catastrophes apart, can be projected with more certainty than total population which is the base for projecting many of the requirements. While long-term projections of population are subject to possible errors of the order of 10%, the number and demographic structure of people of middle and old age can be estimated with reasonable precision. Up to 20 years ahead it is possible to produce reasonable accurate projections of the adult population. As a result, estimates of reasonable precision can be prepared of the number of households and for all the requirements which stem from households, of the size of the labour force, of the number of potential car owners and for other requirements which stem from adults. The further ahead projections are pushed the smaller the proportion of population for which reasonable precision can be obtained.

Thus it is reasonably certain that the greater the increase in the population, the greater the increase in requirements in relation to the size of the labour force and the more necessary it will be to follow a pattern of activities and life styles which tend to increase output per employed person.

The Built Environment

Clearly the total requirements for the built environment depend basically on the size and structure of the population and on its activities. Since so many of the requirements for built environment depend more on the number of adults than on the total population, in the short run, up to about 20 years, there is a basic stability in the projections for the gross numbers of units of facility likely to be required. This element of stability is reduced to some extent by uncertainties about activities and life-styles. The net number of units to be provided depends, of course, on the size of the current stock and its expected rate of obsolescence. This in turn depends on the quality of the built environment which is required in the future.

It is perhaps easier to illustrate the inter-play of these forces in the case of housing than most types of built facility. In order to estimate the requirements for housing, it is necessary to consider rates of household formation, the occupation of dwellings, the standards likely to be required and the stock which is available.

Rates of household formation have been rising for some time and further rises in the future appear likely as real incomes rise. It appears reasonable to expect that in the future most married men and other adults who have been married, and about a half of older single people will form their own households. The proportion of young unmarried people forming their own households is currently very small, about 4% for unmarried men and women of 15 and under 40. Probably this rate will increase three or fourfold. On these assumptions the average household size would be of the order of 2·9 persons, the higher the population, the more children per household and the higher the average size of household. Because of this the number of households will tend to vary with birth rates only about half as much as population. The number of very young unmarried people will tend to be proportionally large, particularly if birth rates are high. The rate at which they form separate households could have a significant effect on the number of households. While many unmarried young people might need or prefer to live away from home, the effect on the number of dwellings required would only be large if they required separate dwellings instead of shared dwellings or hostel accommodation.

The number of dwellings which are likely to be required will depend not only on the number of households requiring separate dwellings but also on the scale on which vacant dwellings will be required and on the demand of households for more than one dwelling each. Not all households require a separate dwelling of their own and not all households require a permanent dwelling. Some households, although not many, prefer temporary homes, for example, boats and caravans. Such accommodation, and older and smaller dwellings, may be acceptable as second homes. At present, about 8% of households move each year; some move more than once.[1] If 10%

of households moved each year and their dwellings remained unoccupied for 5 weeks, just under 1% of the stock would be unoccupied at any time.

The sizes for each type of household can be obtained from the Census data, although the crude figures have to be modified to allow for the effect of changes in birth rates. Census data also provides the best guide to the number of rooms households will wish to occupy. Clearly, it would be incorrect to be guided by the occupation rates of households who are over-crowded or who have excess rooms. In 1961, the balance had on average one room for each 0·69 persons.[1] This rate is, of course, far more generous of space than the minimum standards suggested by the Parker Morris Committee or at which people are initially housed in public authority dwellings. Even so, it appears doubtful whether this standard will be acceptable in future. If people become more home centred and have a greater variety of home recreations, they will probably need more rooms and hence larger dwellings.[9] Thus, while currently there is a need for additional small dwellings, the average size required is likely to rise, especially if birth rates increase significantly.

At the current rate of output, about 400,000 dwellings a year,[10] the number of dwellings available by the early nineteen seventies is likely to exceed the number of households. Of course, not all dwellings would necessarily be located in the areas in which they were most required. During the seventies and early eighties about 120,000 additional dwellings a year are likely to be needed, from the mid-eighties the number required each year appears likely to rise and to have reached 200,000 a year by the turn of the century. Of course, if birth rates were much higher than officially pro-jected, the number required could be much greater.

Currently there are about 18 million dwellings in Great Britain. Of these over 4 million are about 90 or more years old, nearly 3 million are between 50 and 90 years old and another 4 million date from between the wars and are between 30 and 50 years old.[1] The indications are that over 2 million of the dwellings are structurally unsound; these and a further 2 million need extensive repairs and redecoration. While most dwellings have a cold water supply, many lack other basic amenities. There are about 3 million dwellings without an internal water closet, about 2·5 million without a fixed bath and even more without a bathroom and an adequate hot water system. The environment of the housing is unsatis-factory for about 8 million dwellings and very poor for nearly 2 million of them. Only about a quarter of the stock of dwellings have garages and over a half have neither a garage nor a space for one. Generally, of course, it is the oldest housing which has the least amenities and which is in the poorest condition.

The rate at which the stock of dwellings has been improved in the past has been very slow. Currently 80 to 90,000 of the worst dwellings are being demolished each year.[10] In addition about 30,000 a year are demolished to make way for road and town development; only a proportion of these are likely to be in a bad condition. Something over 100,000 unfit dwellings a year are known to have been made fit. Improvement grants are being provided for over 120,000 dwellings a year; some of these may have been for unfit dwellings. Since dwellings are deteriorating the whole time, it is doubtful whether the standard of the stock is even being maintained.

Clearly, even if extensive repair and improvement work were undertaken, many dwellings in the existing stock would become obsolete and need to be replaced before the end of the century. In the absence of information about the types of dwellings in the stock, age, which tends to be correlated with standard and condition, is perhaps the best indicator of the likely scale of obsolescence. Of course, the conveniently planned good quality dwelling is likely to remain in use even though it is old. It will be seen from the figures given earlier, that the rate of replacement is likely to affect the number of dwellings to be built far more than differences in the need for additional dwellings. Between now and say the turn of the century the number of additional dwellings required is likely to be about 6 million.[1] Even if the population was to reach the extreme projection (Fig. 2), less than 2 million more would be required. In contrast about 4 million dwellings would be required to clear and replace the equivalent* of the dwellings which would be over 120 years old by the turn of the century. About 7 million dwellings would be required if the target related to dwellings which would be over 80 years old by the turn of the century. Because of the scale of building between the wars about 11 million would be needed if this group of dwellings were included in the target for replacement.

If the current rate of constructing dwellings, about 400,000 a year, was maintained, it would take to about the end of the nineteen eighties to replace those at present structurally unsound and to end of the nineteen nineties to replace the equivalent of the pre-1880 dwellings. It would not be possible to replace the equivalent of the pre-1921 dwellings until the early years of the next century.

A comparison between expenditure on housing maintenance and the cost of maintenance at the standards adopted by local authorities, indicates that not much more than a third of the necessary work is carried out.[1] This gap is likely to be only partially filled by the work of housing occupiers. Unless considerable additional resources can be found both to provide adequate current maintenance and to make good the backlog of maintenance and upgrading, the housing stock at the end of the century might be no better in quality than it is today.

As mentioned earlier the projections of the number of adults are less subject to prediction errors than the projections for young people. As a result there is reasonable stability in the projection of the potential number of workers in industry and commerce. The rate of increase is lower than for the population as a whole. Over the rest of the century the annual rate of increase appears likely to average at about 0.7%. The probability of error in predicting the growth of each trade is, of course, much greater.

The growth of space requirements depends on such factors as the development of automation and shift working, and the relative importance of

* 'equivalent' implies equal in number since clearly not all the older dwellings would be cleared first—some will be retained indefinitely.

various manufacturing and service industries. To some extent, however, the factors which tend to lead to a reduction in floor areas tend also to lead to higher costs per unit of floor area, so that total costs are less variable than either.

The amount of space required for manufacturing in the future depends on the rate at which demand for the product rises as well as on the technological factors of production. Since population is only expected to rise at about 0·75% per annum, increases in productivity at the levels suggested earlier, would provide for substantial increases in demand per head. Such increases are not required for all types of commodity and many trades are expected to either decline in size absolutely or relatively. As a result the floor space for manufacturing industry is only expected to increase moderately in relation to the current stock. The faster the rate of change in the demand for different products, in technology and in the location of industry, the faster the rate at which the current stock is likely to be rebuilt. An average life of 60 years would imply that 1·67% of the stock would be replaced each year. On this basis building for replacement would be several times as important as building for additional space.

In the retail sector sales per head are expected to rise only moderately in the case of convenience goods, although more substantially in the case of durable goods.[6, 11] Because turnovers per unit of floor area are also expected to rise substantially, total floor area is likely to increase far less than sales per head.[11, 12, 13, 14] In order to obtain such increased turnovers it will be necessary to rebuild and relocate many of the shopping units. Again rebuilding is likely to be an important element in the construction of shops. In contrast, the motor trade has been expanding rapidly in the last few years and is expected to maintain a rapid rate of expansion for some time, so that additional space is likely to be important in relation to rebuilding. Office employment, catering and local government services are all sectors expected to grow rapidly.

Education is likely to be one of the growth industries, particularly that part of it which is catering for people over 15 years old.[2, 3] The educational activity rates for those of 15-19 years old are expected to more than double over the rest of the century; the greatest increases being in the early seventies. The proportion of people attending universities and colleges of advanced technology is expected to have more than doubled by the end of the seventies and to have more than trebled by the turn of the century. The number of students in other higher education is expected to increase even faster.

The average age of school buildings is high and many of them, especially primary school buildings, are obsolete in layout and poorly provided with amenities.[15] Moreover, as housing areas are redeveloped and land uses change many school buildings will be found to be in the wrong location. Thus, there is likely to be a need for both many additional education buildings and much replacement and re-modelling of existing buildings.

The need for health and other welfare buildings is also expected to both increase and change in form over the rest of the century. While the rates at which beds are required for acute cases and psychiatric cases are expected to decline, a greater proportion of births is expected to take place in hospitals.[6, 16] Because of the expectation that births and the number of old will both increase, it is not surprising that the total number of general beds is expected to increase by over a half by the end of the century. The need for surgeries and clinics is expected to double.[6] Substantial increases also appear likely in the number of beds in other residential welfare institutions, particularly, for example, in old people's homes.[8]

On average hospital buildings are about 50 years old,[17] older than school buildings, although not quite as old as dwellings. Moreover, medical science has changed and appears likely to continue to change very rapidly. It is likely to be necessary to replace a large proportion of existing hospitals in the near future. Other social welfare institutions are also very old.

One of the fastest growing sectors of the economy is transport and communications. Over the last decade car ownership per head more than doubled. It is expected to double again by the late nineteen seventies and to continue increasing, although at a slower rate.[18] On the other hand, the annual mileage per car tends to remain fairly constant.[18] Other road traffic is also increasing and it is expected that the load of traffic on the roads will have doubled in 15 years and increased half as much again by the end of the century. Over half the urban trunk and Class 1 roads and about a quarter of the rural trunk and Class 1 roads were already overloaded several years ago.[19] There is thus an urgent need for large scale road development.

Road development in urban areas interacts with the buildings since usually it is necessary to demolish buildings in order to implement road schemes whether for widening or the development of new roads. While usually priority for large scale road schemes is given to those which can be developed the more economically, which tends to be those passing through areas of near obsolete buildings, there is a limit to the extent to which this policy can be followed. Thus urban road development tends to increase the need for building construction and area development.

Apart from air transport, the rate at which traffic is expected to grow is far slower for other forms of transport than it is for road transport.[20] However, the expected rate of technological change is expected to be much greater and to involve a considerable amount of reconstruction of existing structures. Air traffic is expected to have increased four fold by the mid-eighties and fivefold by the end of the century. The amount of aircraft movement is expected to increase until the end of the nineteen seventies and subsequently decline as the larger aircraft come into service. Thus, the major part of development work appears likely to be needed during the nineteen sixties and seventies. In the case of railways, while there is the expectation of a substantial decline in route mileage, a large programme of improvements is planned; this again is expected to be substantially completed by the end of the seventies. Sea traffic is only expected to increase moderately but the rate of technological change is expected to be rapid.[21] Ships are growing larger and mechanical handling is expected to replace manual methods. For manufactured goods the use of containers is expected to have a revolutionary effect on goods handling. A large proportion of port facilities are likely to need to be reconstructed. Again the greater part of this work is likely to have been completed by the end of the nineteen seventies.

The demand for public utility services is increasing both because of increases in demand per head and increases in population. The demand for water appears likely to grow at an average rate of about 2% a year.[22, 23] Over the next two decades the growth in demand may be much higher, particularly for domestic purposes where consumption per head is likely to increase both because people tend to make a greater use of their appliances and because as the standard of the housing stock is improved the number of appliances per head will be increased. Unless an economic method for the complete cycling of water by the user is developed, there is likely to be a need both to substantially increase water storage and transfer facilities, and facilities for the collection and treatment of sewage. Many sewage installations are old and inadequate, particularly treatment works, and will need to be replaced.

Energy consumption is also likely to increase substantially in the future, particularly during the nineteen seventies, reflecting the higher standards of heating and lighting, and perhaps ventilation, which appear likely to be required, the greater use of power in industry and a substantial increase in transport, particularly road transport. It appears likely that in the long run the demand for energy may increase on average by at least 2% a year. Since the use of coal is likely to decline substantially there will need to be a more than proportional increase in the generation and distribution of other fuels, electricity, gas and oil. In addition, the gas network will need to be adapted to the use of natural gas. The telephone service is also expected to increase rapidly; installations are expected to increase at about 4% a year.

Resources for the Built Environment

The amount of resources likely to be required to develop, redevelop and maintain the built environment clearly depends more on the standards and forms of development than on the scale of population growth. While the level of error in predicting the needs for additional units of development can be estimated, the standards and forms depend on human choice in relation to the use of resources and it is possible only to examine the effect of choice.

Over the rest of the century additional housing to meet the needs of the officially projected population would appear to cost on average about £600 million a year.[1] The cost would rise to about £1000 million if sufficient dwellings were also built to replace the equivalent of pre-1881 dwellings. The replacement in addition of equivalent 1881-1921 dwellings would add about a further £250 million a year, while if replacement were extended to include the equivalent of pre-1941 dwellings about a further £425 million would be added. In contrast, the effect of the extreme population projection would only increase the costs by about £200 million.

These estimates are based on 1964 price levels and Parker Morris standards, with an addition of 10% to allow for the incidence of better quality housing. It has been assumed that the current form of development would be used with about 74% houses, 18% low flats, and 8% high flats. On this basis the average density would be about 59 habitable rooms per acre.

The costs of making good the arrears of maintenance and of upgrading dwellings in the existing stock, in so far as this would be economically worthwhile, would be about £8,000 to £9,000 million.[1] While this work would have to be spread over a number of years, it is, of course, all urgent. The total would not be much affected by the proportion of dwellings in the stock which was replaced. In addition regular maintenance to local authority standards would appear likely to cost on average over the period nearly £1000 million a year.[1]

In 1964, new housing work in Great Britain was costing something over £1000 million a year and maintenance on housing probably something about £500 million a year.[1] While occupiers carry out some maintenance work themselves, this is likely to make only a small contribution to the maintenance work covered by these figures. Thus, while expenditure on new housing appears to have been at an adequate level to meet the needs for additional dwellings and to replace pre-1881 dwellings by the end of the century, the level of expenditure on maintenance has been quite inadequate.

The relative importance of building additional and replacement facilities naturally varies from one category to another. Replacement appears to be more important in the case of industrial and health buildings, while additional space appears to be more important for office, education and other categories of buildings except for buildings for distribution for which the importance of the two types of space are relatively evenly balanced. It would appear that on average the annual expenditure over the rest of the century for non-residential building construction would be about £850 million.

Again, the buildings will need to be regularly maintained and from time to time they will need to be refitted and adapted to meet changing needs. An examination of the expenditure on various categories of buildings suggests that regular maintenance averages at about 1·5% a year of the initial cost of a building and that upgrading and alterations averages at perhaps 0·5% a year. On this basis the regular maintenance of non-residential buildings would appear to average at about £600 million a year and refitting and adaptation would average at about £200 million a year. Again the current level of work would appear to be inadequate.

The division between new and maintenance work is even more difficult to establish for civil engineering than for building. Large parts of civil engineering facilities are more or less permanent; they are altered and maintained but rarely completely replaced. Road maintenance generally includes some straightening and widening, and track maintenance frequently includes the substitution of improved components. It is, therefore, better not to attempt a division between the costs of new and maintenance work in the case of civil engineering.

It would appear that the total costs of new and maintenance work on civil engineering facilities over the rest of the century are likely on average to be over a £1000 million a year. Of this main roads appear likely to account for over a third. Public utilities also appear likely to be a large item. Other types of transport appear unlikely to cost more than about a ninth of the total. While civil air transport is expected to expand rapidly, it is comparatively minor in cost. Railways are expected to continue to decline in track mileage and ports are not expected to expand very rapidly. The civil engineering estimates also include allowance for agricultural and extractive industries.

Thus, it would appear that the total for all types of building and civil engineering work might be, at 1964 prices, on average, over the rest of the century, something over £5000 million a year. This is about a third more than is currently produced.

In addition to building and civil engineering resources the development of the built environment would require a considerable use of virgin land. The amount would depend on the densities of development as well as the scale of development and on the extent of redevelopment. In the past the densities of development were generally higher than today and generally fell from the nineteenth century to the nineteen thirties. Thus, the redevelopment of areas originally developed in the last century tends to result in a reduction of densities and in the need for more land elsewhere, whereas the redevelopment of inter-war development would tend to result in higher densities and would release land for additional development. On average, the scale of development visualised would require 40,000 to 50,000 additional acres of land for development each year.

The Availability of Resources

The availability of construction resources for the extension and improvement of the built environment depends on the output of the construction sector of the economy. This sector consists of three parts; the contracting industry, the manufacturers of building materials and the design, administrative and legal groups necessary for creating and managing built environment.

The measurement of productivity in the contracting industry is particularly difficult, partly because of the heterogeneity of the products and partly because of the inadequacy of statistics of output and labour. However, it would appear that over the last 7 or 8 years productivity in new work has risen about 3·0 to 3·5% a year.[1] Productivity in maintenance work has probably risen only about 1·0 to 1·5%. The manufacture of materials and components is spread over many industries. In general, they have probably achieved increases in productivity comparable with those achieved in new construction work. The measurement of output in design and administrative work is very difficult but it is doubtful if productivity in these fields has risen very much.

The supply of innovations in management, construction techniques and component development, which has given rise to the increases in productivity, is by no means exhausted.[24] In established industries the rate at which firms adopt innovations is inevitably slow. It would appear likely that, even in the absence of revolutionary changes, productivity would continue to rise for many years. Some of the advantages from increased productivity might, of course, be lost if hours fall and holidays increase. The effect of sustained rises in productivity over a long period would be quite dramatic, even if the annual increases were only moderate. An annual rise of 2·25% continued to the end of the century would result in doubling the annual output per man, while it would be trebled if the annual rate of increase was 3·5%. Such increases in output may be difficult to achieve unless there are revolutionary changes in the product and in its construction. At present there do not appear to be any firm indications of such revolutionary changes. In fact, with the increase of engineering services in buildings, it would appear that the relative economic importance of structures and of building forms may decline. Substantial increases in the productivity of design and administration only appear likely if the processes are considerably streamlined.

The amount of land in Great Britain is more or less fixed. The amount can, of course, be marginally increased by draining and filling areas of shallow water around the coasts and estuaries but this process tends to be a heavy user of resources. Land for development can generally only be obtained by taking land currently used for some other purpose; this, in the long run, means taking land from agriculture.

The productivity of agricultural land varies considerably. A large proportion of it consists of rough grazing. Such land is of comparatively little value for agriculture or for development and is unlikely to be used for development purposes. Most development is likely to take place on land currently used for arable and permanent grass. About 5% of such land is likely to be required for development over the rest of the century. The output of agricultural land is increasing as husbandry improves, as better use is made of the land available, and as a higher proportion of land is used for the more valuable types of product. Although over the last decade, yields rose only by 1 or 2% per annum, the total value of net output rose over 3% per annum. It will seem that the output lost from farmland taken for development over the rest of the century could probably be replaced within three or four years. Even if the rate of improvement in productivity was only about 1·25% per annum, the remaining farmland would be able to produce enough food by the end of the century, assuming that the present proportion of food was imported, for a population larger than officially projected for that time. Changes in world conditions might, of course, result in it being expedient to import a lower proportion of food. It is, however, clear that the use of farmland for development is of minor importance compared with the size of the population and food import policy.

However, the best farmland produces about three times as much per acre as average land, and yields appear to be rising faster on the better land. It is therefore of some importance to steer development away from the better land as far as this is practical. The better land tends to be flat and well drained, and also the most suitable land for urban development. The costs of drainage and under-building tend to make the use of land unsuitable for development expensive to use. The value of the output from farmland is rarely sufficient to make it economic to save even the best farmland either by developing unsuitable land, or by saving land by using multistorey or multi-level development. Since some regions are endowed with better land than others, it may be difficult in some areas to find sufficient low grade land suitable for development. Similarly there is a very uneven distribution of land suitable for recreational purposes. For these reasons difficulties are likely to be met in finding suitable land for all purposes in some parts of the country, for example, in the Midlands, where land is on average of a high quality.

Scales, Standards and Forms of Development

Some estimate of the feasibility of achieving given scales, standards and forms of built environment can be obtained by relating estimates of the resources which would be required against estimates of probable output of the appropriate resources. It would appear that a moderate annual increase in the output of construction work, about 2%, the rate achieved over the last three years, would be sufficient in the long run to meet the resources required for the development, improvement and maintenance of the built environment at currently accepted good standards. Since if the construction industry maintained its current share of the labour force (this might be difficult since few women are employed) output would rise between a half and three-quarters per cent a year, productivity would only need to increase between one-and-a-quarter and one-and-a-half per cent a year. The level of productivity likely to be obtained will depend not only on the rates of productivity in new construction and maintenance but also on the relative importance of each. It would appear that too little is currently spent on maintenance and that the proportion of maintenance to new work is likely to rise substantially. This would result in a relative shift of labour from new work, in which productivity is likely to be high, to maintenance work, in which it is likely to be low. The average rate at which productivity would be likely to rise in such circumstances would tend to be rather less than the average of the two rates. Even so, the rate of increase of productivity should be more than adequate in the long run.

Clearly, present day standards are unlikely to continue to be acceptable over the rest of this century. The standard of living is likely to rise in step with increases in the productivity of the economy, and with it the standard of the built environment. It is thus likely that a large part of the expected increase in productivity in construction will be needed to meet the additional construction work associated with rising standards in the built environment, and will not be available for meeting the basic load. Over the last decade, the standard of living as measured by the consumption of goods and services per head, has increased by about 2·25% a year;[7] the expenditure per head on housing has increased at about the same rate. At this rate standards would be doubled by the end of the century. This would suggest that most of the likely improvement in general productivity would be needed to meet a rise in standards. It would appear unlikely that productivity in such an old established industry such as construction, much of the work of which is maintenance work, would rise faster than that of the economy as a whole. Thus, the proportion of national resources devoted to construction work would probably need to be raised in order to meet the growth in demand. By the end of the century the proportion might need to be about two-thirds greater than it is today. The larger the population the greater the proportion of national output likely to be necessary.

Housing is the largest category of building. The development, improvement and maintenance of housing and housing areas could account for nearly a half of the total cost of the built environment. While the current expenditure on new housing, if continued over the rest of the century, would be about sufficient to meet the needs for additional housing and to replace the equivalent of pre-1881 dwellings, the level of current expenditure on maintenance is quite inadequate and is declining in real terms.

At 1964 prices regular maintenance work costs £290 million a year, while at the standards adopted by local authorities the cost would be about £850 million a year, three times as much.[1] Nevertheless local authority standards tend to be minimal especially for decorations. The expenditure on improvements to dwellings since 1964 is estimated to be about £60 million a year. Thus, the annual expenditure is not much more than 1% of the estimated value of work outstanding in 1964. Little provision of garages or environmental improvement to the stock of housing is being carried out. In the meantime the physical condition of many dwellings is deteriorating and the number no longer worth repairing is increasing.

Even if the current rate of replacing dwellings was increased threefold it would take over a decade to replace the dwellings in the worst class, those with structural failures and serious physical deterioration. If, in the meantime, arrears of maintenance were not made good and regular maintenance was not carried out at an adequate standard, more dwellings would deteriorate beyond the point at which repair was worthwhile and it might be two or three decades before even the really unsatisfactory dwellings could be eliminated.

The resources required to carry out urgent housing improvement work and to raise the standards of regular maintenance to an acceptable level over the next decade would be equivalent to an immediate increase in the output of all construction of about an eighth and a continuation of increases in output as great as over the past decade. Clearly, even if increases on this scale could be obtained, they could not be devoted entirely to housing maintenance work. Moreover, if as suggested earlier, housing standards rose above those of today, meeting such rises in standard would absorb a substantial part of the annual increases in output.

In the absence of additional resources for housing, an alternative would be to reduce the rate of constructing new dwellings and to switch the resources released to maintenance work. For example, half the additional resources required could be obtained by reducing constructions to 300,000 dwellings a year. Further resources could be obtained by concentrating on the most economic forms of development. Since substantially less resources are required to improve a dwelling than to build a replacement, the rate at which additional satisfactory dwellings would be provided would be faster, even although the number of replacements was reduced. Moreover restored dwellings could be let much more cheaply than those newly built. If productivity continues to rise two or three times as fast in new work as in maintenance work, in the long run more output could be obtained from the same labour force by giving priority to maintenance work in the near future and postponing new work until later, when the comparative level of output in it would be relatively so much greater than today. By switching labour back to new work later in the century when the arrears of maintenance and improvement work had been completed, it would be possible to make good house construction sacrificed in the immediate future. In the long run the number of dwellings replaced need be no less; the stock would be younger and hence more likely to meet future needs.

The social categories of buildings have some features in common with housing. While the maintenance of such buildings has not generally been neglected to the extent of some housing, many of these buildings lack the equipment and amenities now considered essential. Often improvement would be more economic than replacement and lead to a more rapid build-up of adequate facilities. Such a policy would lead to more significant gains for the health buildings category than for the educational category for which the stock needs to be greatly expanded. Again for industrial buildings the major share of resources is likely to be needed for the improvement and rebuilding of the stock rather than for creating additional space. The sector of the economy with the greatest growth is likely to be services and it is there that a great deal of additional space will need to be created.

The extent to which buildings can be improved rather than replaced depends on the extent to which urban roads and town layouts need to be developed, and people and their town facilities need to be relocated on a regional scale. Clearly, none of these activities can take place without the demolition of many existing buildings and their replacement in a new location. The scale on which this work could be carried out would be increased to the extent that the buildings which needed to be demolished were those with the greatest degree of obsolescence. Thus the speed at which urban roads can be improved, by far the largest element in main road costs, depends on the speed at which buildings can be replaced. Similarly, the speed at which new settlement patterns can be created by overspill to new and expanded towns also depends on the speed at which buildings can be replaced. Again this suggests that the priority for building demolition and replacement as distinct from improvement should be given to buildings which both have a high degree of obsolescence and a high priority for road improvement or which house processes which need to be moved to a new location.

The road costs arise largely from the need to expand road capacity, particularly in urban areas. The rate of need depends on the rate at which vehicle ownership increases. Road capacity can also, of course, be increased by traffic management, by the electronic control of traffic and by design of vehicles; all these solutions, of course, have their own costs. Because of the rate at which vehicle ownership has been increasing in relation to increases in road capacity there is already a considerable shortage of capacity. To make this shortage good in the next few years would require an increase in current expenditure on roads of three or fourfold. While the expenditure required for other transport is much smaller than for roads, there is a need for heavy expenditure during the next decade to meet the expected increase in air transport, to modernise the railways and to rebuild the docks to meet the needs of container traffic, other new methods of goods handling and large ships. Public utilities are again a large item and some of the work has a high priority in the next decade, for example, work associated with natural gas installations, water, and drainage.

Thus, while in the absence of a large shift of national resources to construction, the annual output is only likely to increase slowly, there are needs for a considerable immediate expansion in the construction, improvement and maintenance of many categories of built facility. Unless there is a large scale shift of resources in the near future, many needs will inevitably remain unsatisfied and it will be necessary to decide where the priorities should lie. Probably priority will be given to facilities which are related to production since, in the long run, these will tend to result in a larger national output and in the availability of additional resources for the extension and improvement of the built environment. If priorities are decided in this way the scope for choice between better housing, social services and leisure facilities will tend to be limited.

Of course, the standards of the built environment can be raised in a number of ways; by raising the standards at which facilities are currently built; by a faster rate of replacing facilities in the existing stock; by improvements to existing facilities and by higher standards of maintenance. Generally, the rate at which new facilities are added to the stock is rather low. At any one time only 2% or 3% of the facilities in the stock are less than a year old. Raising the standards at which new facilities are built therefore tends to be a slow method of raising general standards. The estimates given earlier were based on the assumption that only 1% to 2% of the facilities in the stock would be replaced each year. Even on this basis it appeared likely that the proportion of national resources devoted to construction work would need to be substantially increased. Unless either a substantially greater share of national resources can be devoted to construction work or new techniques can be found which would allow structures to be built for substantially less than today without a reduction in their expected durability, it seems unlikely that the rates of replacement could be much increased above those assumed. Standards can generally be raised most economically by better maintenance and improvements to the existing stock of buildings.

The resources required for the built environment are also affected by urban form. Dwellings in four-storey flatted blocks outside London are nearly a quarter more expensive than equivalent dwellings in houses and bungalows; equivalent dwellings in twelve-storey blocks are two-thirds more expensive.[1] The provision of garages with high blocks is also more expensive than with houses; while there are savings on development (roads and services) costs of these tend to be small. Maintenance and management costs also tend to rise with the number of storeys. Since densities tend to rise only moderately with increases in the number of storeys, the costs of saving land by building high tend to be considerable, between £40,000 and £50,000 an acre where high blocks are used.[1] This is rarely worthwhile from a national point of view unless either the occupiers place a very high value on living in high flatted blocks, for which there is little evidence, or high density development reduces overspill sufficiently for travelling and other costs to offset the higher costs of development. It is difficult to find situations in which the balance of external economies would make this type of development viable. National housing costs would be raised 10% if average densities were raised from 59 to 80 habitable rooms per acre by using 50% houses and 30% high flats. Financially, this type of high density development is rarely worthwhile because land prices (outside Central London) do not generally reach high enough levels, because site prices per acre tend to rise with density, thus reducing the savings from high density development and because with land at high prices rents tend to be higher than most people can afford.

While costs per square foot rise for other building types as well as for housing, the rise appears to be less steep for wide buildings than for those which need to be narrow enough to be lit naturally from both sides. Even so, it would generally be cheaper to use multi-storey car parks for the cars of industrial workers than to house the processes themselves in multi-storey buildings. It has sometimes been suggested that large groups of people, even complete settlements, should be housed in a single large building. This would involve a large increase in circulation space, either vertical or horizontal, within the building. Such circulation areas would be more expensive to construct and operate than circulation space provided outside. A large proportion of the area of such a building would need to be artificially lit and ventilated. Unless energy became relatively much cheaper than it is today, the costs-in-use of such space would tend to be far greater than that of conventional buildings. Of course, in really noisy situations sealed double glazing and a largely artificial environment is necessary in order to obtain relative quiet in the buildings. However, the number of such situations can be limited by the use of precinct and other planning forms. Moreover, if eventually road vehicles were electrified and aircraft were forbidden to fly low over towns, the problem of noise in towns would cease to be serious.

The multi-level use of space also adds to development and operation costs. Decked shopping and service cores are about five times as expensive as those developed on the ground. Land saved by the use of multi-storey car parks and decking over roads and car parking tends to cost £40,000 to £50,000 per acre. In fact, the amount of land which can be saved by multi-level development is rather small since such a small proportion of land is used for the base of buildings. For example, in a conventional new town only about an eighth of the land is covered with buildings, a further eighth is used for private access, storage and parking, a sixth for roads and nearly three-fifths for gardens and open space.[25] Nevertheless the additional real costs of multi-level development and parking in large commercial centres may be worth accepting because of the convenience obtained by increasing the compactness of the centre. The occupiers will often bear the financial costs of such developments.

The size, shape and form of settlements also affects the resources required to construct them and frequently, even more, the resources needed to operate and use them. It is the main road system and journeys on it which are mainly affected. The costs of the main road network appear to rise with the size of the settlement, although at less than in proportion to size. In a new town situation the costs of the main road network per person appear to rise about 25%, from about £80 to £100 for a doubling in size from 50,000 and by 20% to about £120 per person for an increase from 100,000 to 250,000 persons. It is probable that a further doubling would add about another £10 to the costs per head. The costs of travelling on the network would also be increased. Since travelling costs are incurred throughout the life of the settlement, the effect of increasing the size of settlement on them tends to be five to ten times as important as those for construction. Differences in the shape and form of settlement can have cost effects for the main road network of about the same order. Even without considering extreme urban forms, the costs of development work could be raised by 5% to 10% as a result of using unconventional forms of building and development.

It would appear that over the rest of the century, development on new land may be required for a population equal to about half the current population. About two-thirds of this number would be additional population and the balance would be people who, because of the lower densities obtained on redevelopment, could not be re-accommodated in the areas in which they formerly lived. This population could be accommodated partly by limited growth to existing settlements, partly by large scale forced growth to existing settlements and partly in new settlements. The new and expanded settlements could be organised in different ways and in different locations. While most existing areas of urban development would remain, the urban pattern of Britain could be radically changed.

Regional Resources

As explained earlier land is not of a uniform quality over the whole country. Some regions are already built-up more extensively than others,

and some have far more land than others which is unsuitable for development either because it is too high and steep, or because it is very valuable
for agriculture. Again some regions have a shortage of land suitable for
recreational activities.

Again the availability of building materials and contracting resources is
less satisfactory in some regions than others. The most suitable clay for
manufacturing cheap bricks is mostly in the south-east of Britain, an area
which is also rich in materials suitable for cement production. While the
larger contracting organisations tend to be national rather than regional,
their resources, and particularly their labour, tend to be located in those
areas in which most constructional work has taken place in the past. Thus,
the regions and areas of greatest need, those in which the stock of built
facilities is the oldest and the least cared for, will be those with comparative
shortages of contracting resources. Unless in future such regions grow at a
comparatively slower rate than in the past, contracting resources are likely
to need to be transferred from the better off regions. The greater the
growth of population and development in the regions of greatest need, the
larger the scale on which resources are likely to need transferred. The
difficulty of making such transfers of contracting resources might reduce
the rate at which regional standards could be equalised.

For example, for housing it would appear that the South-East and East
Anglia are likely to have some excess capacity while most other regions
would be short of capacity. The greatest shortages appear likely to be in
the North-West and in Scotland where the relatively poor position in the
case of new construction capacity is intensified by a combination of past
and current poor standards of maintenance.

Life Styles, Values and Finance

So far, attention has been centred on the real resources that would appear
necessary to achieve the various scales, standards and forms of urban
development which have been considered. Real resources have been
measured in terms of land and construction work. The scales of resources
likely to be required have been compared with the availability of land and
with the output of construction work which might be feasible given certain
proportions of the national labour force and certain rates of improvement in
productivity. These proportions and rates have in turn been compared
with possible movements in the economy as a whole. However, the real
resources are unlikely to be moved in the way required unless finance is
available in the required amounts and at the right time. The availability
of finance depends on peoples' willingness to use wealth in this way and on
the existence of a mechanism to enable finance to have the required effects.
If, for example, people preferred to spend their incomes on consumer goods
and services, rather than on built facilities, labour and capital would be
attracted to the industries catering for consumers' goods and services and
the resources available for construction work would be inadequate. Such a
situation might, of course, be modified by government action, for example,

by increasing taxes on other goods and services, and using the revenue to subsidise the finance of construction work.

As pointed out earlier, nearly half the resources required for built facilities are required for housing. Housing dominates both the costs and the quality of the built environment. Inevitably, if the general standard of housing was improved, even only to broadly Parker Morris standards, housing costs would rise. Rebuilding and improving the existing stock of housing to the extent suggested earlier would raise housing costs on average by about two thirds. The poorer households would find it difficult, some impossible, to meet such costs without assistance. Thus, unless action is taken at government level to direct housing grants to those in greatest need, the improvements in the standards of housing would be unlikely to take place.[1]

Moreover, while the ability to devote greater proportions of income to housing would increase as real incomes rose, many households might not value housing sufficiently to be prepared to pay comparatively more for it. It is notable that over the five years 1962-67 expenditure per head on housing only increased about the same as total consumers' expenditure.[7] While expenditure per head on fuel and light increased slightly more than average, that on furnishing increased less that average. In contrast, the expenditure on motoring increased about five times as much as average. The propensity of households to spend on housing could be increased by suitable changes in the incidence of taxation and by simpler market arrangements. For example, local rates are related to the value of the dwelling and are a direct tax on housing quality. A shift of taxation away from housing to other goods and services would reduce the real costs of housing and increase the costs of other goods and services, and hence increase the comparative value for money which housing would offer.

The purchase and exchange of dwellings is complex and expensive. It might be made simpler and cheaper by the extension of property registration, by the provision of a clearing house to facilitate the exchange of dwellings subject to mortgage and by the computerisation of offers to buy and sell dwellings. The availability of housing for rent and of private capital in the supply of housing would tend to be increased if owners could charge economic rents and depreciate capital against tax, and if grants were available to help the needy to pay economic rents. The rate at which existing housing is improved would tend to be increased if more private capital was available, if grants were larger and simpler to obtain and if local authorities guaranteed the future of housing areas and participated in their improvement by undertaking work to the infra-structure.

If the conditions for a supply of housing were to change on the lines indicated above, it would no longer be neccesary for a large proportion of dwellings to be in public ownership.

In the business sector expenditure on built facilities does not depend on the relative values attached to the facilities, as it does for housing and other consumption goods, but on the effect of the facilities on the surplus on the capital employed by the enterprise. Built facilities will be replaced or improved if as a result the total costs of the enterprise are reduced or the revenues increased by a sufficient margin. The standard of the built facilities will vary with the type of business and with its level of efficiency. The amount worth spending will usually be judged after allowance for taxation. Often standards of construction are depressed because of the incidence of taxation and of the difficulty of raising capital. Frequently expenditure on buildings appears to be judged against turnover rather than against the resulting returns, so that buildings housing efficient firms in types of businesses with large turnovers per unit area tend to be opulent while at the other extreme those housing marginal firms in types of business producing little value per unit area tend to be squalid. Low standard buildings will tend to remain in use, particularly where the supply of building is limited, since they provide accommodation for marginal firms. Standards would tend to be raised if taxes on building quality, such as rating, were reduced or eliminated, if grants were provided to stimulate new building and improvements or if minimum physical standards were enforced.

Buildings and development in the public sector are provided partly for the use of industrial and commercial organisations, partly for organisations providing a social or administrative service and partly directly for use by the public. Since nationalised industries and public authority trading services are generally expected to provide something near a commercial return on the capital they employ, their criteria for building standards will not be dissimilar to those of business organisations. Other public organisations tend to operate under conditions which are different both from those in the business and in the personal sectors of the economy. The decisions on standards and priorities are generally made by administrators who are neither responsible for providing the financial resources, which are determined globally, nor experienced as users of the facilities. Consequently, it is in the interests of the occupiers to press for the highest possible standards. All too frequently the standards set for new facilities are too high in relation to the resources available for their national provision and too high in relation to the standards possible with the resources available for maintaining existing facilities. The difficulty of reaching decisions is even greater in the case of the facilities provided directly for public use. In this sector not only is it difficult to measure the full incidence of the costs but generally it is difficult to compare the satisfactions that the community would obtain from different ways of using the resources available. This difficulty appears likely to grow as real wealth grows and urban policy options are less concerned with the scales of provision and more with standards, forms and locations, and as choice increasingly lies between options, some of which provide a basis for new and unexperienced life styles. Despite the difficulties mentioned earlier it might be worth considering whether under conditions of increasing affluence and a greater equality of income the community might be better served if some publicly-provided facilities were transferred to the private sector where the market would indicate where demand lay. Individuals might be prepared to purchase the use of facilities for which they were unwilling to pay through taxation and in this way more resources might be made available for providing the built environment.

The future patterns of urbanisation depend on the future population and life-styles, on technological innovations, on available resources and on the extent to which the community is able to communicate its sense of values and make effective its judgement on the use of resources. The effect of higher birth rates, the fall in activity rates, the greater demand for leisure and a more comfortable industrial life would be to reduce the volume of output resources. The more the resources were limited the more important it would be to improve rather than replace older facilities and the more the past patterns of urbanisation would restrict future patterns. Unless national productivity increases much faster than it has in the past, or a much larger proportion of resources are devoted to construction, the rate of redeveloping the existing urban environment will not be sufficiently rapid to enable either past neglect to be made good and standards substantially raised or sufficiently large to support radical changes in the patterns of urbanisation. Unless the more revolutionary changes in construction occur there would be little possibility of substantially shortening the life of facilities. However, built facilities tend to be very flexible and adaptable. Considerable changes in life-styles could take place without radical changes in the built form. Even if the scale of development was large enough to allow considerable changes in the locational patterns of urban development, the inertia of established communities might impose considerable restraints on such changes. Regionally and locally conflicting claims on land might impose some restraints. Since built form is and appears likely to continue to be relatively permanent and to act as a restraint on future patterns of urbanisation, it is all the more important that decisions in this field should be taken in the light of the best possible predictions about requirements for the future.

REFERENCES

[1] P. A. Stone, *Urban Development in Britain*: Standards, Costs and Resources 1964-2004, Population and Housing, Cambridge University Press (to be published December 1969).

[2] *Statistics of Education 1963 and 1964*, Department of Education and Science, H.M.S.O., 1964 and 1965.

[3] *Ministry of Education Committee on Higher Education* (Chairman: Lord Robbins) 1961-63, Report 1963, Cmnd. 2154, H.M.S.O., 1963.

[4] *Ministry of Labour Gazette*, H.M.S.O., July 1963 and January 1965.

[5] *The National Plan*, Cmnd. 2764, H.M.S.O., 1965.

[6] W. Beckerman and Associates, *The British Economy in 1975*, Cambridge University Press, 1965.

[7] *National Income and Expenditure*, Central Statistical Office, 1968.

[8] B. R. Mitchell and P. Deanne, *Abstract of British Historical Statistics*, Cambridge University Press, 1962.

[9] P. Willmott, 'Some Social Trends', *Urban Studies*, Vol. 6, No. 3, Nov. 1969.

[10] *Housing Statistics, Great Britain,* Ministry of Housing and Local Government, H.M.S.O., various dates.

[11] R. N. Percival, 'Shopping Centres in Britain', *Journal of Town Planning Institute,* Vol. 51, No. 8, Sep.-Oct. 1965, pp. 329-33.

[12] Heather Bliss, 'Local Changes in Shopping Potential', *Journal of Town Planning Institute,* Vol. 51, No. 8, Sep.-Oct. 1965, pp. 334-7.

[13] R. J. Green and R. M. Beaumont, 'The Size of Shopping Centres', *Journal of Town Planning Institute,* Vol. 48, No. 10, Dec. 1962, pp. 311-14.

[14] *Shopping in Coventry,* City of Coventry Development Plan, First Quinquennial Review, Coventry Corporation, 1964.

[15] *The School Building Survey 1962,* Department of Education and Science, H.M.S.O., 1965.

[16] *The Hospital Plan,* Ministry of Health, H.M.S.O., 1966.

[17] B. D. Cullen and J. N. Jeffery, *Running Costs of Hospital Buildings,* Design Series 65, Building Research Station, 1968.

[18] J. C. Tanner, *Forecasts of Vehicle Ownership in Great Britain,* Road Research Laboratory, note June 1965.

[19] *Sample Survey of the Roads and Traffic of Great Britain,* Road Research Laboratory Technical Paper No. 62, H.M.S.O., 1962.

[20] *Transport Policy,* Cmnd. 3057, H.M.S.O., 1966.

[21] *Port Development—An Interim Plan,* National Ports Council, H.M.S.O., 1965.

[22] *Water Supplies in South East England,* Water Resources Board, H.M.S.O., 1966.

[23] *Interim Report on Water Resources in the North,* Water Resources Board, H.M.S.O., 1967.

[24] P. A. Stone, *Building Economy,* Pergamon Press, 1966.

[25] P. A. Stone, 'Housing, Town Development, Land and Costs', *The Estates Gazette Ltd.,* 1963.

[26] P. A. Stone, 'The Impact of Urban Development on the Use of Land and other Resources', *Journal of Town Planning Institute,* Vol. 47, No. 5, 1961.

RESOURCES AND ENVIRONMENTAL CONSTRAINTS

EMRYS JONES

The main aim of this paper is to assess the possible demands of urbanisation
on some of the resources of Britain over the next thirty years, and to suggest
the extent to which these resources may have in them specific constraints
on future urban growth and its location. It is assumed that the emphasis
must be on natural economic resources and manpower, though many
constraints will be social and these cannot be ignored. The starting-point
must be the situation today, when many of these resources are already
being extensively used and contribute to a relatively stable pattern of
settlement which would be difficult to change. Although technology and
society are dynamic, the environmental base is relatively fixed. Our
appreciation and assessment of it is changing but within recognisable
limits, and the result is a general equilibrium which enables us to identify
a broad location pattern together with certain regional characteristics.
Generally speaking this equilibrium, as far as urban settlement is concerned,
is one which emerged in the later stages of the industrial revolution. However much we are moving away from 19th-century technology, its imprint is
absolutely clear. The broad distribution of urban population today is not
radically different from that of half a century ago, or even a century ago.
This is partly due to the fact that most of us are still living in towns and
cities which have grown over a very long time, partly because inertia often
accounts for accretions to existing towns; and partly because much of our
manufacturing industry and service industry has grown up in and around
existing centres, and where population was already dense.

We do not, therefore, start with a clean sheet. We start with a country
which has few parallels in having had most of its surface transformed
physically, its resources exploited, and its different parts having gained
social as well as economic values. The interplay between environment and
society in Britain has been going on for a very long time. But the position
at the moment is one largely dictated by the economic and social demands of
the industrial revolution. This must be stressed because new and future
development must take place not only within a physical framework but
largely within a social appraisal of that framework which is deeply rooted,
and within a built environment which has roots in an outmoded technology.
Moreover, the identification of life modes with specific regions of the
country is well established. The north is not only a direction, but a way of
life. Water carried from Wales to Liverpool has political ripples on its

*Emrys Jones is Professor of Social Geography, London School of Economics and
Political Science*

surface. It is with this in mind that we look briefly at the land and the sort of demands which will be made on it in the next thirty years or so.

The topic of land use in Britain has often hinged on the encroachment of the town on the countryside. The assumption that we must preserve a sharp distinction between these two is not acceptable as a base on which to predict the future pattern of settlement. This is because we are more concerned today with urban process than with urban growth, that is, with the diffusion of amenities, attitudes and values rather than the movement of people into towns. To ignore the dichotomy is naturally difficult, because physically speaking there is still a distinction between town and country, made even more pronounced in the last couple of decades by green belt policies whose aim is the containing of the town. Environmentally speaking about 11% of Britain is urban and the remainder rural. The countryside tradition dies hard, but the old argument that urban spread must be contained and checked because it was threatening agricultural production is now a dead letter. Assuming that this country's policy on importing a large percentage of our food is maintained, and that the equilibrium is not unduly upset by tariff changes and so on, then the part played by our own agricultural areas in feeding the growing population can be more than maintained in the future by its increasing productivity. The average increase in agricultural productivity of 1·3% per annum which we are now experiencing will more than offset the land likely to be consumed by increased building. Trends continuing as they are, agriculture can more than hold its own against the encroachment of towns and the demands of a growing population. What the encroachment is likely to be will be dealt with below.

There are other demands on the land, more particularly recreational. National parks and areas of outstanding natural beauty and other recreational areas in Britain at present account for about three million acres. There is little likelihood of a clash between their use and farming interests. Many areas of natural beauty can exist happily side by side with crop and animal production. National parks are mainly in the highland zone of Britain where farming is either marginal or is dominated by sheep and where forestry is active. There is no clash. Wibberley envisages a future which will particularise rural land use more sharply. Thus land in the richer south-east might well evolve towards a mechanised farming which will make its use increasingly exclusive. Land farmed in this way cannot be used for recreation. This fact could be an important constraint on the type of urban development which would be tolerated in southern Britain in the future. There may be interdigitation of urban and rural, but not the haphazard mixing which would involve multiple use of the land. On the other hand highland grazing combines well with recreational activities, and this might well lead to multiple use. But this delineating of recreational areas, as well as an increase in farm mechanisation, will force the townsman to appreciate the use being made of the countryside. Moreover this positive identification also means that the spread of settlement cannot be indiscriminate over the nine-tenths of Britain that is rural at the moment. This might limit the amount of land available for urban growth. There are further areas in highland Britain where extensive growth is unlikely. Almost all the land over 800′ suffers from exposure, steep slopes and high rainfall. Over the last two thousand years this highland area has, with exceptions, had little or no settlement. It accounts for about a quarter of the land surface of England and Wales and three-quarters of Scotland. Although much of it is ideal for seasonal recreation, it is difficult to envisage conditions where permanent settlements will more than touch the fringes. The seasonal climatic exposure which is a feature of these uplands need not be a deterrent for the summer use of cottages, and these in turn, as they become available to more people, could affect the acceptance of high densities in towns and cities.

Modification of the broad outlines of existing settlement patterns within the next thirty years is unlikely to be revolutionary, although there may be a polarisation of different kinds of urban land-use. If the land area is enlarged by reclamation from the sea, it will be only a marginal addition, and even the possibilities of living over tidal water—or under it—will have little more than strictly local implications within the foreseeable future. The run-down of existing settlement will be very gradual and much of it will be rebuilt within the existing framework of the urban infrastructure. Future change depends more on what form future towns will take than on the extent of that growth.

Another vital resource is water, though it is unlikely that its supply will be critical in relocating urban settlement. Most of Britain's needs are supplied by surface water which is directly related to rainfall. Much of the remainder comes from underground sources, themselves indirectly dependent on rainfall. A simple equation between water derived from rainfall and the present needs of the population of Britain is only fairly reassuring. Although the former comes to about 40,000 million gallons a day and the latter to about 25,000 million gallons a day, there are two causes for concern. Firstly, if we think in terms of the steadily increasing use of water, the margin begins to look precarious long before A.D. 2000. Secondly, nature is not so considerate as to lavish its resources at the spot where it is needed, or at the right time.

Increase in the domestic use of water has been dramatic in the past few decades and is likely to continue so. In 1938 the population of England and Wales used 1,360 million gallons a day, in 1950, 1,770 million gallons and in 1960, 2,470 million gallons, the last an 80% increase on the first. Assuming no more than a marginal change in trend, by A.D. 2000 household consumption will be in the region of 7,000 to 8,000 million gallons a day. The crisis here may be focussed more on storage capacity, which is increasing at a considerably lower speed than the demand, and which really controls the situation.

Household consumption looks small beside the demands of industry. Electricity production is the greatest consumer, using about 15,000 million gallons a day, though much if this is returned to the cycle. The output of electricity has nearly doubled in every decade since 1920, and although the rate of increase may fall off, nothing but a considerable increase can be envisaged for some time. The chemical industry, steel and paper manufacture are other considerable users. The total used by industry is probably about 20,000 million gallons a day. Atomic energy stations are the greatest users of all and this is why their location is coastal with one exception. Sea water is used, thus introducing a radical change in power production location. The exception is Trawsfynydd, where an artificial lake meets demands in a high region where rain is plentiful.

One other considerable use of water can be foreseen—irrigation, which could generate a demand of 10,000 million gallons per day. In the drier south-east there are other demands on water, for example, for compensating loss in canals, for recreation—in particular fishing, which is the sport attracting most people in Britain, and for boating. Water is becoming an increasingly important element in our environment, but so far we have been reluctant to view it as the valuable resource it is. The immediate need is for conservation, otherwise the balance of supply and needs will be upset very soon.

Irregularities in supplies already exist—as the numerous periodic droughts attest—simply because of the uneven regional distribution of this resource. Water is most plentiful where population is most sparse, and the greatest conurbation in the country lies in a basin which has relatively little rain. To some extent lowland England is compensated for lack of ground water by the use of underground resources, but the water table is lowering, an indication that we are locally overdrawn in this particular resource.

As indicated above, the need for water has so far only affected the location of one major energy producing process. For smaller quantities of water, and particularly for domestic consumption, it has been assumed that redistribution can be easily handled. Like most great world cities, our own have had to look constantly to more distant supplies to meet an increasing need, and the Lake District and Wales are already being effectively tapped. There is no reason to suppose that in the foreseeable future with greater conservation and extensive storage and distribution systems, water supply need be a critical element in changing patterns of settlement. Although the location of sources of energy might well show a pattern radically different from that of mid-1960's, the sources which are themselves remote can feed a grid which allows the greatest flexibility. For instance, Trawsfynydd has no industrial significance for North Wales.

The geographical bases of industry in this country have widened very considerably since the heyday of the industrial revolution. The coincidence between economic activity and the major sources of nineteenth-century power (coal) and raw material (iron) no longer holds. Reference has been made to the dispersion of one source of energy—electricity. In the same way an increasing source of energy—oil—can be freely distributed with little locational constraint: but the major associated industries—refining and chemical—are most favourably sited on the coast at the point of import. The third energy source, natural gas, will possibly bring in a new orientation towards the North Sea. It will certainly encourage the setting up of new industrial complexes along this coast. But again, the commodity itself can be easily distributed. In view of this it would be comforting to think that much of the diverse smaller industry of Britain could be located almost anywhere in the country. Growth points are increasingly the creation of transport nodes rather than the centre of a resource. But all industry is not quite as footloose as some planners would like to think. To admit locational freedom in sources of raw material and energy is to deal with only one of the three major locational factors. The other two—labour and markets—do not respond so readily to manipulation, and may be equally strong constraints on flexibility, although manpower is becoming increasingly mobile. Fundamentally a large proportion of manufacturing activity in Britain owes its location to inertia reflecting the outcome of locational forces of half a century ago. This is not unimportant if capital investment has to be taken into account. But there is no reason to doubt that the future pattern of industrialisation will depart more and more from the traditional industrial revolution mould which still seems to shape it.

Control over location does not necessarily imply that in heavy industry, for example, activities will be morcellated. In some activities of this kind there are strong economic arguments for even greater centralisation (e.g. in steel manufacturing), possibly reducing the number of centres quite dramatically in Britain. Location of these few centres is then a matter of choice. Other basic activities will lend themselves more readily to dispersal in smaller units. The locational balance which may eventually emerge will probably embrace the whole country and will reflect economic and social policies rather than environmental resource constraints. Incidentally, this means that if the present trend towards increasing regional control continues, it may have to be resolved by planning the complimentarity of regions rather than by a balancing of industrial activities within each region. That is, we can expect increasing specialising of regional rôles within a national structure rather than the elusive safeguard of diversity within regional structure.

If this is so, it will mean a certain amount of freeing of the resource restraints which have decided the pattern of urbanisation during the last hundred years. In any case these material resources are becoming relatively less important. More consideration must be given to resources less tangible and easy to define, but increasing in significance, more particularly perhaps the desirability or otherwise of certain parts of Britain as locations in which to enjoy life. Recent 'mental maps' of Britain have shown without any doubt that in the minds of most people some areas are much more desirable than others. The southern part of Britain, and in particular the south-east, ranks very high in most images of what constitutes a desirable environment. These ideas are based partly on a desire for more sunshine and warmth, less rain, a less harsh environment, and a vague association with affluence. That cities as such do not necessarily engender the most desirable image is shown by the fact that London does not fully share the very favourable image the south has in the minds of most people in Britain.

But given a complete freedom of choice there is little doubt there would be a considerable redistribution of population.

Comparative freedom of locational choice will in fact increase by virtue of another trend, and that is the relative decrease in the number of people involved in manufacturing (secondary activities). The last century and the first half of this saw primary activities sink to an almost insignificant level as far as the number of people involved were concerned. Now tertiary activities are beginning to relegate secondary to a much lesser rôle in a similar way. Relatively speaking there is a greater degree of locational freedom in the tertiary activities and consequently less constraint. Further, we are now seeing the beginning of the growth of quaternary activities which may have even less constraints. No development of towns and cities in the future will be able to ignore the changing relationships between these classes of activities. As the proportion of workers in services and in communications increases, the freeing from locational constraints could become a real possibility. These are necessary conditions for a Webber type of urban development, though whether they are sufficient conditions for complete urban dispersion is a debatable point bearing in mind some of the social factors which will be mentioned later.

It is now appropriate to return to an assessment of what the likely demands of physical urban growth are going to be on the land and the possible urban patterns that might emerge, with the above considerations in mind. A population growth to about 75 million people in the year 2000 is assumed. Table I gives an estimate of some of the figures which have to be borne in mind.

TABLE I

INCREASE IN URBAN LAND, 1900-2000

	Million Acres	% Total Land Use
1900	2·0	5·4
1930	2·6	7·0
1940	3·2	8·6
1950	3·6	9·7
1960	4·0	10·8
1970	4·4	11·9
1980	4·9	13·2
1990	5·3	14·3
2000	5·7	15·4
	6·0 (Stone)	16·2 (Stone)

The figures have been calculated by Robin Best. Peter Stone has calculated that the projected population increase can be met by a continuing programme of 375,999 houses per annum, and at 50 persons per acre (12-15 households), 1·6 m. acres will be built upon between 1970 and 2000 (Best calculates 1·3 m., area). If the additional building is at half this density, then the need will be 2·1 m. acres (Stone). This is roughly the same as the extent of urbanised land in 1900. The total will increase to 6·0 m. acres and the percentage to 16·2.

Two quite separate issues arise: (a) what form will the new settlement take, and (b) where will the additional building take place?

The first is very closely linked to the problem of densities. The assumption made in Best's table of land use, that we will continue to build at approximately the densities of new towns, may be seriously questioned. In view of the ideas advocated by Webber, even halving current densities may seem only a modest step. In fact, Best himself refers to the new town densities as medium to high compared with average densities in British towns, and they are nearly twice the density proposed by the Reith Committee of 1946. Against this must be placed the trend of tightening up densities even in new towns (from ten households per acre in early neighbourhoods to 14 and 15 in later ones: residential density in Cumbernauld is 27 per acre). This is not a response to the need to save land, but is a result of cost considerations and the architectural appeal of higher density housing.

Low densities commend themselves to planners because they seem to offer a better physical environment: to most town dwellers they represent a more desirable standard of living. In view of the conditions associated with high-density Victorian towns, this is understandable. In Great Britain most of the managerial class, who account for 1 in 10, live at low densities, 22% at over 12 dwellings per acres, 29% at 7 per acre and 40% at 2 per acre: whereas in the unskilled class 32% have no garden and 43% live at over 12 per acre. On the whole the half-acre garden is a sign of affluence, the allotment a sign of need. New towns in the U.S. are being built at 6 dwellings per acre and some are planned at little more than three per acre. In South Africa the upper limit is 5 per acre, though presumably this refers to the white population only! Milton Keynes may aim for an average of about 8 per acre, with a range of between 6 and 10 per acre. We seem set for a very suburban future. The simple equation of low density with good environmental conditions is so naïve that it must be questioned and a more sophisticated approach must surely emerge in the near future. The elaborate range of densities suggested in the South Hampshire study is a recognition of changing needs at different stages in the life cycle which is long overdue. But what is also needed is a more adaptable approach to demands in society which range from the need for full participation to the need for complete privacy.

The average density of new developments, therefore, will encompass a wide range and a great variety of form: but it is safe to assume nevertheless that the average will be low. If one accepts the average of about 8, and assume that the kinds of houses demanded will not change radically, then it means that by 2000 only one-sixth of the surface of the country will be committed to what we call urban functions, and only about one-twentieth will have new developments. This assumes, further, that our cities will not become emptied of residents. Although there is a marked trend towards a decreasing population in city centres, this is unlikely to increase the demand for expansion more than marginally. Moreover, it will be partly offset by the rehabilitation of older residential areas in cities. Looking at the community as a whole, the spatial demands of the next thirty years for new settlement will be comparatively modest even allowing for plenty of flexibility in form.

Physical constraints, though they may be locally significant, will not in any way be critical.

As far as location is concerned, the minimal probable developments of the next thirty years, a modest lowering of residential densities, may be insufficient to change the existing distribution of settlement very radically. There could, on the one hand, be a consolidation of the existing distribution. Milton Keynes will certainly confirm the London-Midland link, and there are other pointers to the emergence of a kind of megalopolis based on a London-Midlands-North axis (this was tentatively outlined in a recent issue of Ekistics, but this is no more than a consolidation of the 'hour-glass' and the 'coffin' with which we have long been familiar). Modifications of this closely-knit urban belt might be coastal and estuarine. Perhaps the most likely are (a) a Severn development linking Bristol and South Wales in a 'Randstad Severn' and (b) city growth on the east coast—possibly linked with a Wash barrage, for example. This would alter the pattern of settlement in the south, but would leave open the traditionally empty parts of upland Britain, though presumably these would be linked with urban development through recreational activities. This assumes the expansion of existing towns, or the establishment of new towns along traditional patterns.

Alternatively, future growth could have a much more broken pattern, less constrained by the existing settlement, possibly of ribbon development or even of great fragmentation. This assumes that the comparative easing of location constraints on economic activities envisaged above will be recognised and exploited. There is little indication of this so far. But if it happens then we can expect a response to the pull of the visually and climatically attractive parts of Britain. Deep-rooted sectional feeling will see to it that this will not be exclusively a pull to the south coast, but it does point to areas outside the traditionally heavily urbanised parts of Britain. There are two constraints on the greater overall spread, one is the advisability of consolidating fairly large tracts of country for agriculture and recreation —though there could be considerable interdigitation of settlement with the latter—and the second is the cost of linking these new settlements and of communications generally. Greater mobility and faster travel may foster concentration or dispersion of activities with equal ease.

Wibberley's view of the possible increase in mechanised farming in the more rewarding south-east would certainly include the need for restricting indiscriminate urban spread here. Urban expansion, in the physical sense, should be no more than confined corridors, linking existing towns and cities with the coast or with inland recreational areas. If anything, Wibberley's model of an urban core, then a zone of mechanised farming, followed by a zone of upland farming with recreation in the highland zone, rather presupposes the greater centralisation of at least some activities.

These minimal changes do not excite the imagination. In a way they represent a 'sensible' forecast. The future envisaged is a familiar one in so far as the present is seen as a point along a continuum from a known past to a probable future. Our response to slowly changing conditions is one of accommodation. Webber has pointed out that in the history of industrial civilisation response comes after the change has appeared. True, we are now in a position to forecast change and we can prepare for it and condition our responses. One of the consistently forecast changes which might stimulate dramatic development is of a threefold increase in G.N.P. and in real personal incomes. This could mean the loosening of one of the major constraints in the past—the economic—but whether this will break the mould of urban living as we know it is doubtful. If it does, then the word urban may become obsolete. Many people may choose to have no more than a *pied à terre* at their job location, which will demand less and less of their working time, and a second home where privacy, solitude and other environmental factors are given first priority. Europe will be drawn into the pattern of our lives, more particularly if the demand for sunshine encourages weekends or seasons out of Britain. Maximal changes are exciting. But within Britain even these will be subject to the kind of constraints with which this paper deals.

The manipulation of future locational patterns and even the forms which urban growth will take, are unlikely to be as simple as the above suggests. It has been assumed that present-day trends will be allowed to continue rather than be drastically revised. The major assumption has been that the industrial revolution has made an imprint which will be difficult to delete. It has also created a set of regional foci which themselves have engendered regional attitudes and demands and these may increase inertia. Metropolitan England persists with a geographical base today which is oddly similar to that of fifty years ago and even 500 years ago. Beyond it the distribution of resources and power are uneven, but the regions, whether they are identified on little more than a statistical basis or on an element as emotive as nationhood, are likely to make demands at variance with a national plan focussed on London. If more power is given to regions in Britain they are more likely to see their rôles as one of presenting and defending local interests. Their concern will be to share equally in future growth, rather than to complement one another in a future pattern suggested by imaginative forecasting.

It is assumed in this paper that any trend in the future of the urban process will not completely over-ride regional differences, because these are imbued with values which will distort the process. The least we can expect is that the urban process will operate in a different way in different places.

In a sense the constraints which have been discussed above are both slight and formidable. They are slight because physically the environment, the amount of land available, the relative clemency of the weather and so on, presents no great obstacle to the continued growth and expansion of urbanisation. They are formidable because of the use we have already made of our environment, because we have inherited a settlement pattern and invested in a complex pattern of cities and industries and transport links. There is too much to undo before we can give ourselves enough flexibility to create an entirely new pattern. Even more formidable, perhaps, are the values with which society has imbued the existing pattern of existence. These are main reasons for suggesting that the area where alternatives will operate in the immediate future will be rather limited at first. Momentum will increase rapidly only when the breakdown of old patterns is deliberately accelerated. We urgently need to know what mechanisms are necessary for this breakdown. Even on the planning side there is little interest in understanding the process of decline. Much time is spent on growth—rightly so because we do not understand this either—but there is hardly a recognition of the need to plan for contraction. But if life styles are going to change very rapidly, then they can only be properly accommodated if we demolish many of our existing man-made constraints—whether they be houses, field boundaries, road networks or habits—extending the possibilities of change in the future and increasing the area where choice will be exercised.

The complement of this picture of resources and the environment in which they are used is the technological/social framework. Although this is dealt with in other papers it might be useful to consider which aspects of the latter impinge most directly on the points considered above. For example, if the so-called geographical constraint—environment and resources—could be manipulated entirely to our satisfaction, theoretically giving an unlimited choice both of location and form of settlement, to what extent would these social considerations still restrict the possibilities? It has been suggested above that location is still strongly governed by inertia, but what makes for dispersion, for example, and what for nucleation?

In rural Britain the distinction between dispersion and nucleation in settlement has long been blurred in spite of the fundamental issues which have supported it historically. In England, although the nucleated village remains as an important feature of the landscape, the scattering of farms which has taken place since the enclosure movement is a significant complementary feature. In Wales the traditional dispersal of farms and lack of villages and towns is partly compensated by the rise of service centres in the last century and this.

Reasons for nucleation are largely tied to services. Small and large towns are held together by the most economic means of distributing water, gas and electricity and of collecting waste. Can we envisage, in the near future, either (a) a free-standing house, completely independent of these services, or (b) a complete network of services to which we can just plug in? Water is the critical element in these considerations. The caravan comes near to the completely independent unit, though the problems of waste disposal are by no means solved. As things are, the economics of services tend to counter any radical dispersion of urban settlement.

Technology must also be considered as having two kinds of effects. It was the techniques of steam power which gave us the industrial towns and cities of the nineteenth century, largely because of the comparative economy of the very large steam power units. Electrical power is minutely sub-divisible, with small units as viable as large: and in addition it is already available for distribution anywhere in a country as small as Britain where even boosting is not essential for the relatively short-distance transmissions involved. Theoretically the use of electricity, from a national grid, could lead to as complete a dispersion of industry as did the water and wind power of medieval England. It has already been noted that manpower and markets militate against this kind of flexibility, but if one envisages a future in which man is both more mobile and more dispersed, then the market follows suit. At the heart of this problem, however, is the extent to which industries are linked. The interdependence of processes has played a large part in the past in the accumulation of industrial plant. In a large sector of industry the advantages are still very great. One must envisage, too, the reduction in total industrial work referred to above and its effects on labour and the amount of work any individual is expected to do. If the time freed from economic activity is devoted mainly to leisure, this will have important repercussions, but one must also envisage that people will be able to travel further to centres of leisure activities.

One of the main functions of the town is the exchange of goods and services. The market has been associated with urbanisation from time immemorial and central place hinges on this. It would be valuable if we could assess to what extent this could be broken down to allow new patterns of exchange. The mail order business—fairly standard in remote rural areas—is one accepted pattern. But is this likely to supersede shops? Shops have lost much of their social function. The self-service system has introduced an element which would not be tolerated in some societies, but which is certainly being applied more and more in this country. Supermarkets have taken a lead in repudiating the town centre and locating peripherally or even between urban centres. They have been forced to do this because accessibility is the basis of their location, not centrality. At the same time their location demands a size and a range—and even linked services like cafés and petrol stations—which is creating new centres. If these were kept distinct from residential areas, dispersal of houses could still predominate, but shopping would have its own nuclei, though not necessarily central or hierarchical.

Planners must also know what are the future needs of education and leisure activities. How far does education involve congregation of people? We are building schools to accommodate 1500 and colleges to accommodate 10,000 students, when T.V. promises to answer a similar purpose with the absolute minimum of centralisation. The University of the Air may be the right pointer to the future. But is the face to face contact still necessary? Can the T.V. interview replace a discussion group? There are 44 universities in Britain—theoretically well dispersed, and giving a good regional cover—but they are not regional colleges. Although there is a strong regional base to some universities, notably in Northern Ireland, Scotland and to a lesser extent in Wales, the majority of institutions draw to some extent on the entire population because they provide for specialist interest.

Leisure has been dealt with in another paper, but it is relevant to note here that some leisure activities already involve complete dispersion, both as a result of increased mobility and of improved communications. The former gives rise to the increasing use of sparsely populated areas and the weekend cottage, the latter has re-focussed much leisure activity at home. But there are many leisure activities which demand group participation and which make complete dispersal unlikely. Some activities involve large numbers of spectators who are only indirectly participating and it is unlikely that the sense of occasion at an opera, theatre, or even a hustings, will disappear. Existing channels of communication are at best a substitute for this.

Perhaps the aspect most in need of investigation is the link which exists between so many of these activities. In emphasising the convenience of having certain activities grouped in the traditional urban manner, planners are only reflecting existing sub-systems. Would new patterns of movement and location throw up new systems?

Doubtless many of the answers to these questions will arise from the differences in attitude of sections of society, and the way by which new concepts are diffused throughout society. The relationship of various groups of people within the existing framework varies enormously. Some are already free from its locational constraints. For an elite, Webber's non-place urban realm is a reality—indeed for a small section of society like the aristocracy, this has been so for a very long time. All Webber is suggesting is that it will become a reality to more and more people, and as it does so the constraints will gradually break down. But until the whole of society is more or less involved we will be operating on several levels. It is a fallacy to assume that this kind of urbanisation is an all-enveloping process, or even that the 'have-nots' of today will want to be exactly like the 'haves' when this becomes a possiblity. There will always be a difference in techniques and in access to them which will affect communication between one group and another. Possession of a T.V. once differentiated a small group of people from the majority who only had a radio. Now colour T.V. differentiates the same kind of groups from those who have T.V. Are we to plan on the assumption that there will come a time whan all people will share in all the most advanced facilities? Or must we be realistic and accept a limitation which may be the essence of our society for some time to come?

FORECASTING 'PLANNING'

A. G. WILSON

Introduction

'Planning' consists of activities, and ultimately interventions in processes, carried out in order to achieve a set of goals. Planning in relation to developing patterns of urbanisation, urban planning for short, ultimately leads to interventions in urban devlopment processes for the greater public good. The Study Group on Developing Patterns of Urbanisation set up by the Centre for Environmental Studies is concerned with all aspects of the process of urbanisation. Urban planning clearly has an influence on the future and so any speculation about developing patterns must include a study of possible developments of the planning system, and the impact of any changes on the developing patterns. This can be seen as the problem of *forecasting 'planning'* itself. Such is the subject matter of this paper. It is hardly necessary to emphasise at the outset that such an attempt is bound to fail; any success will simply be the pointing out of issues related to the future of planning which need to be given more attention.

It is appropriate to set the scene with an abstract characterisation of planning activities, or tasks, similar to that presented in an earlier paper.[1] In this characterisation, there are three main types of planning tasks, concerned with *policy*, *design* and *analysis*. It is also useful to think of the entity which is being planned as a system, made up of many components. Then, policy activities can themselves be classified in three groups: *actions* which have some impact on the system being planned, which can arise from the operation of a control mechanism, or through the taking of firm decisions which determine, wholly or partly, the future of the system; *goal formulation*; and the *evaluation* of alternative plans to achieve goals. Policy makers and implementers may also be concerned with *monitoring* in various ways, to assess the impact and effectiveness of earlier actions. Design is concerned with the techniques of plan formulation and presentation, and with the use of a variety of design methods to generate alternative plans. (A 'plan' has been implicitly defined as the specification of the action (to be) taken in relation to the system being planned.) Analysis is concerned with understanding the system of interest so that the impact of plans on the system can be predicted to the greatest possible extent. Policy, design and analysis activities in planning processes are closely inter-related and sometimes overlap. It is recognised, of course, that this is only one of many ways of usefully characterising planning processes. For this paper, such an abstract characterisation is especially useful in structuring a review of developing planning capability—the new methods which are becoming available to the planner in each of the three main fields of activity. In the end, of course, it proves necessary to return to a more concrete characterisation of planning processes in order to discuss possible developments of existing planning frameworks.

As a further preliminary, it may be worth briefly relating this structuring of planning processes (which rather takes it for granted, implicitly, that planning is necessary and useful) to an alternative analysis, presented in a second paper.[2] The task of planning in relation to a system as complex as a city or a region can be viewed as the problem of the optimal control of such a system. There is in principle an infinitely large number of 'states' which such a system of interest can be in, and it is a requirement for rational and consistent decision-making that the decision-maker should possess a preference ordering over these states. The alternative analysis arises from viewing the urban system as at least in part an economic system, and then drawing on the body of economists' experience in the control of such systems.

The urban system is, in part, a set of markets, and economic theory shows that, under certain stringent conditions mainly related to competitiveness, market systems will follow paths which are Pareto optimal—that is, there is no reallocation of resources that could make anyone better off without making anyone else worse off. So, a part of the optimal control problem is then to ensure that urban markets satisfy the appropriate conditions to guarantee Pareto optimality. Such a system state may be called one of allocational efficiency—resources are allocated in an efficient way.

There are two main reasons why planning interventions are needed over and above those which maintain conditions for efficiency in markets. Firstly, there is the problem of achieving *distributional efficiency*. There are many possible allocationally efficient states, each corresponding to different distributions of real income. The problem of achieving distributional efficiency is that of achieving the distribution of real income which society, in some sense, wants. Secondly, there are two kinds of *market failure* which can only be corrected by intervention. The first of these arises from indivisibilities, or more generally, increasing returns to scale, in the provision of a good. The second arises from the existence of economic externalities. The first type of failure can be tackled by public regulation and control, usually by ensuring that marginal cost prices are charged, with investments being made out of public funds; and the second type is tackled by applying taxes and subsidies so that market prices reflect social costs.

The three kinds of intervention needed, to achieve distributional efficiency, and to tackle the principal market failures, can be related to the characterisation of the planning process presented earlier. Firstly, income distributional effects can only be measured if the planner has adequate analytic capability to measure the distributional impacts of alternative plans, and in the policy making process, these impacts must be related to the current knowledge about society's goals. Secondly, investment policies in relation to public goods also need an analytic or predictive capability, and will be determined by the policy-makers' evaluation criteria. Thirdly, the policy maker, in assessing his response to externalities, also needs the analytic capability to measure the externalities associated with particular parts of his plans.

Thus, a clear need emerges for a substantial analytic capability—to understand cities and regions in order to assess the impacts of alternatives at a level of detail which provides information about the incidence of changes in real income. Attention is also drawn to the notion of planning as a goal achievement process which cannot be fully tackled with the tools of economics. Design capability is needed to get an enumeration of possible states—if the best is to be selected, it must be one of the alternatives to be evaluated! Further, the complexities of policy making tasks are increasingly self evident. It is also clear that the three kinds of planning activity stand in a hierarchical relationship to each other: analytic capability is a necessary prerequisite for both designer and policy maker, and design capability is also a necessary prerequisite for the policy maker.

The rest of this paper is divided into two parts. The next part is concerned with planning capability, particularly in relation to new and improving methodologies. For this purpose, it is useful to retain the abstract characterisation of planning processes presented in this introduction. Thus, successive sub-sections discuss analytic capability, design capability and policy-making capability. In a final sub-section, a portrait is presented of the working methods of an idealised planning team using a range of new techniques.

The final section of the paper, discusses how the developing planning capability could be applied. For this purpose, it is necessary to abandon the abstract characterisations of planning processes, or at least to relate them to institutional practice. Thus, the first sub-section of this part is concerned with the institutions of planning. The second sub-section attempts to set out some of the major issues which are arising and which will arise in the development of planning processes, paying particular attention to the relationship between the planners and the planned (or the consumers of planning). This final section takes its overall title from this topic, which was identified as one of the major subjects for future concern by the Centre's Study Group. Finally, a number of tentative conclusions are drawn in the third sub-section.

It is appropriate to close this introduction with a note about the methods which are employed in this paper, and to request the reader's indulgence and forebearance. It is clear that the field to be covered in the paper is immense, and to do it justice would require several authors with a variety of skills to work for several years and to publish their results in several books! The author has adopted different tactics in the different parts of the paper. This introduction attempts to set down in broad terms a characterisation of planning processes for use in the rest of the paper. A more detailed discussion is available in the two papers already cited. In the second section new methods which contribute to increasing planning capability are reviewed in broad terms. It is not possible in the space available to give detailed references, but an attempt has been made to cite works which themselves have an extensive bibliography. Thus the reader who is not familiar with the material described should be able to gain access to the literature at least indirectly. The discussion of issues and possible developments in the final section is based on an extremely rudimentary analysis of existing institutions in planning. This basis should be formed from extensive survey and study of a vast amount of literature from most branches of the social sciences, especially political science, social administration and sociology. Such a method of working, in this case, has not been possible. Thus, the concepts introduced and used in the final section may occasionally fall short in relation to standards of rigour and precision which the social scientist might apply. Nevertheless, it is hoped that they are adequate to support a discussion of issues and possible developments as these are of such urgency as to need as much airing as possible as soon as possible. Thus, the issues and possible developments discussed in the final section arise from the review of methodological developments in the second, and from a study, albeit cursory, of institutional frameworks in planning in the first sub-section.

This can be put another way. It is assumed that the reader has an interest in, and probably a considerable amount of knowledge of, both developing methodologies in planning (2nd section) and current institutional and political frameworks (3rd section). It is further assumed that the reader with more specialist interests is aware of the issues and questions associated with particular topics. Thus, the purpose of this paper is to study basic underlying subject matter only in sufficient detail to identify a set of major issues about the overall form of planning in the future and to contribute to a discussion of the main alternatives. In relation to more detailed questions, it assumes knowledge on the part of the reader, or alternatively provides an initial introduction for the reader to the relevant literature.

Planning capability

Analytic capability

In the introduction, a need was identified for a powerful analytic capability. Planning involves intervention to achieve goals, and the good planner will design his intervention on the basis of *predictions* of the impacts (which are often felt over a long time period) of his designs. To be able to predict, he needs a good understanding of how urban systems work, and this is what is meant by analytic capability. From a different viewpoint, the principal motive of the planner may be to intervene to solve problems. Again, it can easily be seen that he needs the same analytic capability.

There are two possible approaches to analysis: a first-principles-what-do-we-need-to-know approach, or an investigation of what the various disciplines have contributed to urban studies. These are pursued in turn.

Disciplines can be seen as coalitions of people using particular sets of concepts. As concepts, and theories relating concepts, become refined over time, and as concepts become more or less useful, then the boundaries of these coalitions can change. This has interesting implications for a relatively new field such as urban studies. The first-principles approach studies concepts relevant to particular problems (not represented in single disciplines, such as urban studies and urban planning), and only secondly consider the disciplinary implications.

The first-principles approach is to some extent formalised in what might itself be called a discipline—that of *systems analysis*. This emphasises the need to identify all the components of the system of interest, to consider various ways of grouping the components into (sub) systems and to study behaviour and interaction within and between systems. The main components of urban systems can be classified as objects (especially, people, who are mobile, and physical infrastructure, which is immobile) and activities (especially social, economic and governmental activities); *interactions* take place through what can be called a *communication* sector. There is an initial *taxonomic problem*: to classify the components and systems which have been identified. Then there is the *theory building problem*: to explain and understand the structure and process of development of the components and subsystems. Interactions can be studied in a consistent way by the use of *accounting* procedures. This outline sketch of the first-principles approach will perhaps suffice as a framework for estimating the likely development of the analytic capability of planners. A more extensive discussion is given in other papers by the author.[3, 4]

Ultimately, most disciplines contribute to urban studies. Perhaps the most fundamental disciplines associated with the analysis of cities and regions are demography, sociology, political science, economics, geography and engineering (in so far as it is concerned with the mechanics of operation, and not with design). As professional disciplines, planning, architecture and the other part of engineering contribute mainly to the design and policy aspects of planning processes. The fundamental disciplines contribute tremendously to urban analysis, though the development of approaches such as systems analysis often ensure that research is carried out in multi-disciplinary teams. It should be noted, however, following Mackenzie,[5] that it is often better to erode and extend disciplinary boundaries than to form inter-disciplinary teams: '. . . the best work is being done not by inter-disciplinary teamwork, but in disregard of traditional frontiers.' In other words, important research can be expected both from multi-disciplinary teams and by imaginative disciplinary work. For the purpose of this review, it will be convenient to adopt the first principles' (systems analysis) approach, and to study progress in relation to developing under-standing of the main components of urban systems.

The main task of this section remains to review progress in the field of analysis and to assess likely future analytic capability. The first point to note is that within and beyond disciplines, and in inter-disciplinary teams, there are different styles of research. These range from an essentially inductive approach relying mainly on statistical analysis of data to an essentially deductive approach based on theory building, and comparing theoretical prediction with observation. Many possible hybrid styles can and will emerge, such as the development of mathematical equations which fit data reasonably well, which are theories with a relatively low explanatory power. Much of econometric analysis is of this style. Statistical analysis will support theory building and vice versa. A useful framework within which to assess and predict progress is provided by reviews of *models* of urban systems. A model is a formal representation of a theory, and a model can be tested and made operational for planning purposes if it can be checked against data and all its parameters can be estimated. Present progress is reviewed in two papers by the author which have already been cited,[1, 4] and in papers by Harris[6] and Lowry.[7] There are useful collections of papers in a special issue of the *Journal of the American Institute of Planners*[8] and a more recent Special Report of the Highways Research Board.[9] References on particular models will not be cited in this paper, though further review papers will be cited.

We can now briefly review the progress made so far, and use this as a basis to speculate about the future. Firstly, let us consider spatially aggregated models of population and economic structure. Good matrix models[10] exist for forecasting population structure by age and sex for any large area unit, and these models can be applied at national, regional and urban levels of aggregation subject to assumptions about birth rates and migration rates. Variations in birth rates are relatively badly understood, and it is customary to make projections using ranges of assumptions. Some work has been done on models of migration, however. More difficult problems arise, even at this level of aggregation, in order to understand "structure" in any greater detail. For example, it is necessary to know about occupation structure, so that it is possible to match, at least roughly, the provision of skills from the educational system to available jobs, or vice versa, according to what our goals are. (It is unlikely to be a plank of a planning platform that these totals should not match at national, regional and urban levels, but it is less clear whether social or economic requirements should call the tune—and example of conflicting goals.)

Economic models at the spatially aggregated levels can also be constructed using, for example, input-output techniques.[11] At the national level, models are in use in some countries and considerable progress has been made in Britain. At the regional and urban levels, the area can be treated methodologically as a 'country', or it can be treated as a part of an inter-regional system. The first alternative is the simplest (though of course it offers less information) and some operational models of this type exist; the second is more difficult because there is rarely much available data on inter-regional flows to calibrate a model, though a considerable amount of theoretical work has been done. Thus, at the spatially aggregated level, at least the beginnings of good models exist, though more empirically based work needs to be done.

Models in the field of intra-urban structure are much less advanced, and the problems of model building are correspondingly more difficult than at the spatially aggregated level. The only model which is anything like adequate is the transport model.[12] Mathematical models of urban transport flows have been used in many planning studies, including those being carried out in all the major conurbations of Britain. These are the only intra-urban models at present being used continuously by planners. Attempts to model urban systems vary from being comprehensive in scope to being very partial. At present, the price which is paid for comprehensiveness is loss of detail. Models of the retail sector[13] are being built with increasing success, and are now being used by some planners for work on planning new retail centres. The residential and workplace location fields have proved more difficult. Rudimentary models exist but a better understanding is needed of certain fundamentals, such as individual preference structures, before much more progress can be made. For similar reasons, the whole social sector is very difficult to handle; the provision of urban public services and social facilities have been dealt with according to 'need' and various rules of thumb adopted by the agencies who are responsible for their provision. (And this is much less than half the story: much of the success of social provision will be the returns measured by individual utility functions if we get everything else right; that is, a large part of a social success will be determined by achieving the best provisions of residence and workplace.) Considerable progress has been made in the understanding of the social structure of the population, however. Some progress has been made with industrial location models on the theoretical side,[14] but this has been taken a relatively little way on the empirical side, mainly because the kind of data demanded by the theories is not easily available. At the intra-urban level, the usual measure of economic activity in the models discussed so far is jobs. It is important also to be able to develop models of the distribution of infrastructure, and this is perhaps the most difficult modelling sector of all, mainly because buildings have long lives and can change their use many times during their lifetimes. A considerable amount of effort has gone into studies of the service and commercial sectors, some of which is now coming to fruition. This sector does illustrate the sort of classification problems which sometimes arise, however: we are often interested in offices per se, and useful studies have been carried out on offices. However, this, as a sector, is a compendium of parts of almost all the other economic activity sectors. This illustrates again that there is probably no way (except at an impossibly fine level of disaggregation) of classifying activities so that any *type* of activity which could be of interest falls clearly into one sector.

There are various ways in which we can speculate about likely progress. Let us first consider progress in relation to the styles of research discussed earlier, ranging from the deductive/theoretical to the inductive/statistical. The first point to note is that there will be progress, and there will be a shift: there will be theories about subject areas which are today susceptible to statistical analysis only, but there will also be new subject areas which move in to fill the gaps in the statistical-analysis only category. Issues of interest have an unhappy knack of shifting towards problems where one's analytical capability is deficient.

The present position could be summarised by a statement saying that very few subject areas of interest are covered by adequate theories, some can be described by sets of mathematical equations and good classification systems, and most are susceptible to statistical analysis though, in many subject areas, the data are very poor. Each of these situations will improve. There should be a theoretical understanding of the main location subject areas: residential location, industrial location and retail location. A good theoretical understanding would imply that at least the broad outline of the preference structures or utility functions of individuals in each of these sectors would be known. This will be of crucial importance for improving problem solving capability. At a more aggregated level, but at a level which remains useful for many planning purposes, there should be good mathematical descriptions of development phenomena, at least as accurate as models of transport flows at present. The better and more detailed theories which will develop will serve to refine these, and they will also facilitate evaluation of alternative plans since, when preference structures are understood, it will be possible to measure benefits arising from plans. Statistical analyses should be facilitated by the existence of computerised data banks and more easily available statistical analysis programmes of the most advanced kind.

Of course, it must be recognised that the models which are currently available are not very accurate predictors, especially over long periods. The level of accuracy should improve for conditional prediction, but it is important to recognise that a high error level will persist, more in some sectors than others. This will represent one contribution to the planner's uncertainty when he makes his forecasts. It does not mean, of course, that the models are useless; the alternative of not using models simply means that the planner relies on his intuitions, which in most cases would give rise to even greater uncertainties. What it does mean is that uncertainties should be explicitly recognised and accounted for in the planning process, using such techniques as statistical decision theory.

To summarise: theoretical and statistical developments will stimulate and follow each other. We shall begin to solve classification problems on the one hand, and the development of operational information systems, such as co-ordinate referencing systems, for storing many kinds of spatial data, will be available on the other. The solution to the classification problems will also facilitate theoretical advance in a more direct way: it will enable sub models to interact and communicate with each other more easily than at present, possibly through an accounting framework.

Design capability

What is design? Alexander[15] defines design when he writes: 'The ultimate object of design is form . . . every design problem begins with an effort to achieve fitness between two quantities: the form in question and its context.' This can be put another way: the 'form' can be taken to mean the form of the city, socio-economic as well as physical, and the 'context' the goals to be achieved, and so design is "finding forms which achieve goals in the best way". In terms of the use of models, this design, a specification of the form, is an assignment of specific values by the planner to those variables which he can control. Alexander goes on to point out the seeming impossibility of achieving good designs in a self-conscious culture where the possible number of forms, because of the number of possible combinations of the components, is astronomical. Thus, consider the simple example of designing a transport network: there are an enormous number of possible ways of connecting nodes with links, and of defining the characteristics (such as road widths) of each link. This is a typical combinatorial problem which arises in design, and the large numbers involved means that the designer cannot find the best design by simple enumeration of alternatives with an analysis of each to find the best. The way out of the dilemma is to seek a number of organising concepts to reduce the dimensions of the problem. Thus it has been argued, in the case of the example of designing a transport network, that there are only three basic forms: the grid, the directional grid, and the centripetal radial system, for an urban area.[16] This may or may not be seen, ultimately, to be an over-simplification, but it can be seen how this simplifies the problem: the only *sensible* combinations of links to examine are those which form one of the three patterns, and design then becomes a matter of thinking about spacing of parallel links or radials, in relation to land use. To test the alternatives, the models outlined in the previous section will have to be used to test the impacts of various designs and the alternatives can be analysed using an evaluation procedure which will discover which design(s) come(s) nearest to meeting the goals. It is clear even from this very sketchy outline that design is always likely to be an evolving process and that there will perhaps never be 'final' answers to design problems. This is partly because goals will be continually evolving, and the designer will have to take account of technological change, but also because of the essential element of inventiveness in design: the urban design process is so complex that it will be possible in the indefinite future (especially since the context is continually changing anyway) for people to invent new organising concepts which would have a major impact on design, and hence on developing patterns.

Thus, to summarise: the designer uses a mixture of understanding (and hence prediction) and imagination to build organising concepts for design, and then he generates good alternative designs to achieve policy goals. The alternative designs are compared using some evaluation process (and the criteria used are themselves part of the policy area—a function of the goals adopted). In cases where this process could be fully formalised (which means that, literally, where nothing is left to the imagination!) some optimising procedure could be used to produce the best plan, but the cases which arise in urban planning are unlikely to be sufficiently simple for this method to be applicable. Above all, it should be emphasised that in a context of shifting goals, and increasing understanding, the designer will be continually learning.

Policy making capability

The policy making part of planning contains three inter-related elements: firstly, the tasks of implementation and control, secondly, the task of goal formulation, and thirdly, the decision taking role of selecting a plan from a number of alternatives according to appropriate criteria.

Policy making capability relates in an obvious way to analytic and design capabilities: in the end, analysis will have to say enough about preference structures for the policy maker to be able to evaluate correctly; and a good plan can be chosen only if designers have a good plan among the alternatives they produce. The assumption will be made for the present that no special problems are presented by implementation and control. This leaves us with the task of exploring in more detail the problems of goal formulation.

It is a crucial element of policy making that goals should be precisely articulated and the subject of public debate. It could be argued that it might not be in the interests of some community groups to make goals public, but a number of currently developing techniques do contribute and force a trend towards explicitness. In particular, the development of planning, programming and budgeting (P.P.B.) systems explicitly relates the contribution of inputs to various outputs, and these outputs are (at least approximately) explicit statements of goals. In a field such as urban planning, all goals cannot be made explicit and measurable, but procedures which are equivalent to those used in P.P.B. Systems are being developed. Examples are Lichfield's planning balance sheet[17] and Hill's goals—achievement matrix.[18]

Increasing analytic and design capabilities give considerable scope for extending the nature of plans themselves. Plans can cover several time horizons (and a wider range of functions) with all the appropriate inter-actions incorporated in the planning machinery. It is then possible to distinguish between short run and long run plans (and hence, using terms from other branches of planning and operational research, between tactics and strategy). It becomes possible to measure flexibility: to what extent does a decision about the short term contribute to the 'firming up' of the long term strategy. Further, these developments relate in an obvious way to goal formulation and enable exploration of the latter concept in more depth. One can distinguish, for example, between short term goals (more specific, and perhaps called targets) and longer term goals aimed at various time horizons. Thus, it should be possible in the not too distant future to integrate policy making capabilities over different time horizons. Statistical decision theory can be used to help take account of uncertainties, as mentioned earlier.

Problem solving can often be related to policy making in one obvious way: a 'goal' may be 'to solve a problem'. However, it may not always be possible to make such an identification without a lot of analysis. In particular, the planner will sometimes have to employ his analytic capability as a diagnostician.

Finally, note that it has been implicit throughout this section, that the planner will rarely have an optimising capability. His task is to use various techniques to find good solutions to problems, to devise good policies. The situation will usually be too complex to lend itself to optimisation procedures in the manner, for example, of the planning of some industrial processes.

Portrait of a future planning team

As an example, consider the workings of a local planning authority in the year 1980. It will be a large authority, brought about through local government reorganisation a few years earlier; suppose that it is a metropolitan authority, but sub-regional, and so it has relations with other tiers of government at regional and national levels. Firstly, consider the facilities which are available to these new planners. It is unlikely that the authority will have its own computer; its computing equipment is likely to consist of terminal equipment only which hooks into some national computing grid, and which supplies it with virtually unlimited (and cheap) computing facilities. The nationally provided facilities will consist of software as well as hardware which means that extensive packages of computer programmes, which facilitate data collection and monitoring, and which contain all the basic models, will be available.

Many of the authority's goals will be specified as output targets in something like programme budgeting procedures; programmes (or plans) specifying these targets (and other related actions) will be available, and planning work will consist of rolling them forward for different time horizons. Planning for the longer term time horizons (15, 25 and 35 years) will create possibilities just as wide and exciting as those of today; it would be wrong to suggest that this sort of planning would become anything like routine. The targets, at the different time horizons, would have specific degrees of 'firmness'; each target might be expressed as a range of possible values and a probability distribution be associated with each range. Paths to each possible target value (and there would be many for each value) would also be specified and analysed through the techniques of statistical decision theory; a continual monitoring procedure would indicate which path was at present being followed. The paths themselves (and the possible future paths) would be subject to continuous amendment as the planners' knowledge of the system increased through time, and the underlying models were improved and as society's goals changed and evolved.

The technical aids available to the designers in the planning team would be considerable. They would be designing city structure in what amounted to an experimental lab situation, and alternatives could be examined at great speed. The designers of a transport network for example, would be able to sit at a map and draw on links of different transport modes and different travel characteristics with a light pencil linked to a computer, and instant computer output, produced via a model system, would say what the impact of the design was, how it related to the targets and forecasts specified (by their probability distributions) by other planners in the department, whether it was 'better' than any previous effort and if so how, and so on.

There would be corresponding teams of planners with similar facilities at regional and national government levels, each upper tier constraining lower tiers by fixing (possibly probabilistically) quantities to satisfy national or regional goals (which had been negotiated with lower tier interests). It could also be that some scale economies were achieved by the upper tiers of government providing the teams to do much of the research work on the model system, then used by all through the computer network. The facilities which have been outlined would also be available to various community groups who would themselves be employing professional resources in complex public participation procedures.

The striking thing about the predictions of this section, aimed at 1980, is that many, if not most of them, are technologically possible now. The main weakness at present would be in the model system, but even in that case, a rudimentary system would be available which would be good enough to begin this kind of planning framework. Indeed, it may be that this kind of planning framework is necessary to the rapid development of appropriate models. It is interesting to see that some local authorities are already beginning to set up the beginning of planning systems of the kind outlined here.[19]

The planners and the planned

Institutional frameworks

It is now necessary to study institutions in more concrete terms. It is possible, as a first approximation, to consider separately the institutions of the planners and those of the planned. This will facilitate a discussion on the development of the interaction between the planners and the planned—one of the major issues to be aired in this paper.

In order to classify in general terms the types of institutions associated with planning, four basic dimensions can be distinguished:

    i) type of activity
    ii) functional responsibility
    iii) geographic scale of responsibility
    iv) nature of public responsibility

'Type of activity' covers two basic classes, one of which can be further subdivided. The first is activity associated with the implementation of plans (executive agencies), and the second that associated with innovation in planning technique. The latter class can be subdivided into strictly *research* activity, as distinguished from *developmental* activity (making research discoveries operational for use in executive agencies). Each group could be further subdivided into responsibility for policy, design and analysis aspects of planning.

'Functional responsibility' refers to the particular functions of the urban system which an institution is responsible for. This responsibility may be broad (say, 'city planning' covering many urban functions) or quite specific and narrow (as with a public transport authority responsible for one mode within the transport sector).

'Geographical scale of responsibility' can be defined in areal terms, and considerable variety is possible, from international to very local.

To define 'nature of public responsibility', at least three groups can be distinguished which can be called governmental, public and private. An institution will be governmental if it is responsible for taking or implementing planning decisions in the public interest; it will be public if it is not directly concerned with decisions, but is none-the-less in some sense under public control; it will be considered private otherwise, which implies control by an individual, or small group, not responsible to the public at large.

It is appreciated that these categories are not always precisely defined, but they will suffice for present purposes. The four categories generate an infinite variety of type of institution arising from the variety of mixes of type of activity, functional responsibilities and degree of public responsibility at a variety of possible geographic scales.

The institutions of the planned are included in the 'private' sector of the above classification. Each individual or household is in a sense an institution. Such units take a variety of decisions (such as location decisions), which are often heavily influenced by the planning system, and which, in the end, determine much of the shape of the patterns of urban development. Further, nearly all organisations of individuals, such as firms, are similarly consumers of planning. Individuals, households and organisations are thus the main client of planners. The final group could involve ad hoc pressure groups specifically formed to discuss planning matters. There are, in addition, institutions of interaction between the planners and the planned— in essence the entire political structure, but including ad hoc institutions such as Commissions and Inquiries.

Any categorisation of institutions of the above type must, of course, be an over-simplification. It is beyond the scope of this paper to pursue an analysis in more depth, but it is perhaps worth noting a number of ways in which the analysis should be expanded. Firstly, for all kinds of institution, a well known, but important distinction should be noted, which is well stated by Mackenzie[5]: '. . . one must admit into the discussion the awkward distinction between "formal" and "informal" organisation.' In other words, when institutions or organisations are analysed by political scientists, the actual behaviour is often found to be different than would be expected on the basis of the formal constitution, and so it will be important in analysing the role of institutions in planning to study informal as well as formal operations. Much careful research has been carried out on this topic. For example, Meyerson and Banfield,[20] in a now classical study, have described a conceptual framework to study political processes associated with public housing decisions in Chicago; Griffiths[21] has made a detailed study of the relationships between central and local government, in a general context, but including a study of urban planning matters; more generally, Maass[22] has constructed a detailed model of the constitutional democratic state; Levin,[23] in Britain, has tackled a similar analytic problem from a different viewpoint, by analysing how decisions are actually made in urban planning; Friend and Jessop,[24] in a recent book, present a detailed case study of planning processes in Coventry. It will obviously only be possible to begin to resolve some of the issues raised in this paper through detailed analytic work of this kind.

It is even an over-simplification to assume that it is sufficient to categorise institutions and to go on to discuss the roles of particular types of institutions. Stringer[25] has introduced the concept of multi-organisations as those parts of several organisations which play a role, formally or informally, in a common decision field. He argues, as discussed by Friend,[26] that the most striking practical successes of operational research to date have been within the setting of a single organisation, but that if operational research is to make a comparable impact on the processes of public planning, then conscious steps must be taken to adapt its approach to the special problems created by decision processes which impinge on the responsibilities of several organisations. Further, it is also useful to take into account what are in effect special kinds of formal multi-organisations—Commissions (super-institutions) or similar organisations, which are being set up almost continually to review forms of institutions and their appropriateness for the current period.

Issues

It will by now be clear to the reader that the issues to be raised in this paper are issues *about* urban planning, as distinct from issues *within* urban planning. (It is essentially a paper in the field of meta-planning as distinct from planning, in the same way as one enters the field of meta-mathematics to discuss issues about mathematics.[27]) Issues within planning are extensively discussed in the other papers of this special issue. It has been shown that the planner *professionally* has a developing and increasing capability; he can analyse and predict increasingly effectively, and he is becoming a more self-conscious (following Alexander[15]) and effective designer. He has improved tools for policy making. However, all this stops short of more effective policy-making! If urban planning is about *society achieving it goals,* then the main issue about planning is whether the professional planner can link with society sufficiently effectively to ensure that it is society's goals which are being achieved, and not his own. It is, of course, an over-simplification to maintain this distinction between the (professional) planner and the planned. Another way of stating the issue is whether society can plan for its overall ends effectively. However, the distinction between planner and planned is convenient for the purposes of this paper and will be retained. The main issue about planning, linking the planner and the planned, can then be subdivided into issues about

    i) goals
    ii) conflict resolution
    iii) communication
    iv) public participation

These are all issues about the workings of *democracy*. It is taken as read that within urban planning, capabilities will be developed to be as *efficient* as possible. The four sets of issues are closely interrelated, but it is convenient to begin by discussing them separately.

It is perhaps best to begin discussing goals with the conjecture that planners at present are rather ineffective in articulating society's goals as distinct from their own ideas about society's goals. Crick[28] expresses this in writing about planners as follows: 'They are our sort, particularly dangerous, sometimes almost disgusting, in a propensity not merely to know what is best for ordinary people, but to say that this is what ordinary people want.' It is necessary to find systematic ways of finding what society, as individuals and collectively in groups of various kinds, wants: from within the political framework (voting), by listening to shouts (pressure groups, market research) and, most effectively of all, observing what people do in circumstances where they have choices (in markets and through various kinds of revealed preferences).

It is possible to distinguish between goals for individuals and community groups on the one hand, and a group of economic units on the other. This represents a distinction between the social lives of individuals and groups living within an economic environment, and the units which create income and wealth in the latter environment. The community has obvious needs for workplaces, residences, shops, social facilities and a variety of public services, many of these being linked through a communications sector, and goals could be articulated, at least in broad terms, in relation to these needs. Economic units, at the present time, often appear to have growth as the critical goal. The implications of this can be articulated in various ways.

Of course, not all of the goods and services required by society are publicly provided. Indeed, one important question in relation to goals is the extent to which goods and services can be or should be provided through private market mechanisms, and to what extent through public planning. This issue was discussed in broad terms in the first part of this paper. More specifically, it appears that planning requires an increasing amount of information about individuals and organisations, both in the drive for greater efficiency and in order to be able to calculate the detailed incidence of the impacts of plans, than has been necessary or possible hitherto. This in itself is sometimes considered to be a major issue as a possible infringement of privacy or freedom. This issue is explored in some depth in a paper by Michael.[29] For example: 'Complementary pressures from those who would use information about the private person are likely to be great.

The real or imagined need to use people efficiently will increase as more organisations find themselves in the throes of complicated and disrupting reorganisations, remodelling people and procedures to meet requirements imposed by the use of automation and computers. Thus, executives and decision makers, responding to emotional and practical pressures, will try to squeeze the utmost from available personal information as clues to efficient job assignments.' This is written about privacy with respect to employees in firms. However, it does not need too great a stretch of the imagination to see the 'executives' as the planners, and the firm as the city. In other words, there will be considerable pressure merely as a result of the existence of new methods, on individuals, both on their privacy (and in particular on their private goals) and on their range of opportunities. Planning which threatens privacy is often also considered to threaten freedom. The issue now is: whose freedom? The 'freedom' of one individual (or indeed the privacy) often threatens the 'freedom' (or privacy) of others—consider, for example, the 'freedom' to drink and drive. This, then, all relates to the first issue about the determination of societal goals, but offers a further pointed example that goal formulation will almost inevitably generate conflicts.

It is clear in a general sense that the more planners can help society to articulate its goals, the more evident will be the conflicts between different sectors of society. And, of course, the institutions which play roles in the articulation of goals, will also inevitably play major roles in the resolution of conflicts. At present, goal articulation is imprecise and, along with the tasks of conflict resolution, is largely carried out within political institutions as they now exist. The next and final section of this paper will take up the question again in relation to possible developments.

Problem of goal articulation and conflict resolution each raise issues of communication, especially between planners and planned. This raises issues associated with language and general availability of information. If planners are, for example, using the language of mathematical modelling, it is important that the resulting information can be communicated to the planned. This can be achieved in one or both of two ways in different circumstances: either by making a simplified presentation of results if nothing is lost by this, and/or by ensuring that experts are also available to the planned. An even more important point is the need to make all relevant information about planning issues available to the planned as well as within planning teams. There is a tendency at present for governmental agencies to use expert advice in forming decisions or plans, but then *not* to make this expert advice generally available in any public debate which follows.

This all leads naturally to the issue of public participation in planning. It is clear from the above discussion that effective public participation means creating an institutional framework which ensures the articulation of society's goals, and the provision of machinery for effective communication and conflict resolution. It is equally clear, even from this outline sketch of the complexity of these tasks, that effective public participation needs more than a series of public meetings (which tends to be the only accepted implication of the phrase in Britain), and also more than advocacy planning[30] (one of the steps towards public participation in the United States).

Some possible institutional developments which might help resolve some of these issues are discussed in the next and final section.

Possible developments for planning

Two related streams of development in planning have been discussed in this paper: the first relates to increasing planning capability in a technical sense and is concerned primarily with *efficiency*, the second to public participation, and is concerned primarily with *democratising* planning. It could be argued that the second stream is related to the first: that the existence of a deeper knowledge and understanding of how urban systems function coupled with an increasing capability to plan such systems inevitably becomes public knowledge and so moves more firmly into the political arena with corresponding demands for more public participation then hitherto. It may be possible to trace a connection between the development and use of mathematical models of urban systems and the student riots!

The key to possible developments in planning lies in the possible developments of institutions associated with planning. A number of obvious points can be made in relation to the types of institution already categorised. There is likely to be an ever increasing drive for more planning capability. Thus, in the long run, more professional planning effort is likely to develop in a number of different kinds of planning institutions. The numbers of professionals concerned with implementation and control substantially exceeds those involved in development and they in turn substantially exceed those in research. For example, many people are involved in the implementation of transportation engineering schemes in cities (typically in local government), a substantial number, but considerably fewer in the practical development of new transportation planning techniques (typically in firms of consultants or in central government) and even fewer in research (typically in universities and specialist institutes). These numbers are all likely to increase in absolute terms, but relatively more new effort should develop in research and development if the trend in urban planning follows trends in other fields. It is important to recognise that development work does use up more resources than the related research work; one of the evident weaknesses in urban planning at present is a relative lack of resources in development.

In terms of functional responsibility, institutions at present tend to be concerned with transport modes, housing, land use, health, education, and so on. As awareness of the strong inter-relationships between functionally-defined sectors increases, there is a strong trend to merge to form units with wider responsibilities. A similar point can be made about geographical scale or responsibility: there is a trend towards bigger areas units because of the strong interactions and spillover effects crossing many existing administrative boundaries. One recent example which illustrates both trends is the creation of Passenger Transport Authorities by the Ministry of Transport in Britain. These have extended functional responsibilities in having to plan for several transport modes, and cover a wider geographical area so that conurbations can be planned as integral units. Many other examples could be cited to bear out both trends.

The fourth institutional category defined nature of public responsibility. The analysis of this paper suggests that both public and private institutions will grow and develop to facilitate public participation in planning. Some existing institutions, such as universities, may contribute in such roles. For example, if a governmental agency has carried out a transportation study using mathematical models, then one or two local universities may work with the same or similar models and data which would fulfil some of their own educational and research functions, as well as helping the community to check and extend the governmental work.

With this background of obvious possible trends, it is now appropriate to discuss more systematically the *requisite variety* of institutions associated with urban planning. It has already been noted that a tremendous variety of institutions exists. This notion can be developed: urban systems are extremely complex and the whole planning system (including the institutions of the planned as well as the planners, to allow for public participation) aims to control this complex system. The theory of control in complex systems is studied in cybernetics, and cyberneticians, such as Ross Ashby,[31] state a law of requisite variety which, roughly interpreted, means that a control system must be as complex as the system it sets out to control. This paper is not the place to discuss such concepts and laws in precise terms, but they offer a relevant guide. It is a safe conjecture to interpret the law of requisite variety for urban planning systems as implying the need for a wide variety of institutions. It is interesting that Friend and Jessop[25] make a similar point, also quoting Ross Ashby, in relation to the function of elected bodies in planning processes. They argue that a local council, for example, *cannot* be sufficiently complex (i.e. have requisite variety) to effectively represent the community, and this is what many of the present demands for increased public participation are all about. The law of requisite variety can probably be applied separately to planners, planned and the institutions of interaction.

As an example, it can be shown how the law of requisite variety might work out in a specific research context. Research units tend to take on the style of a relatively small number of their senior staff. At any given time, the results sought in a particular research context could probably be derived most quickly from a particular style. In the nature of research it would probably be impossible, a priori, to choose the 'winning' style correctly. So, if a problem is important, several research groups should attack it to guarantee quicker solution. An analogous need for institutional variety arises in relation to public participation: the more institutions there are representing the 'public' interest, the more likely it is that the interests of specific community groups are communicated to the planners.

In the discussion of issues in the previous section, it was noted that this paper was essentially a paper in meta-planning. So, it is possible to stand outside planning in the discussion of possible developments and to apply the general notions of planning developed in the introductory section to planning itself. That is, the processes of analysis, design and policy making can be applied to urban planning itself. Analysis in this context would refer to the study of behaviour of institutions associated with planning, and was previously discussed in a rudimentary way. Design refers to the invention in institutional frameworks (with impacts checked out through analysis) which will make appropriate impacts on the issues raised in the second part of the third section. Policy making refers to the possibility of society having a policy *about* its planning frameworks, which in general terms may be stated as the need for requisite institutional variety to achieve control of urban systems in such a way that society efficiently achieves its goals. The importance of these statements is that it is possible to be systematic in relation to devising and using planning frameworks. It is obviously beyond the scope of this paper to carry such a systematic study much further, but it is appropriate to conclude with a brief examination of institutional design problems raised by the issues previously discussed. These thoughts can then be added to the analysis of the more obvious trends in institutional change already presented in this section.

Issues were raised under the general headings of goals, conflict resolution, communication and public participation. Goals can be articulated, as has been indicated, in relation to each of the functional sectors of governmental agencies—needs for housing, workplaces, access through the transportation system, and so on. It is important to recognise that this is only one way of articulating goals. It may be more effective to state societal goals in relation to needs to redistribute real income, and to create greater access to a wider range of access to opportunities (which is an example of a degree of freedom which can be created by effective planning), and the like, rather than in relation to functional sectors. This would then have implications for the design of planning institutions. Conflicts are resolved in what is usually called the political arena. Institutional variety is obviously important, and Stringer's research[25] on multi-organisations is also relevant in this context. This set of issues also illustrates the possible use of legislation: if a better system of compensation for gainers to pay losers could be devised and instituted for example, then conflicts would be easier to resolve. Methods of resolving communications issues were indicated in the previous section. It is interesting to note that Friend and Jessop recommend to local authorities that they should form within the authority a 'communications research unit'. The key point to emerge about public participation which has emerged is the need for professional resources to be available on the public side as well as the governmental side. It was suggested in one example that universities might play a role in this context. If developments of this type took place, the implementation of plans may be achieved more quickly and easily than hitherto, as the ground would have been thoroughly prepared for conflict resolution. It is often thought that public participation involves slowing down the rate of implementation of plans, but this probably only happens in circumstances where the public do not have expert help available, so that far from the ground being prepared for conflict resolution, the opposite is true: it is known that there are conflicts, but they are not clearly understood and specified, and so the public can only use whatever power it has to block implementation. Such a situation would be especially acute when there was no efficient compensation system.

Above all, one final conclusion should be noted. It can be deduced from the law of requisite variety if it is not already obvious: the problem under discussion is so complex that it would be wrong to *expect* to find simple solutions. Such discussions as this represent a preliminary scratching of the surface of a set of very deep problems.

REFERENCES

[1] A. G. Wilson, 'Models in Urban Planning', *Urban Studies*, Vol. 5, No. 3, 1968.
[2] A. G. Wilson, D. Bayliss, A. J. Blackburn and B. G. Hutchinson, New Directions in Strategic Transportation Planning, Working Paper 36, Centre for Environmental Studies, London, 1969.
[3] A. G. Wilson, 'Research for Regional Planning', *Regional Studies*, Vol. 3, No. 1, 1969.
[4] A. G. Wilson, 'The Integration of Accounting and Location Theory Frameworks in Urban Modelling', in A. J. Scott (ed.), *Studies in Regional Science*, Pion, 1969.
[5] W. J. M. Mackenzie, *Politics and Social Science*, Penguin Books, 1967.
[6] B. Harris, 'Quantitative Models of Urban Development', in H. Perloff and L. Wingo (eds.), *Issues in Urban Economics*, Johns Hopkins, 1968.
[7] I. S. Lowry, Seven models of urban development, in Special Report 97, Highways Research Board, 1968.
[8] *Journal of the American Institute of Planners*, Vol. 31, No. 5, 1965.
[9] *Special Report 97*, Highways Research Board, 1968.
[10] J. Willis, 'Population Growth and Movement', Working Paper 12, Centre for Environmental Studies, London, 1968.
[11] T. A. Broadbent, 'Techniques for Regional Economic Analysis', Working Paper 13, Centre for Environmental Studies, London, 1969.
[12] A. G. Wilson, D. Bayliss, A. J. Blackburn and B. G. Hutchinson, *op. cit.*
[13] M. Cordey Hayes, 'Retail Location Models', Working Paper 16, Centre for Environmental Studies, London, 1968.
[14] D. B. Massey, 'Some Simple Models of Industrial Location', Working Paper 24, Centre for Environmental Studies, London, 1969.
[15] C. Alexander, *Notes on the Synthesis of Form*, Harvard, 1964.
[16] C. Buchanan and Partners, *The South Hampshire Study*, Ministry of Housing and Local Government, 1967.
[17] N. Lichfield, 'Economics in Town Planning', *Town Planning Review*, Vol. 39, No. 1, 1968.
[18] M. Hill, 'A Goals-achievement Matrix in Evaluating Alternative Plans', *Journal of the American Institute of Planners*, Vol. 34, No. 1, 1968.
[19] E. L. Cripps and D. H. S. Foot, 'Evaluating Alternative Strategies', *Official Architecture and Planning*, Vol. 31, No. 7, 1968.

[20] M. Meyerson and E. C. Banfield, *Politics, Planning and the Public Interest*, Free Press, 1955.

[21] J. A. G. Griffiths, *Central Departments and Local Authorities*, Allen and Unwin, 1966.

[22] A. Maass, 'System Design and the Political Process': a general statement in, A. Maass (ed.), *Design in water resource systems*, Harvard, 1964.

[23] P. H. Levin, 'Decision making rules for Urban Planners', *Journal of the Town Planning Institute*, Vol. 38, No. 12, 1967.

[24] J. K. Friend and W. N. Jessop, *Local Government and Strategic Choice*, Tavistock, 1969.

[25] J. Stringer, 'Operational Research for Multi-organisations', *Operational Research Quarterly*, Vol. 18, No. 2, 1967.

[26] J. K. Friend, 'Inter-organisational Decision Processes in Town Development', mimeo, IOR/382, Institute of Operational Research, 1969.

[27] S. Korner, *The Philosophy of Mathematics*, Hutchinson University Library, 1960.

[28] B. Crick, 'What People Want from Planning', paper presented to S.S.R.C./C.E.S. Joint Conference, Glasgow, July 1968, in Working Paper 5, Centre for Environmental Studies, London.

[29] D. N. Michael, 'Speculations on the Relation of the Computer to Individual Freedom and the Right to Privacy', *The George Washington Law Review*, Vol. 33, No. 1, 1964.

[30] L. R. Peattie, 'Reflections on advocacy Planning', *Journal of the American Institute of Planners*, Vol. 34, No. 2, 1968.

[31] W. Ross Ashby, *Cybernetics*, Chapman and Hall, 1956.

LEISURE AND RECREATION

BRIAN RODGERS

As human productivity increases and labour inputs decline, the advanced industrial nations seem to be moving inevitably towards societies based rather on leisure than labour. This is a social revolution for which we are ill-prepared, yet it may be upon us well within the limits of the planning time-scale. Mass under-employment in an age of abundant, perhaps superabundant, leisure may pose problems just as serious in their way as those of mass unemployment in the past.[1] Certainly these changes, whatever their pace and nature, will throw a large new increment of demand on recreational resources of all kinds. Not all leisure is spent recreationally, nor does all recreation express itself in a demand for space and facilities, but the outdoor pursuits which are probably the chief growth sector are prodigal in their demand for land, and they lead also to difficult problems of management where recreation is involved in the multiple use of land. For these and other reasons (the problems of the 'carrying capacity' of recreational resources, of access, of investment and pricing, of seasonality and periodicity in use) recreation must now be seen as one of the primary social needs for which the planner must make detailed provision. There is no 'laissez faire' alternative to public direction.

Part I

Leisure and Recreation : The National Pattern and its Trends

The Research Background

Serious research into recreation as a function of planning is in its infancy in Britain. A research 'explosion' is in progress, but the great bulk of the work is still 'in the pipeline'. A pattern of research is beginning to shape itself. The proposition that the first step in planning for anything is to measure (and if possible predict) the demand for it has brought into being two considerable national surveys (based on random household samples) which attempt to measure the national pattern of recreation and its variants across sectors of the population. These two 'demand surveys' are in part complementary. The Government Social Survey study is concerned with the recreation of urban populations and is orientated especially towards physical recreation and formal sport:[2] The University of Keele—British Travel Association survey is more general,[3] for though its chief concern is

---

Mr Rodgers is a Reader in Social Geography, University of Keele

with outdoor recreation, it attempts also to quantify the amount of leisure among the sample and its use in both passive and active pursuits at home and away from home, and it examines the recreational use of the private car in some detail. Together these two general surveys outline the national pattern of recreation with reasonable confidence. Whether either can be used predictively, in any exact sense, is dubious; neither has a sample big enough for sophisticated treatment.[4]

National random sampling is a very blunt instrument for this purpose: most recreations are minority activities, and low-ratio sampling is at its most vulnerable in this context. Interest is therefore shifting towards major regional studies. These have two great advantages: the sampling fraction can be higher, and at the regional level (but not at the national) it is possible to examine the supply side of the equation as well as the demand side. Since opportunity creates so large a part of the demand in recreation this is a crucial advantage. Stocktakings of recreational resources and facilities have been completed for several regions (in particular the North, the West Midlands, the North-West) and several counties.[5] In one region, the North, a demand survey has also been made, and its results are awaited. Sophisticated analyses of the interaction of supply and demand should become possible at a regional level: one such study, methodologically orientated, is in progress.[6]

Most recreational research in Britain so far has taken the form of studies of particular types of facility, often coupled with user surveys.[7] Some of these are national in scope: a general study of the coastline as a recreational resource has appeared in draft.[8] At a lesser regional scale there has been a large scale use-survey of the Peak Park[9] and another of the Loch Lomond area.[10] But much of this work has been fragmentary in scope and idiosyncratic in method. The result is a curious conglomerate of research, not easily quarried from to establish general principles. Much of this detailed work is directed towards the problem of carrying capacities and saturation points in the use of recreational facilities; but few answers have yet emerged. Very recently, empirical local work of this kind has been given a new direction by the first attempts at developing demand-predictive models.

Labour, Leisure and Recreation: the present pattern

If the results of the Keele—B.T.A. study can be trusted (and they check well against other data) we are not yet a leisured society. As 'official' working weeks have shortened (to 41 hours for the men in the sample) people have become more prepared to barter leisure for income: 1 in 10 of all men have second jobs, about 1 in 3 factory workers do regular overtime. Despite his 41-hour week the 'average' man commits at least 50 hours to economic ends. Working days are long: in all but its least demanding forms, recreation is an activity of weekends and holidays. Leisure varies surprisingly little with income, occupation or education: the rich are not also leisured (except for their longer annual holiday, often spent abroad). The only leisured class is the very poor, who are also the old, but the old are recreationally passive. Thus those with the slightest recreational appetite have most leisure, while those with the greatest capacity for generating recreational demands often opt out of leisure. A self-cancelling situation exists, and acts as a brake on demand.

Any attempt to look at the time-budget of individuals is confused by semantic obscurity: many of the words one uses have imprecise meanings and even looser usage. From 'waking time' one can subtract 'economic time' (the compulsory demands of an occupation) to leave 'disposable time'. Not all of this is leisure: the chores of life absorb some, and part may be used to increase income: what remains is leisure, by no means all of which is used, in any real sense, recreationally. Recreational time itself takes various forms; it may be spent at home or from home, indoors or out, actively or passively. The planner's overwhelming concern is with a quite small fraction of time (even of leisure)—the part spent outdoors, actively, away from home. This fraction polarises across the socio-economic scale. Its likely changes are one of the central predictive problems.

Overall activeness in outdoor recreation varies with a number of social parameters: it diminishes with age, with a sharp break at marriage; it increases with income and with income-associated variables like occupation, education and car-ownership. These trends are true for almost all outdoor pursuits: but some show slight decrease (or even growth) with age, the 'old men's' sports like bowls. Others show only a slight increase with income (the poor man's sports) while some respond only at the highest steps on the income scale, the pastimes of the rich. Some sports seem education-sensitive: others are almost monopolised by car-owners. But beyond a list of about a dozen pastimes, neither of the two national surveys can yield detailed profiles of participants, for sub-sample sizes are too small.

What clearly emerges is that a pattern of constraints, varying between individuals and changing over the life-cycle, shapes recreational idiosyncracies. Three broad phases are identifiable. To the young and single adult constraints are fewest: he has a combination of physical capacity, disposable time and 'free' income which he will probably never again enjoy. This is overwhelmingly the most active phase, generating much the greatest demand: yet it is a demand largely channelled to relatively formal recreations and to sport in a narrow sense; so that space requirements are quite limited. After marriage, in the 'family' phase in recreation, uncommitted income diminishes and so does disposable time: the physical capacity of the family unit is that of its feeblest members, so recreation becomes informal and undemanding physically, focused on coast, countryside and park. The car becomes a crucial factor. As families age, both leisure and income may increase, but age sets increasing physical restraints: most people leave most things until too late: if they did not then demand would swamp facilities. Old age is a phase of excess leisure, of recreational passivity, undemanding in terms of space and facilities. Very often the needs of these three basic stages in the life-cycle conflict, and their reconciliation is one of the chief tasks of the planner.

So recreation is closely adapted to and conditioned by the life-cycle. But it is also determined by—and itself an expression of—the life style. Life style is discussed at length in another paper (Willmott p. 291): it is compounded of income, education and occupation, though by no means a mere amalgam of these, and its recreational expression is relatively subtle. Some pursuits are, for obvious reasons of cost, the monopoly of the relatively rich: sailing, winter sports, golf and the second home are among these, some of which represent an 'escape' environment of one kind or another. But some of the recreations most characteristic of the upper-income life style are cheap: hiking, hill-walking, camping, the 'field' interests, like natural history, all show (in the Keele-B.T.A. data on the costs of recreational 'trips') a low ratio of cost to time spent. Conversely some of the favourite recreations of the low-income sample, indoor sports and fishing for example, are relatively expensive. Life style in general, not income in particular, is the essential key.

For most families a critical break in life style follows the acquisition of the first car, and the impact of this on the use of leisure is probably greater than on any other aspect of life. From the very large mass of material on the recreational use of the car assembled in the Keele-B.T.A. study two broad conclusions emerge. The car enormously stimulates recreational demands, but its use varies markedly across the income ranges. The first of these is obvious: access problems are resolved by the car, especially during the 'family' phase in recreation. Camping, sailing, riding, moorland recreations and golf are all reported in very great excess by car owners. Part of this, of course, is merely a concealed income effect. Conversely sports without a great access problem (bowls, cycling and team games) are not reported in great excess by car users. To a degree, car ownership is therefore a predictive variable, and could be so used. However, the use of the car varies considerably with income. Low income car owners use their vehicles less often and over lower mileages recreationally; among them acquisition of a car depresses holiday taking, though the car is used most strongly at this income level as a family vehicle. In brief it would be unsafe to deduce from the present leisure patterns of middle and high income car owners what the recreational impact of the car might be on families (chiefly from lower income ranges) who will become motorised during the next decade.

There is an obvious danger in generalising, at the national level, about recreational patterns and their determinants. In fact the use of leisure varies both regionally and at a lesser scale, and no discussion limited to national archetypes is realistic. Spatial contrast in recreation exists at three levels: on a regional scale, between communities of different size, and between housing areas of different age and type. The regional differences which show (very dimly) in the data at present available seem geared chiefly to access. For example the North has a particular interest in moorland recreation, the South and West in sailing, the Midlands in fishing.

Conversely, some pursuits are stunted in some regions, and for these clearly a suppressed demand may exist. A rather confused set of contrasts distinguishes conurbations from smaller population units, and again access factors seem to be crucial. Very sharp differences occur between house-types (obviously reflecting a range of social variables) though it is difficult to discern the true impact of urban environment alone. This system of spatial contrast probably has less relevance to prediction in time, than to spatial 'forecasts' of recreational demand in communities of different type.

In summary, the two national household surveys sketch out at least the broad shape of the national profile of recreational activity and some of its social and spatial variations. The results scarcely paint a picture of frenzied activity; about 1 in 10 had swum in 1965, about 1 in 20 had camped or fished, played tennis or team games, hiked or sailed during the year. The rest are minority interests. Not surprisingly, some of the home-based and passive recreations threw up much larger proportions of participants: about a quarter had gardened during the week before survey and two-thirds or more watch television on a weekend evening. In short the home is still the frame and setting for most of our leisure; but with increasing income, educational and occupational status we break away from it more frequently in satisfying our recreational needs. The simple, home-centred recreational life style of the past is giving way quite quickly to the more mobile, more sophisticated life style of the future.

Growth and Change in Recreation

Any attempt to predict change is very uncertain, if only because so many factors of chance and fashion are involved. There are two approaches to prediction. One can ask the sample what they would like to do (and firmly plan to do) in the future. Discounting fanciful replies, this yields a few reasonably credible signposts to the changing shape of future demand. Secondly, the association of particular pursuits with specific socio-economic attributes (themselves crudely predictable) provides a theoretical basis for forecast, though it would be statistically foolhardy to push this far at present. From both exercises a number of pointers emerge. Some recre-ations suggest little growth. Low income pursuits are not likely to respond much to a rise in real wages: thus the growth of demand for bowls among the elderly or cycling among the young is unlikely to be huge. The sports of young adult life (those which fade in the twenties and rarely survive marriage) like team games or athletics have a certain growth potential geared to changes in national age structure, but few are strongly income sensitive (and so should not respond quickly to rise in incomes) and the trend to early marriage is a damping factor. Other sports which, conversely, are income sensitive (especially over the middle steps) but not strongly age selective have enormous growth potential. Golf and the cheaper forms of sailing are obvious examples: some minority pastimes (winter sports, perhaps riding) may fall in the same category. But in so many recreations demand is so geared to supply that it seems unprofitable to guess about their prospects. Whether swimming has growth potential depends largely on the volume of latent demand which lies interstitially between catchment areas of existing pools (or perhaps only attractive modern pools). A study recently mounted should illuminate this. Tennis has the profile of a stagnant sport, but colour television may promote a revival.

A group of recreations stands out as likely to generate great increases in demand, the coastal and water-based pastimes, and some of the countryside pursuits. Sailing in all its forms figures very strongly in the wishful thinking of the Keele-B.T.A. sample; so does fishing (a much cheaper pastime). Interest in countryside recreation (hiking, camping, moorland recreations) is especially strong among the better educated and the car owners, and for these if for no other reasons is likely to grow. A conclusion which develops, strongly if imprecisely, from all of this is that many of the recreations with least growth potential (team games, tennis) make very modest space demands, while others with far greater capacity for growth (golf and the water group) require far greater space allocations and become involved in complex conflict situations.

It is an inherent danger in this kind of tentative prediction that changes in taste and fashion will reverse what appears to be the logical trend, and this risk is certainly greater in attempting to discern the future of urban recreation than in the context of the relatively stable pursuits of coast and countryside. We have seen, in a single decade, the rise and decline of ten-pin bowling. Over a somewhat longer time-scale the theatre (in the Provinces at least) has been miniaturised, while the massive cinema industry of the 'forties has been dismantled and converted to gambling in its simplest form, the bingo-hall. But now the mini-cinema and the multi-cinema offer new prospects of growth, while the development of the casino-club offers an obvious challenge to bingo. Surely a more numerate society will prefer its gambling in the more sophisticated form. In a different dimension of urban recreation, the last ten years have seen a considerable investment in multi-purpose indoor sports centres, often associated with a good modern swimming pool, while the traditional outdoor facilities for team games and the like have attracted less interest. Only one conclusion seems possible, that the changing nature of urban recreation is impossible to predict, and that therefore facilities should whenever possible be adaptable, not inflexibly purpose-built. But there is a second general characteristic of simple outdoor urban recreation, and that is that it is becoming ever more difficult to distinguish it rationally from general countryside recreation. There is now developing a hierarchy of open space that transcends the urban-rural dichotomy, extending from neighbourhood open space to national park. Whether the regional park within the conurbation, the country park on its fringes and the area of open-access countryside beyond will be put to different uses and purposes seems unlikely: they are simply alternative offerings within the same system, and a mobile society will use them all indifferently.

Part II

*Policy objectives in recreational planning; the development and
management of recreational resources*

Fortunately the great bulk of the leisure of the British public is absorbed
in pursuits for which the planner need make little specific provision. Most
recreation is passive and undemanding—reading, viewing, visiting and
gossiping—and when the majority of people venture away from home for
recreation they gather compactly on the few acres that is all the cinema or
bingo hall, the football ground or the dance hall need. Agreed, an improvement in real income, education and car ownership must lead to a
shift towards more active and less gregarious pursuits, but the present rather
passive majority pattern is scarcely likely to undergo quick and revolutionary change. In fact some present trends may strengthen the recreational importance of the home itself: gardening, car maintenance and
home improvement all absorbed considerable quantities of the leisure of
the Keele-B.T.A. sample, particularly in the middle income ranges. Many
low-income families will doubtless soon acquire their first car to clean,
cherish and tinker with, their first garden and their first home worth the
effort of improvement. Home-based recreation involves the planner only
marginally, though his decisions clearly establish a framework for it,
especially in the context of the density and form of housing.

Though recreation focused on the home will continue to dominate the
leisure patterns of the majority, there is no doubt that the pastimes with
the greatest potential for growth are the active outdoor recreations which
not only generate enormous demands for land and for investment by either
private or public entrepreneurs, but which also, because they lead to
difficult conflict-of-interest situations, involve the planner in complex
problems of management. All the available evidence shows that the relatively poor are not only recreationally passive, but their active interests
make little demand for land. Bowls and team games are 'compact' sports
in total contrast with the space-hungry recreations of the rich—golf, riding,
sailing and winter sports. All of these are still, in varying degrees, minority
pursuits; but some have an obvious potential for quick and massive growth
(if facilities to meet rising demand can be created) for they are sensitive
to increments of income over the middle ranges of the scale. Because they
are, presently, minority interests, even a slight proportionate increase in
demand among the national population could quickly clog existing facilities;
but because they are also space demanding even a modest growth in
facilities might involve an impossible scale of land allocation. Golf for the
conurbation populations is the obvious example, and perhaps the most
urgent real need.

The problem of 'carrying capacity'

How quickly the growth of demand for particular types of recreational
facilities overtakes and saturates the existing supply depends obviously

upon their maximum use-capacity. This is the essential calculation on the supply side of the equation and in some senses the nub of the planning problem.

There is no insuperable difficulty in estimating the use-capacity of some sorts of recreational facility, particularly for the formal sports and especially, rather unfortunately, for some of the pursuits with relatively slight growth potential. Playing fields for the team games, bowling greens and tennis courts have a finite capacity, though this is never realised because of the strong factors of seasonality and periodicity in recreation. But at least there is a basis for a calculation. In the case of most of the coastal, countryside and moorland recreations which are so clearly a great growth sector, no firm basis for a calculation of carrying capacity exists. It is difficult even to describe or define the needs of the user, let alone invent a unit of measurement of use that permits some sort of approach to the problem. The carrying capacity of a beach, an estuary used for sailing or a moorland valley depends entirely on what the user wants to do there and expects from it. Capacity is sensed empirically by waiting for obvious signs of over-use. These may ultimately be unequivocal, for example the physical destruction of the sand-dune environment on the Lancashire coast by an excess of picnic parties.

In fact almost any open country or coastal recreational location is used as a multi-purpose facility, and its capacity depends largely on the varying mix of purposes among its visitors. A beach which may, without gross congestion, allow a thousand families to sunbathe and build sand-castles would be crowded if three sand yachts had the exclusive use of it. Attempts have been made to quantify beach capacities in terms of different classes of user, with a view to using car parking as a mechanism of control, and this perhaps coupled with segregation of incompatible types of user (the concept of the 'sports beach') may provide an empirical basis for guiding and developing the use of the coast as a recreational resource.[11] The mountains and moorlands pose even greater problems, for their recreational rôle is so indefinable. They offer the last illusion, in Britain, of escape from the civilised world. Presumably this is what the 'serious' visitor seeks from them, but if his view from the upland slopes is of the ribbon development of picnic parties along the valley road he leaves dissatisfied. In one sense all but the remote cores of the British uplands are already used far beyond their carrying capacity, during most of the summer season. In another sense a fivefold increase in the number of visitors could easily be tolerated in many upland valleys, even in August, before the average visitor began to feel he was merely one of a crowd. In short we must assign a purpose to the uplands—and to specific parts of them—before speculation about carrying capacities begins to make sense. So far much planning for the upland regions has embodied the principle of escalation: demand grows and clogs existing access routes; these are improved thus generating an increment of previously suppressed demand, and so the process continues. All our data suggest that this kind of almost inflationary process in the growth of demand can scarcely be satisfied, short of the 'motorway over the Kirkstone Pass' type of solution, if the expression of a mass demand is permitted to lead policy making to its logical conclusion in this direction.

The management of outdoor recreational resources

If in the long term it is unacceptable to allow the growth of mass demand to dominate the recreational use of the coast and countryside, leaving minority interests unprotected, then complex problems of management arise and perhaps unpalatable principles have to be accepted. All the fundamental resources that are the setting for the major growth sectors in recreation—the coast and country, water and wilderness—are more or less inelastic: indeed they are diminishing in supply as the apparatus of an urban-industrial civilisation makes irresistible demands for land. Within a shrinking total resource, and against the background of a rising pro-rata demand among a growing national population, the sophisticated needs of a minority have to be balanced against the simple needs of the mass of users. And more commonly than not, the total complex of recreational needs must be reconciled against the claims of other forms of land use, for recreation rarely has sole rights to the spaces it uses. It would be entirely pretentious to suggest that these management problems can be explored in a few paragraphs. It is intended merely to outline three principles that may be adopted in segregating irreconcilable components in the total mix of demand, giving each its opportunity for expression. Pricing is an obvious management mechanism, so is the principle of the valve, while lastly the concept of the hierarchy of facilities, sieving demand into its components and guiding each to an appropriate setting, is being explored by some planning authorities.

The Price Mechanism

Pricing is the most obvious, and perhaps also the easiest and most effective, way of regulating demand against the existing supply of facilities. Give the majority the simple facilities they need at low cost, but charge the more demanding minority user a higher price appropriate to his needs and to the much lower carrying capacity of the facility as he proposes to use it. In short let people hire the space they need, within a logical price structure. Applied to a swimming bath, the 'splasher', the learner and the family party would be able to satisfy their needs at low cost, while at stipulated times the serious swimmer and diver could hire the greater space allocations they need, paying a higher price calculated to keep the 'splasher' away. The use capacity of the bath is enormously greater when it is satisfying a simple mass demand than when put to more sophisticated uses, and so there is some economic equity in the principle of selective pricing. Without such a price structure the 'serious' user may never in fact have the chance to satisfy his particular needs at all. Against this may be set arguments based on social justice: the high income splasher may attend at the wrong time, the low income (or young) serious swimmer may be priced out of his sport. In some pursuits the principle of management by a club is an attractive alternative to management by price control: most golf facilities are at present governed in this way, so are some sailing facilities. But the broad mass of countryside and coastal recreation lies outside any possible application of the 'club' principle. Whatever the balance of advantage may be, pricing is widely applied as a regulator of recreational demand. All the best things in life are certainly not free. Golf is an obvious example. Pricing not only restrains total demand, but selectively sorts it between a number of sectors (public and club courses, 'fashionable' and 'popular' courses). Without price restraint, the demand for golf would probably grow far beyond the capacity of existing courses, or indeed any likely addition to them. Without price restraint in any form, what will be the growth of demand for those recreational resources that have been traditionally free, the coast and countryside in all their varied forms? In fact some element of price control is already at work shaping the pattern of demand in these recreational environments. The countryside is free, but not the 'stately homes' and many country parks: in fact much of the countryside to which there is public access is priced. The hills are free, but not to the camper or caravan owner. They must often rent space: should not the casual visitor by car pay also, at least for his parking? If the principle of paying to use the countryside is accepted in some contexts, then is it positively immoral to use pricing creatively, as a policy instrument? Large low-cost car parks at the mouth of a mountain valley would provide the mass of visitors with the picnic places and the backcloth of upland scenery they want: small high-cost parks at the valley head would provide the climber or fell walker with access to a protected environment, but at a price. Thus two different carrying capacities, geared to different forms of use, are reconciled by the medium of price control. None of this is too visionary: the question of putting a price on the use of even the major tourist roads through the Lake District at peak periods has already received serious attention.[12] Whether pricing can be used, in a sense non-commercially, to implement policy decisions is debatable. But it is plain that people must be prepared to pay the high cost of creating new facilities to meet rising demand, and that these may be available only at much higher price levels than have been traditional. Sailing provides an example. The sea is free (though the boat itself may be expensive) and access charges have been low or even absent. To keep a yacht at swinging moorings, or to keep a dinghy at a dinghy-park (if it is not trailed home behind a car) are all low-cost ways of storing a boat. But the capacity of dinghy-parks on many popular estuaries is beginning to be exhausted, while the hundreds of yachts at swinging moorings (in terms of the space consumed, a very uneconomical way of 'storing' a boat) are seriously eroding the available sailing space in sheltered waters for small boats along the southern coasts. In short there is already a critical 'parking' problem, and this is one of the major growth recreations. The answer is the marina, with jetty moorings for yachts, dinghy and power-boat parks and a mass of other necessary facilities. But access to the sea via the marina is likely to be a good deal dearer than in the traditional ways. There is, potentially, a serious conflict of interest in this situation: the sailor using the marina may find part of the space to which he has bought access occupied by boats parked 'on the cheap' at swinging moorings. Some rationalisation of the use of sheltered waters seems inevitable in the long term, and it must turn on the question of pricing.[13]

In other regions sailors may have to help to pay, not merely for access to the sea, but for the very water they float on. The Northwest is a poor coast for the sailor, and this is a sport of stunted growth in the region.[14] The smooth, exposed shore is broken only by a few estuaries, most of which dry completely to enormous spreads of sand and mud on the falling tide. In the restricted channels, pleasure sailors and commercial vessels get in each other's way. But almost every Northwestern estuary except the Mersey has been suggested, at one time or another, as capable of enclosure behind a barrage. This might provide, apart from reclaimed land, both protected areas of non-tidal water within the barrage for small boat sailing and marina access to the open sea for larger craft. The only project that has reached the stage of serious inquiry, the Morecambe Bay barrage, is seen primarily as a huge fresh water reservoir for the supply of industrial Lancashire. Granted that small-boat sailing is seen as a compatible use (as it is, increasingly, by water supply authorities) then this could also become one of the largest areas of sheltered water in the country, and the region's resources in the development of one of the major growth sports would be transformed. Surely recreation must be seen as one of the dominant terms in the cost-benefit equation for such a project, but by the same token the sailor must be prepared to meet some part of the capital cost through pricing. The moral that seems to lie in all of this is simple enough. In many recreational contexts free access inevitably means limited, congested and unsatisfactory facilities. The acceptance of the need to pay for what one uses makes possible both the creative development of resources and (if a further, perhaps unpalatable principle is accepted) their selective use so that people may hire what they need. In short, pricing is one approach (though by no means the only or a universal approach) to the carrying capacity problem.

The physical metering of demand

There is a radically different approach to the problem of managing recreational resources so that they are not destroyed or debased by over-use, the principle of the valve metering demand to match the available supply. This, too, is widely adopted—consciously or by happy accident—in many recreational environments already. It is in essence the display of the 'house full' notice, familiar enough in urban recreation and in many sports for which facilities have a finite capacity, but now beginning to appear in the countryside and the uplands, though rarely on the coast. If car access and parking facilities are limited—whether by design or merely by default—to the maximum use-capacity of the environment they serve, then destructive over-use is avoided. The principle may be seen in operation any day during the peak season at Tarn Hows, an attractive lake in an upland setting near Coniston. Single track roads of low capacity operate, in effect, as a one-way 'scenic circuit', serving car parks with a capacity for about 300 vehicles. Illicit parking is virtually impossible, and the site can easily absorb the thousand or so visitors who may secure access to it at any one time. Admittedly, this may mean some frustration of part of the potential demand at peak periods, but this is inherent in any system of metering demand. Access to Loch Katrine is similarly (and very effectively) regulated: at the forestry estates at Glen Trool in Galloway both progressively narrowing access roads and limited parking meter the flow of visitors.

Once on a site of this broad type the flow of visitors is self-regulating and self-selecting. Any car park in an upland area serves a very small effective hinterland. Most visitors stay within a few hundred yards: the proportions penetrating to successively greater ranges diminish quickly, probably curvilineally, stepping down at any minor physical obstacle. The illusion of the wilderness is only a few minutes walk from the parked car, for those few who want it. Given the principle of the valve as a restraint on total flow, the several elements in demand, from the family picnic to the rock climber, can be left to segregate themselves, aided perhaps by intelligent site-design.

Provided that pressures to improve road access are resisted, this kind of metering of demand clearly protects the semi-wild environment effectively and permanently. But this is negative planning: it does nothing to meet the enormous potential increase in demand for access to the uplands, not only one of the most strongly seasonal sectors in the recreational market. The extra demand can be accommodated merely by opening the valves a notch or two: this is what has generally been done in the past, usually disastrously. The alternative is the opening of new metered access systems to presently inaccessible locations, and this will bring its own storm of protest.

In fact there is little prospect of effectively regulating the flow of visitors by physical constraints except to the remoter parts of the wilder uplands. Most of the moorland regions are too well intersected by through routes to protect against over-use in this way. Almost every major 'beauty spot' in the Peak District is served by excellent high-capacity roads (especially when industrial traffic is thin at weekends) except perhaps Dovedale and the Kinder-Bleaklow moors, and the latter are rather an acquired taste. Much of upland Wales, too, is wide open to the expression of a mass demand. There can scarcely be any question of metering flow into areas like these (short of charging entry tolls) but the principle of the scenic circuit, punctuated by parking provision at appropriate places, would provide some slight measure of guidance and control.[15]

The hierarchy of facilities and the filtering of demand

Lastly, in this outline of approaches to the management problem, recreational facilities may be seen as structured into a hierarchy, so arranged that the mass of simple unsophisticated demand is filtered off close to its origin, while the more specialised elements in demand pass through to the sorts of environment they need. There are many simple applications of the principle: the learner pool alongside the competition standard pool, the short nine-hole course as an alternative to the full-scale golf course, while in the urban setting the hierarchy of children's playspace, the larger park offering a basic range of sports facilities and the sub-regional park simulating a rural environment is a familiar and long-established one.

The filter principle has been explored in recreational planning for Staffordshire, a county which, by geographical accident, lends itself to this kind of strategy.[16] The main mass of recreational demand is generated on its southern threshold, in the West Midland conurbation; from here the county straddles a variety of recreational environments of contrasted potential culminating in the Peak District National Park along its northern border. A hierarchy of facilities, extending from the conurbation to the wilderness, should sieve the components in total demand and accommodate them in appropriate settings, though the simplicity of the model is obviously disturbed by the corridor of urban growth across the county to the smaller Potteries conurbation in the northwest.

The Black Country green-belt in the south, in fact mostly very grey and scarred, would contain facilities for relatively intensive use, for example major concentrations of playing fields, sports centres with athletics facilities, golf courses, and water recreation areas based on old reservoirs, flooded mineral workings and the intricate canal system. Beyond the main mass of the green-belt would lie country parks, 'stately homes' in their estates, areas for walking, riding and the picnic party, in short a wide range of settings for simple family recreation. Some parts of mid-Staffordshire also offer long term prospects of development for water-based recreation, especially in districts of wet-pit surface workings. This kind of complex of countryside facilities already exists in the forested upland of Cannock Chase. Here a local filter system provides peripheral zones with full public access, while the core is protected by an interceptor ring of car parks. For those who want a more dramatic setting (probably a minority) for their day in the country there are, at greater distance, the limestone uplands and grit-stone crags of the National Park. All data on the mileage covered on the day or half-day excursion suggest that the filter role of Cannock Chase (and its equivalents elsewhere, as in some senses a regional park) will be an effective one in localising simple sorts of recreational demand that would otherwise seek to express themselves in environments more appropriate to other purposes.[17]

None of this, quite obviously, is intended as a detailed appraisal of contrasted approaches to the development and management of recreational resources. Nor is it suggested that the principles of pricing, management through clubs, the valve or the filter system are mutually exclusive. All have their appropriate applications, often in association. Conversely none of them need be applied, to the bulk of outdoor recreation, for the greater part of the time. In applying any kind of control or guidance to the use of outdoor recreational facilities, one is legislating for a few fine summer weekends. If the seasonality and periodicity of recreational demand can be smoothed many problems are minimised. There are hopeful trends: holiday taking is becoming a little more flexible with a tendency to spread over four months rather than two, while continuous processing in industry will certainly mean that the four- or five-shift week, will blunt the distinction between working week and weekend. Real progress in these directions would in effect enormously increase the use-capacity of our present recreational resources.

Conclusion

Trend, change and the time-base

The phrase 'the future' has no meaning unless it can be defined, at least approximately, in terms of a time base; and this must be attempted for the trends and changes discussed in this paper, though the difficulties of trying to 'time' changes in recreational habits and preferences are clearly greater than those in most sorts of predictive problem. The most that can be attempted is a distinction between a short-term future, of about the next decade, and the long-term future, of about the next quarter century. The future of the next 5 to 15 years is in essence the extended present, a period likely to be dominated by 'trend' rather than 'change'. The probability is that the present determinants of recreational performance—chiefly aspects of social structure and socio-economic attributes—though differently quantified ten years hence will produce patterns of recreation identifiably similar to those of today, though particular recreational 'mixes' will have moved along the social spectrum. Perhaps within a decade the typical patterns of leisure associated with a working class life style will be closer to those currently associated with the middle class, but they will still be interpretable in terms of the present system of linkage between recreation and age, income, education and car ownership. But it would be over-simple to argue that the short-term future is predictable in terms merely of a general shift upwards a rung or two along the ladder of life styles. Much depends on social attitudes: as much depends on the working class wife learning to drive as on the working class family acquiring a car, and even more upon the adoption of a middle class attitude to the apportionment of the car between rival uses. The working-class car today seems to be much more committed to journey-to-work than to general leisure purposes. Despite these open questions, it is only over the short term that predictions about changing leisure patterns may be made with any confidence, or projections calculated geared to present associations. The comments above on the growth capacities of particular recreations can only be applied with any confidence to the short term; and the general conclusion, more golf, swimming, camping, open-country recreation and sailing refer primarily to this period. But in the short term 'trend' may easily be disturbed by 'incident'. Our present economic debility has slowed the growth of incomes and leisure and probably of social mobility as well.

The longer term of the next two or three decades is one in which radical change may overtake and overturn conclusions derived merely from the present trend, and in which therefore the process of prediction—in the ordinary sense—may have little validity. For example within this period we can surely expect the workshift to replace the workday—perhaps in the office as well as the factory—so that the distinction between weekday and weekend disappears. But will leisure be taken in doses of three or four days—or one week in three or four, or as extended holidays? The quantum of leisure is at least as important as its overall amount in determining a recreational response. Perhaps more significant still is the likely change in the next generation or two, in the life cycle (see Willmott p. 16). If the age of marriage falls, progressively, much further, it will have radical effects on the general distribution of leisure over the life cycle. Late-teenage marriage would eliminate or greatly modify what is presently the most active recreational phase, the period to which interest in competitive sports is largely confined. But teenage marriage in a second generation would produce virtually childless couples in their mid-thirties. Will this shift the period of maximum recreational activity from late adolescence, as at present, to the thirties and forties, to a post-parental phase in which physical capacity for quite demanding recreations is undiminished but coincides with maximum financial capacity and a superabundance of leisure? Perhaps therefore the recreational explosion is to be seen in terms of the preferences and tastes of early middle age. If so, what form would it take? Probably not the most demanding, most disciplined, of the competitive and team sports, but the time-absorbing, countryside and water-based pursuits—golf, boats, second homes, moorland recreations, and doubtless travel abroad on an enormously increased scale.

Other radical changes with a powerful recreational impact seem likely to come in the 25-year time scale. Home ownership is spreading and doubtless will spread over a broader income band; and housing quality is improving. Will this mean a trend towards a more strongly home-centred society, content with home-based recreation (Willmott p. 17)? To offset this is the obvious progress towards universal car ownership: but will we, in twenty years' time, be able to use cars (or their successors) under much the same conditions as those that apply today, or will we have to submit to restraints (see Hall p. 138)? The 'mobility versus stability' argument produces no obvious conclusions for the future of recreation except that there is room, in a half idle society, for the great growth of both home-centred and mobile leisure pursuits. But the need for re-education and locational re-training may place serious constraints on the volume of leisure available in middle life.

One last question of the 25-year time scale deserves brief comment. At present we can interpret recreational patterns in socio-economic terms and this is the chief predictive tool. Will society retain anything like its present structure a quarter of a century hence? Will 'class' differences persist? Will life styles have become almost standardised within the framework of the life cycle? Our present thinking about recreational patterns as a dimension of social contrast may have no relevance in a differently structured society, so that our present conclusions can bring little comfort to the recreational planner interested in the long time-scale. Willmott (p. 9) shows that inter-generational occupational mobility is only slowly accelerating. Does this mean a process of levelling up? But how will occupational differences express themselves in a social sense in a mobile society? The 'blue collar–white collar' distinction is already blurring. If these trends are correctly predicted and if life styles come ever closer to a norm, the socio-economic parameters are a feeble tool in predicting the changing shape of recreational demand, and the influence of change in the life cycle the surer guide.

REFERENCES

[1] The social aspects of these changes are taken up by Peter Willmott in his contribution to this volume, 'Some Social Trends', pp. 8-30.

[2] The Government Social Survey's study of leisure and recreation was conducted among the urban population of England and Wales, with separate sub-samples for inner London and the New Towns: the national sample totalled 2,682 members, the other samples were 1,732 and 1,321 respectively. K. K. Sillitoe, *Planning for Leisure*, H.M.S.O., 1969.

[3] British Travel Association—University of Keele, *Pilot National Recreation Survey, Report No. 1*, 1967. A second report, on the chief differences in recreation between six major divisions of Great Britain, is in the Press. This survey, on which the reports have been written by the present author, was based on the relatively small national sample of 3,167 individuals. Broadly speaking, its salient conclusions have been confirmed by the results of the Government Social Survey inquiry.

[4] A pioneer attempt to use the data of a 'demand survey' predictively is contained in the first of the major regional recreational studies, the inquiry into *Outdoor Leisure Activities in the Northern Region*, by National Opinion Polls, which uses the technique of discriminant analysis to establish a relationship between recreations and those demographic and socio-economic characteristics that appear to be their chief determinants. This report is not yet published, and so comment is inappropriate. There are two obvious hazards in this—or any related—technique: the relationship between a recreation and its 'determinants' is often too loose for confident calculation, and there is often great difficulty in projecting those socio-economic factors that seem to be the chief influences on recreation.

[5] See, for example, K. O. Male, *Recreation in Cheshire*, Cheshire County Council, 1967; and *Cheshire Countryside*, 1968. The former is a facilities survey and the latter a stocktaking of resources for countryside recreation, on a sub-regional basis, related to estimates of demand.

[6] This and other problems in the methodology of recreational research are discussed in T. L. Burton and P. A. Noad, *Recreation Research Methods: A Review of Recent Studies*, University of Birmingham, 1968.

[7] Among the chief exceptions to this are two more general studies: T. L. Burton and G. P. Wibberley, *Outdoor Recreation in the British Countryside*, 1965; and T. L. Burton, *Outdoor Recreation Enterprises in Problem Rural Areas*,

　　　1967. Both are Wye College Studies in Rural Land Use, Nos 5 and 9 respectively.

[8] M. F. Tanner, *Coastal Recreation in England and Wales*, Sports Council, 1967.

[9] British Travel Association and Peak Park Planning Board, *A Survey of the Peak District National Park*, 1963.

[10] D. C. Nicholls and A. Young, *Recreation and Tourism in the Loch Lomond Area*, University of Glasgow, 1968.

[11] F. P. Tindall, in 'The Care of a Coastline', *Journal of the Town Planning Institute*, Vol. 53, 1967, p. 387, deals with the problems of capacity, conservation and development on a varied coastline in Scotland.

[12] N. W. Mansfield, Traffic Policy in the Lake District National Park, *Journal of the Town Planning Institute*, Vol. 54, 1968, p. 263.

[13] See M. F. Tanner, *op. cit.*

[14] This is clearly shown by the regional data of the Keele-B.T.A. survey.

[15] See N. W. Mansfield, *op. cit.*

[16] Staffordshire County Council, *Recreation Plan for the County*, n.d.

[17] A related concept, that each major city region must have easy access to a recreational 'lebensraum' in its hinterland to which the great bulk of pleasure trips is made, is explored in B. Cracknell, 'Accessibility to the Countryside as a factor in Planning for Leisure', *Regional Studies*, Vol. 1, 1967, p. 147.

RACE AND HUMAN RIGHTS
IN THE CITY

NICHOLAS DEAKIN

Race relations is, if not unique, unusual among social questions in that although it comprehends issues of great complexity, in debate these are almost invariably reduced with great rapidity to the crudest over-simplifications. This is a process to which not merely individuals but even governments are subject: not many pieces of legislation in recent years have been as rushed as the three-day Commonwealth Immigrants Act of 1968 and not many so misconceived.

This tendency to view the issue in (in both senses) black and white terms is matched by the tendency of opinion to coalesce round opposed alternatives; and tensions between these opposite poles help to add to the overcharged atmosphere. For example, there is a constant tension between the concept of the coloured newcomer as an equal citizen and the notion that he is admitted solely by virtue of the contribution he makes to the economy; or between the recognition that newcomers may come from a variety of cultural backgrounds and the undifferentiated stereotype of the black stranger. This tension recurs in slightly different form between the accurate perception of a migration criss-crossed with differences of social class and degree of familiarity with the urban environment, and a common view that it is composed of helots, of uniformly low status. These concepts in turn interlock with the wider public debate, in which there is a sharp division between those who conceive of the issue in terms of immigration and those who think in terms of a domestic race relations situation. A subterranean version of the same debate also rages among race relations specialists and shades into the dispute between the cheerful school of prophets and the gloomy school.

This paper examines some of these opposed concepts and makes a tentative attempt at resolving some of them, but before this, it might be convenient to define the central issue under consideration. It is the question of the entry into our society and the consequences for both parties of the entrance of over one million non-white* Commonwealth citizens. The most reliable estimate available for total numbers is 1,406,000 on 1 January 1968[1]: but any estimate—for reasons given later—is subject to a degree of error.

* The term 'non-white', disagreeable though some of its overtones are, is consciously chosen, since the question of nomenclature is itself *en cause*, as is made clear later.

Nicholas Deakin is Director, Joint Unit for Minority and Policy Research, London

Classical studies of race relations in Britain derive essentially from two perspectives. The first draws upon the colonial experience, and in particular its significance both for the colonising minority and the colonised majority, in material and psychological terms, in order to explain the series of responses set in motion where members of that majority, themselves now a minority, enter a metropolitan country. The general approach is essentially a Marxist one. Like Dr Williams,[2] those who employ this perspective for migration from the West Indies see the original colonial situation in terms of an exploitative relationship based on demands generated by capitalism and the new relationship arising out of migration as a continuation of the colonial situation albeit on somewhat different terms. The white majority in Britain categorises the coloured newcomer as a member of an un-differentiated subordinate group, and gives practical expression to this view by evolving a system of *de facto* segregation in which the newcomers are confined to poor living accommodation in narrowly demarcated areas and permitted access only to unskilled employment. This relatively straightforward view of race relations, in which colour categories cor-responded to class categories and evoke—perhaps in exaggerated form— the response appropriate to a rigid system of class categorisation, was confirmed by a number of studies carried out in British port-towns in the late forties and early fifties.[3] However, with the growth in size and changing composition of the migration which from the mid-fifties began to be directed to differing goals and satisfy different needs in the receiving society, the situation changed and the original rationale for the colour-class interpretation began to lose its force. It is worth mentioning here, however, because there are elements in the analysis which retain their relevance— and may in fact have become more apposite, despite the now marginal relevance of the fieldwork data on which these studies are based.

The view that supplanted this earlier two-category model of race relations derived from the colonial situation was one that emerged from observation in the case of fieldwork undertaken among the West Indian settlements in London in the later fifties. This was based on a comparative view of the processes of immigration, and the effect that the entry of 'newcomers' (as Mrs Glass chose to describe them in her very influential study of that name)[4] has had both on British society and on the new arrivals themselves. It was hypothesised that the West Indians were ultimately an assimilating group, in that their system of values derived in most respects from the version of British culture current in the colonial system, reinforced by the educational system and the practice of Christianity. The factor of colour was admitted as a complicating element, both insofar as it constituted the basis for a complex system of power and prestige in the sending society and to the extent that it might determine the response of the receiving society. However, it was assumed that the 'strangeness' (the key concept in Mrs Patterson's analysis and her title)[5] would in due course be modified by experience and the British would come to accept the West Indian in much the same way as they had accepted, after initial hostility and revulsion, the Irishman. Thus the old building site joke about West Indians as 'toasted

Irishmen' would become a reality. It was not part of Sheila Patterson's case (though West Indian critics misrepresented her on this point) that the logical terminus of this process would be assimilation, in the full sociological sense. In the final statement of her case she anticipated that the eventual condition might be one of pluralistic integration, in which the primary institutions of family and social network might remain confined within an identifiable, if vestigial community, while the institutional structures of society would accept and deal with the coloured minority on a basis of parity.[6] Once again, this is an analysis which still has a good deal of relevance.

In some ways Glass went further still. She argued that since the West Indians were an energetic, skilled and well-equipped migratory group, their relative failure to carve out a secure foothold in British society could only be attributed to pathological weakness in that society. The hostility that they encountered would be likely to be (in the first instance) verbalised, and based on irrational or malicious stereotyping; it would be disseminated and eventually translated into action by right-wing organisations and, ultimately at one remove (partly as a result of entryist tactics), by politicians of major parties. Evidence from opinion polls was adduced in favour of this thesis,[7] although the conclusion reached was disputed by Banton, who had found in his own investigation that the level of verbal hostility was comparatively low, but that of rejection in most social situations high.[8] He postulated a form of British Dilemma, in which high standards of behaviour towards minorities and verbal expressions of good intentions were at odds with actual behaviour. Glass's view, valuable because it focused attention on the receiving society as a crucial determinant, received further reinforcement when the special tabulations on Commonwealth immigrants from the 1961 Census were published. These showed, in her words, that:

> the social and geographical distribution of coloured immigrants
> is rather similar to that of the local population. They are
> certainly not all in menial jobs and shabby streets. And there
> are hardly any coloured ghettos. Commonwealth immigrants are
> more widely dispersed throughout British society than is
> realised.[9]

Further reinforcement for this view was obtained in Peter Collinson's reanalysis of Census data for the city of Oxford. After careful examination of the spatial distribution of those born in the West Indies and the Indian subcontinent he concluded:

> We think it is now time to question the assumption that
> immigrants are necessarily and everywhere underprivileged and
> to consider seriously the hypothesis that British society is more
> open so far as immigrants are concerned than is generally
> supposed and that the energy and enterprise often shown by
> immigrant groups can carry them rapidly up the social hierarchy.[10]

Taken together, these verdicts might be said to epitomise the case of the cheerful school among students of race relations. Crudely paraphrased, this is that the new immigration, composed on the whole of the most enterprising elements in the sending society, was encountering unusual obstacles deriving from the factor of colour, but these obstacles were in many ways no more serious than those encountered by their Irish predecessors entering an intensely competitive labour market and unsupported by any structure of welfare services, or East European Jews at the turn of the century facing overt anti-Semitism. Unless irrational hostility infected both the politicians and the institutions of British society to such a degree that it became the sole determinant of policy, the new migrants would in due course pass through a series of processes of progressively more complete adaptation analogous to those undergone by their predecessors.

The context in which this view first came under close critical scrutiny was in relation to the Asian immigration. This had at first constituted a negligible element in the migration, but in the late fifties it had begun to increase rapidly and in the eighteen months before the introduction of control, in 1962, the numbers entering reached almost one hundred thousand (see Table I). Although this was in fact still slightly less than the numbers of West Indians coming in, the situation altered drastically after control of immigration was introduced. The system placed a premium on the possession of professional skills; indeed, after 1964 all provision for the admission of unskilled workers, except those with jobs already arranged, ceased. As a result, the intake of men entering for employment was from that point almost exclusively composed of those coming from the Indian subcontinent: the only West Indians have been students or dependants of men who had entered previously—mainly in the 'beat the Act' rush of 1960/1.[11]

TABLE I
NET INWARD FLOW OF COLOURED COMMONWEALTH IMMIGRANTS BEFORE CONTROL

	West Indians	Indians	Pakistanis
1955	27550	5800	1850
1956	29800	5600	2050
1957	23000	6600	5200
1958	15000	6200	4700
1959	16400	2950	850
1960	49650	5960	2500
1961	66300	23750	21500
1962	31800	19050	25080
(first 6 months)			

Source: Home Office statistics

The Census figures (for 1961) for those born in the Indian sub-continent at first sight appear to lend support to one limb of the 'cheerful' school's hypothesis; they show this group well distributed through the occupation and social class categories, if in an 'hourglass' pattern, with under-representation of the skilled and lesser white-collar categories. Three points have however been made, which tend to modify this picture. The first is a mainly technical one. Since the Census records are kept by birthplace and not by ethnic group, a substantial proportion of those enumerated as Indian-born are in fact white (or perhaps red) skinned. This group of children of Indian Army and Civil Service personnel are likely to be disproportionately concentrated in the higher socio-economic categories. The Registrar-General's office has unofficially estimated their numbers at 100,000 in 1961 on the basis of data on citizenship: but there is no wholly reliable way of disentangling them from the 'genuine' Indians when it comes to detailed analysis of occupational or spatial distribution. Second—and this is a point of general application—the Census was taken at a particularly awkward moment from the point of view of the student of race relations, when the tide of rushed entry before the coming into force of the Commonwealth Immigrants Act, fifteen months later, was at full flow. There are good grounds for believing that the processes of introducing control not merely accelerated entry but brought in people who would not otherwise have chosen to enter. Among these were large numbers of unskilled men from rural backgrounds, both in the Indian subcontinent and the West Indies; their arrival diluted the composition of the migration (in terms of skills) and complicated the already complex problems of adjustment. Third, although those who entered from the Indian subcontinent after control were mainly graduates, this did not necessarily imply that they exercised their professional skills in employment in this country. Either directly as a result of discrimination, or because the material rewards in industry are greater, a process of sharp occupational downgrading has taken place. Stories about graduates working as bus-conductors, in textile mills or rubber factories are common; and usually true.

The picture of the coloured newcomer as well-equipped for coping with his new situation, to the extent that the limits set on him by the receiving society enable him to do so, therefore requires some modification. But the crucial implication of the growth in the Asian migration is that the other limb of the 'cheerful' case could not be applied to these newcomers. The basic cultural similarities on which the case for the West Indians was founded, do not exist in their case. There are religious differences, for instance, which are particularly marked in the case of Pakistani immigrants. Recent investigations have suggested that the significance of the Muslim religion for adaptation is marked, although the same investigators seem less sure precisely what the implications are.[12] Other culturally based differences have proved, in the case of the numerically largest component in the migration, the prosperous Sikh peasants from the Upper Punjab, to be of equal significance. Communal institutions have proved to possess viability in the new context and to provide protection for newcomers confronted with a double problem of adjustment—to the urban situation and the new values and imperatives of urbanised society and to the idea of being categorised as coloured in a white man's world. In turn, the capacity of British society to accommodate itself to the presence of distinct minorities was put under too great a strain: the jelly-fish (the image of that society employed by one investigator[13]) could not ingest this new catch.

Paradoxically, running alongside this marked trend towards diversity in the migration, an increase in hostility within the host community was generating and continually reinforcing a negative and essentially un-differentiated stereotype of 'the coloured immigrant'.[14] This increased rejection of newcomers can be traced back to the Fascist 'groupuscules' described by Glass: but the main reason for the growth and legitimation of hostility lay in the *volte face* of the politicians on this issue and the manner in which it was executed. By first proclaiming the inalienable right to equality based on total absence of significant differences, then amending this position by the Act of 1962 and finally introducing a series of new restrictions on entry, in the White Paper of 1965, based on the proposition that the immigrants were placing an intolerable strain both on the social services and the tolerance of Britons, successive Administrations invited the electorate to designate a scapegoat for the admitted inadequacies of the amenities and services of the inner city areas. By presenting the immigrants as a threat, and the process of immigration as a constant drain on national resources (not, as it actually was, an economic asset[15]) the Government made sure that the positive measures belatedly introduced to promote integration were largely nugatory in effect. In this situation, the practice of discrimination—especially on the part of those who 'operate the clumsy strings of the housing market'[16]—became entrenched, and rejection, often initially excused by reference to the attitudes of third parties (neighbours, other tenants or employees), a common experience. As the P.E.P. in-vestigation[17] of the extent of discrimination, carried out in 1967, revealed, this was a particularly painful experience for West Indians, whose expecta-tions had often been cast in terms of acceptance on the basis of common citizenship and culture and who found neither honoured in practice.

Younger fieldworkers, carrying out their investigations in this atmosphere of increased hostility on the one side and increased consciousness of, and resentment of, rejection on the other, tended to find that the immigration perspective was inadequate for their purposes. By stressing the significance of immigration as such, politicians and publicists had defined a new role—that of 'immigrant', who approximated, in the subjective perception of the majority, to the coloured helot identified by Little in his pioneer investigation.[18] Not merely the individual, with his distinctive cultural characteristics, but the objective evidence of the diversity of the different immigrant groups were submerged in this new category. And although this role of 'immigrant' has a number of different resonances, it boils down essentially to a mealy-mouthed way of designating a minority distinguished purely by the factor of colour. That the status of immigrant is seen by some people as something fixed—possibly even immutable—is revealed by references to 'permanent immigrants'.

In this situation these investigators preferred to define the situation as one of 'race relations'. By this, as one of them put it, they meant:

> a reciprocal relationship, between groupings, but an
> asymmetrical power relationship in which the 'racial' minority
> grouping is subordinated.[19]

The immigration perspective, as employed by other social scientists was:

> confusing awareness of the position of coloured people by
> focussing attention on the recency of the settlement, by
> distracting attention from evident concern about their
> pigmentation and by obscuring the nature of the white-coloured
> relationships which are being increasingly categorised and
> institutionalised.[20]

As employed by politicians it was hastening and entrenching in policy a polarisation into two categories.

All this was not to suggest that the processes of adaptation to change in the various different migrations, the adjustments made to the demands of the majority society and comparisons with the experiences of earlier ethnic groups were irrelevant to the situation: merely that the major determinant had become the categorisation employed by the majority and the action taken on that basis. And an important additional element was brought out by Banton, in his synoptic study of race relations in the cross-national perspective.[21] This was the significance of change in the social structure of the receiving society in restructuring the contact situation and revising the assumptions of those who participated in such situations.

These insights, and others, were systematically applied by John Rex and Robert Moore in their study of the Sparkbrook area of Birmingham.[22] Their argument was in essence that a race relations situation existed in Birmingham, and that the developing pattern was determined by the distribution of power and access to resources of various parties to this situation, which defined their bargaining position.

The functioning of the housing market has created a series of housing classes who had reached and sustained a position by means of their capacity to mobilise power. A private suburban class had achieved the highest degree of security and autarchy. This group is protected from the possibility of the entry of coloured settlers by the activity of wardens, in Denton's terms—estate agents—who manipulate the stereotype of a threat to property values to exclude undesirable newcomers. If this fails, defensive organisations are created. As the Chairman of one of these said of 'immigrants': 'You may say they're the same but I tell you they're different in ways we don't understand.'[23] An equivalent public suburbia has been created, largely as a result of the activity of the skilled working class to mobilise political resources on its own behalf. Entry to this class is controlled by the local authority, which is of course in turn generally controlled by the political representations of this group. The justification for the exclusion of coloured newcomers is in this instance cast in terms of qualification, based on a system that emphasises length of residence at the expense of need; the ultimate sanction is the hostility of public opinion, which, it is assumed, would not tolerate the allocation of housing to recent arrivals, although there is evidence to suggest that this hostility is not as great as Chairmen of Housing Committees imagine.[24]

Third, and diminishingly significant, is the stable working-class enclave in the private rented sector. This consists mainly of the back-to-back post-Industrial Revolution working class housing, with some model workmen's dwellings constructed at the end of the last century. Entry to this category, once considered highly desirable and controlled on a dynastic footing, is the subject of less competition as the opportunities for entering the publicly-owned sector or even—in the West Midlands at least—embarking on owner occupation become greater and the stock of housing in this category diminishes through slum clearance.

Faced with these entrenched classes, the newcomers are in practice restricted to the inner ring of Victorian or Edwardian housing abandoned by the middle class after the First World War. Here the size of the houses and the basic soundness of their fabric invites sub-division and the incursion of the landlord. The group that has had the resources to turn this situation to advantage, in the Birmingham situation, is the Pakistani entrepreneurs. Yet although this group caters not only for their own needs for accommodation and that of their kin and fellow countrymen but for the socially disadvantaged of all colours who are forced for a variety of reasons to resort to this area for accommodation, the local authorities' response towards this situation has generally been disapproving, even punitive. Often this punitiveness assumes a ritual form: landlords are paraded before a special landlords' court and fined for a practice which all parties accept will continue. The overall policy has been one of containment—in the case of Birmingham by special legislation introduced by the Corporation to limit the areas within which lodging houses can be established—and control, through the increasing efforts of the Public Health Inspectors to reduce overcrowding.

This solution is bound, at least in the short run, to intensify the pressure in the inner areas. It has been devised regardless of the fact that the situation derives from the distribution of resources determined in part by the local authority itself which intensifies the problems of newcomers by excluding them from access to alternative solutions.

Rex's analysis is worth quoting in detail, because it is the most significant contribution so far to an understanding of the key issue in the recent development of race relations, that of access to housing. Although, as Peach has conclusively demonstrated, the initial determinant of the distribution of the newcomers between different areas of settlement was the employment opportunities available,[25] the existing housing situation remains the factor chiefly responsible for structuring the social situation, and deciding the extent to which the individual immigrant has access to services and is capable of exercising those rights to which, on paper and in political rhetoric, he is entitled. The importance of housing circumstances is not merely material: it is also psychological. Lyon, reporting a study carried out in an inner area of Bristol, describes the cumulative effect of the loss of esteem suffered by the inhabitant of such areas, which affect the attitudes of both white and coloured:

The disadvantages of the settlement areas—and this includes

their low status—tend to consolidate the low 'racial' status of coloured immigrants; . . . within the settlement areas English people so resent and withdraw from coloured neighbours that the coloured settlers become defensive about their traditions and fearful of dispersal.[26]

Of the factors specifically affecting the coloured minority in these areas the most important is discrimination, of which there can now be little argument. Although the P.E.P. investigators unfortunately missed the opportunity of making a comparative study of the response to different immigrant groups, striking evidence of rejection specifically on grounds of colour was found. Situation tests in the private rented sector showed an overwhelming tendency to reject the coloured applicant for accommodation, and there was no reluctance to express that rejection in explicit verbal terms. If there is a dilemma here it merely consists of finding the most convenient way of ridding oneself of a tiresome and potentially difficult applicant. The P.E.P. evidence is unfortunately less satisfactory for the public housing sector, but there we have the study by Burney which demonstrates clearly how the various factors at work in obtaining access to local authority accommodation, though each stage is innocent of any explicit intention to produce racial discrimination, combine to produce a situation of *de facto* segregation. Such a situation is clearly revealed for Birmingham by P. N. Jones, in a re-analysis of 1961 Census data.[27] He shows that there is almost no correspondence at all between the areas of substantial immigrant settlement (which the extent of local authority activity would lead one to suppose that poor housing conditions existed) and the designated redevelopment areas. Taken together these trends crystallise in the concept of the coloured ghetto as a present or future phenomenon in major British cities and form the basis for the diagnosis made by the 'gloomy' school of race relations.

If this notion of incipient or actual ghettos is to be sensibly discussed, it must be examined at two levels: first, the objective and secondly, the subjective. On whether the concept can satisfy tests at both levels or at only one or none depends the credibility of the 'gloomy' interpretation.

It can be said straight away that the objective evidence for the existence of ghettos in the Wirthian sense is not strong. Glass's analysis of the 1961 Census data has already been quoted, with the qualification that the data for the Asian-born must be approached with caution: the situation that she describes had not radically altered at the time when the 1966 Sample Census was taken. Although detailed analysis of the later data at ward level is not available at the time of writing, it is possible to say that in no ward in the Greater London area was the proportion of Commonwealth-born residents over 30%. For the distorting effect of the factor of visibility is such as to exaggerate the extent of concentration, even in the case of experienced observers. Somerleyton and Geneva Roads, in central Lambeth, had for ten years in local folklore been all-black streets. When the Council came to conduct a census of the inhabitants, on assuming control of the property in 1967, they found that about half of them were white. This experience could certainly be paralleled in any number of local 'Little Calcuttas' and 'Burma Roads': or rather, it would be if the local authority took the same initiative taken by Lambeth. Perhaps more interestingly, there is little evidence for the existence in this country of a number of key factors in ghetto formation in the United States—the existence of a 'tipping point', for instance, or the universal rule that once an area has passed into Negro occupation it remains a black area. The phenomenon of middle-class re-entry to city centre areas, still largely confined to London but growing in scope and intensity has created a situation in which there is sharp competition for the type of housing which previously provided the opportunity for coloured househunters to find some relief from the pressures of the housing market. It is by no means uncommon in any of the areas of transition in the throes of what Glass calls 'gentrification' for houses to pass from white to coloured ownership and back again over quite a short period. In a quite different setting, studies in the West Riding of Yorkshire show that the cheap back-to-back housing in the city core also changes hands in the same way.[28]

But if there is some feasibility left in the situation, which allows individuals to examine a degree of choice, the limits on this choice have hitherto been rigidly set. Peach's vision of a future in which 'the map of British towns will add black belts and white rings to established features such as green belts'[29] will probably turn out in practice to have been too pessimistic; Eversley and Sukdeo point out that the proportion of immigrants from the three main countries of origin to be found in the six major conurbations decreased—in the case of the Jamaicans by over 10%—between 1961 and 1966.[30] In London, the 1966 data shows, besides a marked improvement in the housing conditions of most minority groups between the Censuses, growth in population distributed comparatively evenly between inner boroughs (within the old L.C.C. area) and those outside it, reflecting a degree of movement outwards (see Table II). It is particularly interesting to see how comparatively low the increase has been in Kensington and Chelsea, the area often connected with the 'ghetto' stereotype. However, such dispersal as has taken place is largely contained within the conurbations; and the movement has occurred despite a number of clearly marked obstacles.

That immigrants are able to compete at all in such a competitive market underlines another crucial factor likely, if taken by itself, to militate against ghetto formation. That is the capacity of the newcomers to raise sufficient capital to enable them to purchase housing. This phenomenon was first observed among West Indians by the second wave of investigators: Patterson saw this process developing in the Brixton settlement, where they were able to buy the ends of leases comparatively cheaply in the early and middle fifties before the sharp inflation in London house prices, and compared it to the similar process by which post-war Polish immigrants were able to establish themselves. The initial capital was obtained partly through co-operative savings schemes—called 'pardner' or 'sou-sou' schemes

TABLE II

CHANGES IN POPULATION FROM THREE MAJOR IMMIGRANT GROUPS IN SELECTED
LONDON BOROUGHS, 1961-1966:

Inner (inside old L.C.C. area)	% of total population in 1961	% of total population in 1966	Index in 1966 (1961 = 100)
Camden	3·0	3·6	121
Kensington & Chelsea	4·4	4·6	105
Lambeth & Wandsworth*	3·6	5·5	150
Tower Hamlets	2·6	3·9	151
Westminster	3·5	4·3	122
Outer (outside L.C.C. area)			
Brent	4·1	7·4	180
Bromley	0·6	0·9	150
Haringey	2·7	5·6	209
Havering	0·4	0·5	139
Kingston-upon-Thames	0·3	1·0	345

Source: 1961 & 1966 Censuses

* Boundary changes make it necessary to consider these boroughs together.

according to the island of origin—and partly through intensive saving by individuals. The fact that West Indians were able to establish themselves in the labour market without too much difficulty—and that among women a far higher proportion have been economically active than in the general population*—meant that although wages have tended to be at artisan level, earnings together with overtime (where, as good trade unionists, they were able to obtain it without friction) made raising deposits a possible, though uphill, task. However, it was also likely to involve obtaining further funds from one of the suspect building societies or investment companies which specialise in providing loans at high rates of interest for coloured house-purchasers—unless the individual concerned was lucky enough to live in London, where it was possible (at least for three years) to profit from the G.L.C.'s immensely significant 100% mortgage scheme. The results of this process can be seen in Table III, based on 1961 Census data, which shows that in seven selected inner boroughs in London, Jamaicans are three times likelier to be owner-occupiers than natives. The same pattern emerges from an analysis of data from the 1966 Sample Census for the same areas.

A broadly similar process has been at work with the Asian migrants. Burney has perceptively commented that whereas the average West Indian is interested in property principally as a means of containing and keeping possessions, the Asian house-owner sees his property as a symbol of social position, a source of financial profit and a means to discharge his social obligations to family and kinsfolk.

With such a powerful drive towards house-ownership in all immigrant groups—and especially among the brown bourgeoisie—there is clearly a strong probability that aspirations will collide head-on with the obstacles

* 62%, as opposed to 39% of the English-born at the Census of 1961.

TABLE III

PROPERTY TENURE IN SEVEN SELECTED LONDON BOROUGHS, 1961

	English %	Jamaican %	Indian %	Pakistani %
Owner-occupiers	14	40	24	33
Renting furnished	5	45	35	39
Renting unfurnished	50	13	28	17
Renting from Council	28	1	10	8
Other	3	1	3	4

Source : Adapted from Table 27 in R. B. Davison, *Black British*, I.R.R., 1966

Rex and others describe. Conflict of some sort seems inevitable. The resolution of this conflict might be supposed to be a task for central Government. In practice, the Ministry of Housing have not thought it right to make any systematic intervention in this field. The broad priorities which had been set for local authorities at the beginning of the period of migration involved the clearance and replacement of slum housing. The Macmillan Administration saw council accommodation as a safety net and the main thrust of policy as being directed towards the creation of a 'property-owning democracy'. The homeless family scandals which broke with increasing regularity at the end of the fifties and the early sixties compelled the Department to recognise that all was not well in the twilight areas not touched by the slum-clearance programme: the Housing Act of 1961 was the result. Not until the West Indian Lucky Gordon's revolver bullet set in train the Rachman scandal and led at one remove to the production of the Milner Holland Report, did the notion of direct intervention gain much ground with Whitehall. Indeed, the opposite process took place. The complicating and illuminating factor of the presence of coloured immigrants in the areas in question brought into play the official orthodoxy that in any matter involving immigrants no specific action should be taken over and above that already provided for in general policy. This doctrine may be glimpsed at its most Olympian in the White Paper on Immigration of 1965.

Since then, wiser counsels have prevailed. Official policy, embodied in the 1968 Housing White Paper *Old Houses Into New Homes*, now envisages a direct attack on the problems of blighted areas, taken as a whole rather than in penny packets, with rehabilitation rather than wholesale use of the bulldozer as the instrument. In this direction, at least, the willingness of the Ministry not to be Bourbons and to learn from past experience—not only in this country but in the United States, where the bitter equation has in the past been made between urban renewal and Negro removal—is encouraging. Seen from the perspective of the interests of minorities, the White Paper provides an implied recognition that settled communities, which might otherwise qualify for obliteration, will not necessarily be broken up. Further, alongside these changes in housing policy there is a recognition that the aspirations of those who are potentially mobile (both upward and outward) must be allowed free play. The Race Relations Act of 1968, amending and extending its predecessor of 1965 (which applied only to public places but had the merit of demonstrating that the principle of conciliation through a statutory Board was workable), now makes discrimination in the field of housing a civil wrong, the victim of which may seek redress through statutory conciliation machinery. This provision covers both the public and private sectors, and includes the sale of housing on the open market. All other things being equal, this should be a powerful instrument in checking any tendencies towards ghetto formation.

Other factors in the general situation may work against these welcome trends in official policy. In brief, there is a real risk that a ghetto psychosis will emerge among the minorities. Clearly, the open expression of hostility among the majority plays a large part in this. The avalanche released by Enoch Powell's speech of April 1968[31] represented the abandonment by the majority of their remaining inhibitions about the overt rejection of coloured minorities. But what may be more significant in the long run is the experience over time of rejection in practice, particularly by local authorities. Elizabeth Burney has shown how the sanitary tradition of English local government, with its locus in the office of the Medical Officer of Health, generates a restrictive and at times punitive attitude towards the immigrants and their difficulties of adjustment. This approach was summed up by one Medical Officer of Health, who observed that newcomers 'shared a preference for living in overcrowded houses in multiple occupation with few hygienic facilities and tended to bring deteriorating urban districts to the level of some of the worst slums'.[32] The underlying assumption is apparently that residence in a twilight area in sub-standard accommodation is a matter of choice. The irony is that the repetition of such assumptions may in fact lead to a situation in which the reception area, whatever its disadvantages, is in fact preferable—'Nobody bother you here', the saying goes.

Extreme adherents of the 'gloomy school' would see this process of withdrawal, and shrinking from rejection into a psychical if not a physical ghetto, as the first step towards total de facto separation. Some would welcome this. Prophets of doom have been employing the American parallel to this end for some years now: violence being the inescapable corollary of such a process. For some of them, it cannot arrive here fast enough. 'Riots will certainly take place,' observes an Indian poet, apparently with no more concern for the implications than for any development which might provide suitable subjects for his heroic couplets. For others it would serve as the best possible confirmation of the lurid version of the racial apocalypse which they have been peddling to complaisant journalists for the past couple of years. In this version a black minority (for which they naturally provide the leadership) composed of all the non-white ethnic groups will eventually respond to the oppression of the white majority by violent insurrection. In this they join hands with the jeremiahs of the opposed extreme: for example, Enoch Powell. Writing in 1967, he observed:

The best I dare to hope is that by the end of the century we

shall be left not with a growing and more menacing phenomenon
but with fixed and almost traditional 'foreign' areas in certain
towns and cities, which will remain as the lasting monuments of
a moment of national aberration.[33]

Although they might no longer care to admit it, there are those members
of the Wilson Government who would agree with this analysis. Their
answer is, broadly, that we must admit to having failed to satisfy the
aspirations of the migrants themselves and content ourselves with ensuring
that their children, the so-called 'Black Britons', enjoy equal access to all
those rights available to their white peers. This view is embraced with
almost religious fervour, as if our sin in rejecting the fathers will be re-
deemed by acceptance of the sons. There is evidence to suggest that this
line might be acceptable to public opinion:[34] the difficulty is that in the
form in which it is professed and from the hands of those who offer it this
solution might no longer be acceptable to the black teenager. Politicians
may be able to compartmentalise in their minds the raven croaks in which
they lay repeated emphasis on stringency, harshness and toughness
towards immigration and the sucking dove cooing about social justice for
coloured minorities: to them it is obvious that each speech is addressed to a
different audience. But the black Englishman can hardly help hearing both
and is likely to assess the content of one message by the tone of the other.
Certainly the bizarre arrangement by which one man, a Parliamentary
Under Secretary at the Home Office, is responsible for both strands in
policy and must utter speeches alternately in one mode and the other is
calculated to inspire the least possible confidence in official intentions.

There is, however, another alternative. This is based essentially on the
view that the structure of society will have to undergo radical modification
if we are to negotiate the process of accommodation successfully. Taking
Roy Jenkins's definition of integration as 'equal opportunity, accompanied
by cultural diversity in an atmosphere of mutual tolerance' as a starting
point, an attempt could be developed to build respect for cultural diversity
into the institutional structure without limiting freedom of choice or
opening the door to the provision of 'separate but equal facilities'. This is
a particularly delicate exercise in social engineering and it cannot be
claimed that it has progressed very far or very consistently. The crux of
such an approach lies in the recognition that the initial policy of equality by
proclamation is a failure and that a wholly justified reaction has taken place
on the side of the minorities. Such a reaction is the basis for a process of
withdrawal which can be recognised without being institutionalised.

A programme of this kind must start with the assumption that there are
certain aspects of the life and circumstances of coloured minorities which
relate to policy goals which have had a universal application and should be
handled on that basis.

First, attention must be given to the physical environment. Thus there is
considerable significance for race relations in the new Urban Programme,
which will attract £25 million of central government funds over the next

four years to deal with the material difficulties of the inner urban areas as a whole. A start will be made with the nursery schools (on the lines of Plowden recommendations) but work will extend ultimately to housing and education, where the post-Plowden educational priority areas scheme will also attract additional resources for the improvement of educational facilities in such areas. Second, it is clearly essential that education should be provided on a universal basis, and that the educational process should embody values common to society as a whole. To say that is not merely to pay lip service to the virtues of multi-racial experiences, both for their value in the classroom and in equipping individuals for life in a multi-racial society, real though those may be. The fact is that there is hard evidence that integrated schools are more satisfactory in terms of the educational performance of their pupils.[35] It is perhaps worth adding that in advertising integration in education it is necessary to avoid patronising implication that is it only the black children who stand to profit: in many inner city areas they are better motivated and more enthusiastically supported by their parents than their white schoolmates. The ethos widely prevalent in the fifties, of education as an instrument to anglicise, in which the limit of recognition of the special needs (indeed, of the existence) of new minorities was confined to language instruction, went beyond reasonable limits. If there is to be respect for minority cultures, it will have to start in the schools, and with teachers.

Third, there are the other services whose provision in such areas has in the past been so inadequate. Contrary to a widespread myth, as Mrs Jones has shown,[36] the immigrants make less use of the social services than the population at large, but those services which they do use are often substandard in quality and personnel, and their special needs are insufficiently clearly recognised. This applies both to health services and local authority welfare services. The provision of the latter on a co-ordinated basis, as the Seebohm Report recommends, would do a good deal to overcome this difficulty for majority and minority alike—if sufficient resources were made available.

Other institutions in society are open to newcomers on a universal basis. There is good evidence to suggest that in the workplace situation, integration has already gone a good deal further than it has in the neighbourhood: equal access to membership and benefits of trade unions are two important factors in confirming and consolidating this process. At one point it seemed possible that at least one of the political parties might be prepared to perform a mediating rôle on behalf of the newcomers. Like the Democratic Party in the United States, the Labour Party appeared to be providing a means for articulate and ambitious West Indians to participate in the political process and for the expression through them of a form of communal commitment to that process. This process, which had only progressed as far as producing the odd Parliamentary candidate and Councillor, has now been snuffed out and is unlikely to revive. Individuals hold elected office, on both sides of politics, but their success is a product of special factors—of personality or the local situation.

But the best efforts of the school, the trade union branch, and the social worker may not necessarily convince the coloured citizen that dispersal from an area of immigrant settlement is the most desirable goal. Nor, in fact, need it necessarily be so. The Milner Holland report rightly inveighed against the 'rubbish sold dear' in inner areas which was the only choice which discrimination left open to the newcomer anxious to invest in house-ownership. But if anti-discrimination legislation led to a situation in which decent accommodation sold cheap in the same sort of area, became accessible and was chosen, there is nothing in this which should necessarily alarm those responsible for policy formulation, provided that the infra-structure which will guarantee equal status is available. There are, after all, a number of good reasons for choosing the familiar surroundings in preference to the dubious honour of integrating a housing estate, with the possibility of hostile or at best anxious neighbours, on which one's children are likely to be the butt of good-humoured but nonetheless hurtful teasing. It may be convenient to live near work—and many West Indians in London are shift workers who need to have easy access to their place of work. It is psychologically supportive to have neighbours from a familiar background and the kind of facilities which most migrant groups are now evolving for themselves and whose success in turn depends upon a degree of concentra-tion—shops, barbers, driving schools, even cinemas (in Southall) and banks (in Bradford). The function of these institutions is not merely to provide a foothold for the immigrant entrepreneur; they also form the basis of a social network through which individuals can exchange information and opinions on issues that affect them. This is particularly true for Asian women, who may be in purdah and particularly isolated without women friends and shopping facilities which they can use without language difficulties. For the community's leaders—or those claiming a leadership rôle—concentration may also be important. It provides a basis for oper-ation in terms of mobilising a following, either to gain prestige appoint-ments in voluntary or statutory bodies set up to promote integration, or, in some exceptional circumstances, for an incursion into politics. By mobilis-ing the appearance of an ethnic block vote, it is possible to wring favours from the local political establishment and in one or two cases to obtain representation on local political bodies.

Such 'coloured quarters', in order to be viable, must be open: that is to say, they must permit the ambitious and the potential assimilators to move on, and not obstruct the entry of members of the majority who wish to take advantage of cosmopolitanism which such areas are likely to possess. They will also need to be economically viable, not in the sense of generating their own employment opportunities, but by providing access through geographi-cal proximity to sufficient jobs to sustain the community. It may be that changes in the industrial structure will eventually force the abandonment of those areas of minority settlement in the inner city that are not cleared. A decline in the number of unskilled and semi-skilled jobs available, per-haps through the introduction of new industrial processes or the stream-lining of old ones is an obvious passibility. On the other hand, the expansion in the service industries and the security of the niche they have carved out in the public sector may protect the minorities from the consequences of change.

There is a distinction that needs to be made at once, between a bohemia and a coloured quarter, in which an incoming ethnic group adds diversity to the environment. The former provides the ideal circumstances for the footloose under twenty-fives to experiment with various styles of behaviour at the stage in his or her life cycle when he can best afford to do so (what Donnison calls the 'lair' use for such areas). By suggesting that immigrants were a natural ingredient for such an area John Rex gratuitiously confused the former with the latter.[37] What the coloured head of household requires is the kind of environment which is suitable for bringing up a family, in the kind of circumstances which will seem to outsiders exotic only by virtue of the way in which the majority respond to other cultures. The hipster element in the stereotype of the black man in the city has obscured the intense puritanism of the ordinary West Indian, to whom respectability is of immense importance.

There is an obvious danger that the stereotype of such bohemias as disorganised areas associated with certain kinds of behaviour—drug-taking, promiscuity—will be transferred from the area to its black inhabitants, who will be stigmatised by reference to it when (or rather if) they manage to move out. While they remain in the district, the visible signs of their presence, in the form of shops selling unfamiliar goods that produce unaccustomed smells when cooked, touched-up brickwork or eccentric variations on curtains, become signals of a threatening exorcism. Changes of this kind, along with others more reasonably resented (the late-night drinking or gambling club, for example) are relatively simple to make. This is one way in which minorities can make an immediate impact on their environment. They are also easily misconstrued. In fact, the drinking-club phase seems to be almost over: the life style of the urban West Indian has come to approximate with remarkable fidelity to that of the respectable English working class. Whatever external differences may suggest, coloured minorities, in their widely different ways, are often successful (perhaps even more than their white neighbours) in creating a form of stability in initially unpromising circumstances.

Such stability is a necessity if these areas are to provide supporting elements for the adjustment problem of the second, and indeed the third, generation. It is one of the strengths of the immigration perspective that it functions as a healthy corrective to the commonly-held expectation that the second generation will turn out to be de facto Englishmen. Past experience shows that the tensions arising from collision of different cultures are profoundly difficult to resolve, not merely for the children of migrants, but for their grandchildren. The importance of a viable coloured quarter lies in demonstrating that the presence of coloured people is not automatically associated with slum housing and squalid schooling.

On the other side, a majority within most ethnic groups is still likely to see its ultimate future lying in the wider community. All other things being equal, the West Indians, chiefly skilled artisans with a small but growing white-collar element but largely without the entrepreneurial skills so characteristic of the Asians, are natural clients for public housing. The forces of the market have frequently turned them aside into house purchase and at present the aspirations of the majority still lie in this direction, but the owner-occupiers are still in a minority and if the obstacles were removed there is no reason why they should not make the same kind of transition to such accommodation as the Irish have done before them. There is good evidence, from Lyon's work in Bristol, to show that West Indians can be accepted on, and make a good adjustment to life on council estates, provided that the operation is conducted with some degree of forethought on both sides. Such difficulties that have arisen can be traced to the systematic rehousing of immigrants as a potential problem group, in low-status housing in close proximity to tenants classified as problem cases for more objective reasons. In the same way, the potentialities of the New Towns as areas for ambitious West Indians, unrealised at present (partly as a function of the basis of operations of the Industrial Selection Scheme) deserve to be systematically explored as soon as possible.

By the same crude cultural analogy, there is no reason why the rapidly developing brown bourgeoisie should not begin to move away from areas of settlement in perceptible numbers in the fairly near future, as the Jews did from their initially far denser areas of settlement in the East End of London. Once the obstacles to house-purchase in the form of discriminatory practices are removed—assuming that legislation is effective*—such a process could be expected to inject a new ingredient into suburban life, people ferociously ambitious for themselves and even more for their children: Free Enterprise Man incarnated, in a brown skin. Such an exodus might have surprising consequences both for white suburbia and the brown bourgeoisie. Before the exodus is complete the Asians may pass through an interim stage in which they have found new areas of residence, but their commercial interests are still centred on the area of settlement.

Even considered as an interim solution, coloured areas will not possess the stability to launch and sustain such movement unless they achieve parity of esteem. If they do not, the processes described by Lyon come into play and the settlement areas become, in concept and practice, semi-delinquent zones with a transient population. In order to obtain parity they have to receive an equal investment of resources, and possess facilities of an equal standard. The implied judgement in the Department of Education and Science's circular 7/65 that no school which contains more than a certain proportion of coloured children can be up to adequate educational standards—it proposes that local authorities disperse coloured children if they form over 30% of the population of any one school—is a perfect illustration of an official attitude which links low standard of

* The Act of 1968 does not extend to sales made between private persons, without advertisement. Their proved capacity for organising such sales is one of many reasons why certain residents' associations would make interesting subjects for research.

performance with the bare presence of children of different skin pigmentation. In fact, a careful study by the I.L.E.A. shows that there is no such connection.[38] A new approach does not, of course, preclude the provision of separate services on a purely educational basis to deal with specific linguistic difficulties: what it does rule out is what Rex labels with brutal accuracy the 'nigger bus'—that is, an institution which perpetuates and reinforces a sense of inferiority.

The title of this contribution suggests a perspective derived from the concept of human rights: the format of these papers calls for an attempt at a scenario for further developments in this field. Obviously, one crucial determinant of such developments is political. It has been the contention of all politicians from the outset of the migration that newcomers from the Commonwealth possess all the rights of full citizens. Once, these were assumed to be the automatic birthright of all those born within the Commonwealth who were endowed with latent privileges, Roman-style, which sprang to life on his entry to the British Isles. Subsequently, a series of inroads began to take place: not only citizens of Commonwealth countries, but those possessing citizenship of the United Kingdom and colonies if their passports were issued by the colonial authorities, not the British Government, were by the Act of 1962 deprived of the right of free entry to Britain. In 1965 new administrative restrictions were placed on the numbers permitted to enter, on the plea of excessive strain on the social services and proposals made for the supervision of those who had actually entered. These proposals were not enacted, largely as a result of opposition within the Labour Party; but three years later a further category of British citizen, those holding U.K. and Colonies passport issued by the British Government but not having a substantial connection with the United Kingdom by birth (either of parent or grandparent) was also deprived of freedom of entry. This legislation, the Commonwealth Immigrants Act of 1968, was directed chiefly to slowing up the rate of entry of British citizens of Asian origin from Kenya. Its critics contended that it was in breach of five international covenants or declarations and had, according to the assessment made by the International Commission of Jurists, created numerous *de facto* stateless citizens.

The important positive initiative of the Race Relations Act 1968, designed to secure the enjoyment of certain civil and social rights, has since been balanced by additional measures of restriction upon entry: fiancés of Commonwealth citizens already resident here are the chief group affected. After acrimonious disputes between Government and opposition on immigration policy in the autumn of 1968 and early 1969, the probability of further restrictions on the entry of dependants was freely canvassed—but had not materialised at the time of writing.

The dangers of prophecy have already been demonstrated, as Enoch Powell has justly pointed out, by the totally unpredictable progress of events in this field over the past dozen years. In fact, the only merit of any attempt at predicting future policies is that it may help to clarify the determining factors in the current situation. The first of these is the fact that the process of immigration from the 'New' Commonwealth is almost over. No political party can be expected to reintroduce it in the foreseeable future, even though the case for a policy of selective immigration is strong. In practice, the Dutch auction between the parties in severity of control will continue. Granted these policies, the entry of dependants of past immigrants will also cease in the near future, whether formal steps are taken to terminate their previous right to entry or not. As Eversley and Sukdeo demonstrate, their numbers will be quickly exhausted.

Such growth as the coloured population of the United Kingdom will experience will therefore stem from natural increase. This growth has been the subject of a number of forecasts of dubious reliability. The most that can be said of these is that they have always in the past been proved wrong, no matter how respectable the source that made them: the manner of their use tends to tell one more about the user than about the future of race relations.

The second underlying factor is the final emergence of a system of categorisation purely in terms of colour—although one complicated by the use of the increasingly misleading term 'immigrant'. This has in turn provoked the beginning of a process of counter-stereotyping around the equally misleading term 'white', often coupled pejoratively with 'liberal'. Such a process leaves several questions unresolved, centering on the position of the second generation. Although this may be seen as a single unit by the host population (a hostile perception in some cases; a guilty one on the part of the policy makers pledged to make of them 'first class citizens') their own perception of their position is far from clear. The wide differences between the various ethnic groups clearly persist in this generation, but might be swamped by the pressure of events. One point of reference may come to be Negro ghetto youth—though the problems of the coloured British teenager pale into insignificance beside those of the ghetto school-leaver facing catastrophic rates of unemployment. Or it may still be his white English contemporaries. Certainly the grip of the universal youth culture seems to be as strong upon black teenagers as on white. A situation may be created in which values, tastes and yardsticks by which success is measured all come from different directions: tastes from the international teenage cults, flavoured with distinctive elements, values from parents (whose attitudes towards the majority may also be changing) and yardsticks of achievement from white contemporaries. Without the pressure endemic in the current situation, this generation might develop a style of life which would have a good deal to contribute, in terms of vitality and variety, to that of the majority. But while hostility, both individual and institutional, imposes a ceiling on achievement and limitations on social contacts, their energies may be frustrated and turn to apathy or forms of violent rejection. In the second case, the model for action seems less likely to be black leadership in this country, pedestrian in style and limited in effectiveness, than the glamorous international symbols of the rise of the third world.

One hypothetical situation, already touched on, may illuminate the function of this second generation. If entry into the Common Market does

result in large numbers of (say) Sicilians using their new right of free entry
to come to a Britain in which the long-delayed economic miracle has taken
place, a new, unskilled sub-proletariat, culturally alien and linguistically
ill-equipped will be inserted into the competitive situation of the big cities.
Under the pressure of their entry, the British might at last accept the claim
of the coloured Briton to a genuine equality of treatment. Alternatively,
they might prefer to exalt the white newcomer at the expense of the black
native. The current signs are that rejection on a basis of colour is likelier:
if so, it would be the final rejection for the Black British—who would
discover that to be termed 'British' is an artificial substitute for a real
identity.* They would become 'non-belongers', in the literal sense of the
legal phrase. Enoch Powell's prophecy that a child of West Indian parents
born here can never be anything but a West Indian—would be proved half-
true: he could become a black and experience a cruder rejection on grounds
of colour.

The alienation of a talented minority that would result—of the existence
of a substantial reservoir of talent there is no doubt—might have incalcul-
able consequences. Such a group might serve as a trigger for other minorities alienated on different grounds. University students, whose reverence
for a black skin exceeds even that of British jazz musicians in the previous
decade, would certainly be prepared to accept such leadership. But the
possibility of such a process taking place would depend on how other crises
are resolved within society as a whole—the means adopted by the other
minorities in the struggle for a bigger place in the sun, and in particular the
resolution of the debate about planning and participation.

A Utopian solution which relates to these broader issues has already been
sketched in: the introduction of a co-ordinated programme of 'social
growth', whose objective is to eliminate squalor (and which is related to
need rather than to minority status) and to create a situation in which the
exercise of free choice by members of minority groups is limited neither by
racial discrimination, cultural imperialism nor racial patronage (by which is
meant encouraging minorities to base behaviour on distinctions which have
no real significance): a society where differences can be accepted, not used
as a basis for divisions; where public men do not think it fair game to use
minorities as scarecrows to make flesh creep, nor minority spokesmen are
impelled to taunt their allies with hypocrisy.

In such a set of circumstances one might even find that some of the old
goals still made sense; that the negative stereotype of the coloured immigrants is not as powerful as was thought, and that with the gradual
disappearance of language differences and the educational and commercial
success of the second generation (leading to a breaking-down of defensive
communal solidarity) integration is after all a viable objective—if over a
rather longer time-scale than was once expected. Colour would no longer
blot out reason. But this would require a revolution in attitudes of the

* Curiously, no-one has ever referred to the second generation as 'Black
English'. One suspects that 'British' is still—as it has been in the past—an artificial,
not a natural term.

most fundamental kind, and its consummation is one prophecy from which this writer shrinks.

REFERENCES

[1] D. Eversley and F. Sukdeo, *The Dependents of the Coloured Commonwealth Population of England and Wales*, Institute of Race Relations, 1969, p. 56.
[2] Eric Williams, *Capitalism and Slavery*, Deutsch, 1964.
[3] For examples, K. Little, *Negroes in Britain*, Routledge & Kegan Paul, 1947; Michael Banton, *The Coloured Quarter*, Cape, 1955; and S. Collins, *Coloured Minorities in Britain*, Lutterworth, 1957.
[4] Ruth Glass, assisted by H. Pollins, *Newcomers*, Allen & Unwin, 1960.
[5] S. Patterson, *Dark Strangers*, Tavistock, 1963.
[6] *Ibid.*, Ch. 1.
[7] Glass, *op. cit.*, Appendix.
[8] M. Banton, *White & Coloured*, Cape, 1959.
[9] R. Glass, Articles in *The Times*, 30 June and 1 July, 1965.
[10] Peter Collinson, 'Immigrants & Residents', *Sociology* Vol. 1, No. 3, pp. 277-92.
[11] The latest summary of the position can be found in Eversley & Sukdeo, *op. cit.*
[12] J. Rex and R. Moore, *Race, Community & Conflict*, Oxford University Press for Institute of Race Relations, 1967.
[13] E. Huxley, *Back Streets New Worlds*, Chatto & Windus, 1964.
[14] Data from opinion polls is presented in E. J. B. Rose, *et al.*, *Colour & Citizenship*, Oxford University Press for I.R.R., 1969.
[15] See M. H. Peston in Rose, *et al.*, *Colour & Citizenship*, *op cit.*
[16] E. Burney, *Housing on Trial*, Oxford University Press for I.R.R., 1968.
[17] Published as W. W. Daniel, *Racial Discrimination in England*, Penguin, 1968.
[18] K. Little, *op. cit.*
[19] Michael Lyon, unpublished paper read at Conference of Eugenics Society, September, 1968.
[20] *Ibid.*
[21] M. Banton, *Race Relations*, Tavistock, 1968.
[22] J. Rex and R. Moore, *op. cit.*
[23] Quoted by Burney, *op. cit.*
[24] Survey of attitudes in Rose, *et al.*, *Colour & Citizenship*, *op. cit.*
[25] C. Peach, *West Indian Migration to Britain*, Oxford University Press for I.R.R., 1968.
[26] Michael Lyon, *op. cit.*
[27] P. N. Jones, *The Segregation of Immigrant Communities in the City of Birmingham 1961*, University of Hull, 1967.
[28] V. Karn, 'Property Values amongst Indians and Pakistanis in a Yorkshire Town', *Race*, Vol. X, No. 3, January 1969.
[29] Peach, *op. cit.*, p. 100.
[30] Eversley and Sukdeo, *op. cit.*, p. 15.
[31] Reprinted, *inter alia*, in *Race*, Vol. X, No. 1, July 1968.
[32] At the Royal Society of Health, International Conference, The Hague on 8th September 1966, on *The Health & Care of Immigrants*.
[33] Daily Telegraph, 10 February 1967.
[34] From the opinion polls cited in Rose, *et al.*, *op. cit.*
[35] *Racial Isolation in the Public Schools*, U.S. Commission on Civil Rights, 1967.
[36] K. Jones 'Immigrants and the Social Services,' *National Institute Economic Review*, 41, August 1967.

[37] Prof. J. Rex, in a speech to the Town and Country Planning Summer School of the Town Planning Institute, quoted in *The Times*, 9 September 1968.
[38] A. Little, C. Mabey and G. Whitaker, *The Education of Immigrant Pupils in Inner London Primary Schools*, Race, Vol. IX, No. 4, 1968.

TRANSPORTATION

PETER HALL

Introduction

In this paper, I am going to make a fundamental distinction between intra-urban transportation, and inter-urban transportation; though in the last section, I shall argue that the distinction is steadily becoming more artificial. By intra-urban or inter-urban transportation, writers may mean different things; I mean transportation within one city region, or between two different city regions. City regions may have various definitions, for various purposes, in terms of different quantities of different attributes. Thus we may define city regions in terms of specified amounts, or densities, of activities within them; the number of employees per square kilometre, for instance. Or we can define them in terms of the network which connects the activities; in terms of the numbers of people travelling to the central node of the network to work or to shop, for instance. Or we may define city regions in terms of the number, or density, of the physical structures within them: in terms of the density of rooms or dwellings per hectare, or the percentage of land that is given over to those uses we have defined as urban. Commonly, definitions of city regions are in terms of one of these sets of attributes, or in terms of a combination of them. Thus the American Standard Metropolitan Statistical Area is defined partly in terms of all three; the British conurbation, almost wholly in terms of the third.[1]

Thus a city region may be defined narrowly, or broadly. The sort of city region I want to examine here is broader than the British conurbation, which is a narrow physical definition. It could be defined in terms of a certain density of population and employment in each of its constituent areas, and in terms of certain flows along its communications network. It corresponds approximately to the concept of the Standard Metropolitan Statistical Area. In North America, such an area would have a particular physical form: a densely built up, more or less densely populated central city which was stagnant or declining in population and economic activity, surrounded by rings of progressively lower density suburbs, of which some outer ones (but not, as a rule, the outermost) are showing rapid population growth; within the outer rings, there are still many pieces of land not yet built up, but not used for agriculture either. In Britain, since the operation of the 1947 Planning system, such an area has a different form: a conurbation or free-standing city, of which the inner, more densely built-up area rep-

Peter Hall is Professor of Geography at Reading University

resents growth before 1914 and the outer, medium-density area represents growth between 1918 and 1939 or a little beyond, surrounded by a green belt, which in turn is surrounded by a scatter of separate towns and villages exhibiting more or less rapid growth. This growth predominantly takes the form of medium-density single family homes. In this, context high density means roughly over 20 houses to the net acre; medium, between 10 and 20; and low, below 10. Examples of the phenomenon I am trying to describe would be London and the ring thirty or so miles around; Birmingham and a similar ring; Leicester City and much of Leicester county.

The reason for being interested in this sort of area is that it is where most people in Britain live now, and will go on living in the conceivable future. According to the definition used in the P.E.P. study of Urban Growth in the British Countryside, which is as close as possible to the concept of the American Standard Metropolitan Statistical Area, some 36·4 million people, or 77·1% of the population of England and Wales, lived in exactly 100 Standard Metropolitan Labour Areas at the 1966 Census.[2] These were areas where a substantial proportion of the resident labour force—15% or more—travelled to work into a major urban employment concentration. The proportion of English people who lived in such areas has barely changed over the last thirty years; since the second world war, the very rapid growth of the population has largely passed into them. By focussing on them, we shall see more clearly some critical relationships between urban transportation, urban functions, and urban physical form.

Intra-urban Transportation and Urban Form

Historically, there is a close interrelationship between the available forms of urban transportation, and the form of urban growth. At any point in the city's development, its form affected the available choice of transportation; but then, the available transportation affected the subsequent growth. This mutual relationship is fairly well documented and well known. There was the pre-public transport city, with a very dense concentration of people and activities within walking distance of the centre: London and Manchester, at any time from 1801 to 1851, are good examples. There was the early public transport city, dependent on the horse bus and horse tram and steam railway, with characteristic tentacular growth along the main radial arteries: London or Birmingham in 1901 provide good illustrations. There was the later public transport city, dependent on the finer-grained accessibility of the electric train and motor bus, with an overall spread of medium density housing, but with employment still concentrated at the centre or in well-defined factory or warehouse areas; the classic example is the London of 1939. In such a city, where employment was more concentrated than homes, the prevalent direction of work journeys was inwards in the morning, outwards at night. These journeys were gathered into big radial traffic flows along a few radial routes. Since few families, even middle-class ones, owned cars, work journeys were by far the most numerous journeys, and other journeys perforce were made by public transport. All this helped to support a frequent, cheap, efficient public transport system, both in London and in the provincial cities. Such a system reached its apogee during the 1930's.

This past history is important, because in our city regions today, a very large past legacy remains. There is a legacy in the pattern of activities, in the network, and above all in the physical structures. There is also an obvious imbalance, brought about by the familiar fact that in cities, structures can be changed less rapidly than activities or networks. The results of transportation studies show that the greatest concentrations of jobs are still in the central business districts, that densities of employment still fall away from these sharply but fairly regularly (with high-density projections following the radial factory or port belts), and that the greatest trip attraction rates correspond to these concentrations of employment. Because of the very high trip generation or attraction rates, per acre or hectare, and because of the tendency of the work trips to concentrate into short peak periods, it only proves possible to accommodate the resulting flows by carrying most people on public transport. In medium-sized cities —and this includes even the biggest provincial conurbations—most of these mass transportation trips are bus trips; these may be described as bus-based cities. Such cities may have between 50,000 and 150,000 workers in their central areas, and between 70 and 90% of their central area work trips are made by bus. In the factory zones outside the centres, a higher proportion of work trips may be made by car, though generally only at the cost of acute local congestion. London, in contrast to all provincial cities, has such a great concentration of workers at the centre (1·38 million) and such great radial flows in consequence, that it can no longer depend on the bus for most movements: 90% of all commuters use public transport—a little more than in Manchester or Glasgow—but no less than 75% of all commuters use rail. (Tables I(a) and I(b)). It is interesting that Meyer, Kain and Wohl made the same distinction in their economic analysis of urban mass transit systems; only very large cities with big central employment concentrations, like New York and Chicago, they concluded, could normally justify large-scale investment in rail systems for commuters.[3] (This has not gone unquestioned. The Manchester Rapid Transit Study indicates that an underground railway, built partly overground and partly underground, would be justified for that city (total population of the urban area, 2·5 million). It is significant though that a central government capital grant would be needed to guarantee the viability of the operation.[4]) American commuting figures are set out in Tables II(a) and (b).

In all large city regions in Britain, it is possible to develop a common model, within which individual features of individual cities will fit. Rail trips, when they occur at all in any quantity, are largely focused on the very centre; often they are longer-distance trips. Bus trips are focused on a slightly wider area, embracing the centre and the innermost suburbs; they are predominantly short trips, a product of the low average speed of most urban buses. Lastly car trips are extremely scattered over the whole urban

TABLE I(a)

COMMUTING TO CITY CENTRES, BRITAIN, 1962

	Populn. (Urban area) 1956	*City Centre Workers 1962**	*Total*	*public transp.*	*private motor*	*other (incl. transp. walking)*	*public transp. rail*	*road*
						of which:		
	000s	*000s*	*000s*	%	%	%	%	%
Cardiff	597	40	40	53	27	21	23	30
Coventry	547	18	17	59	24	16	—	59
Darlington	152	11	10	54	23	23	20	34
Doncaster	180	20	20	38	35	27	—	38
Glasgow	1897	159	154	90	8	2	26	64
Leeds	1000	70	69	80	19	1	14	66
Leicester	440	50	50	81	17	22	2	79
London	12491	1270	1210	89	9	—	73	16
Luton	156	30	25	60	40	?	8	52
Manchester	2499	?	138	92	8	?	25	67
Newcastle	1137	70	70	83	17	?	12	71
Norwich	218	30	27	48	22	30	4	44
Southend	190	19	15	57	7	3	3	54
Sunderland	235	23	22	80	17	4	5	75
Walsall	130	12	12	67	33	—	2	65

Source: National Institute Economic Review, May 1962.

* From Kingsley Davies, *op. cit., The World's Metropolitan Areas.* The figure for Leeds is an estimate only.

TABLE I(b)

COMMUTING TO CITY CENTRES, BRITAIN, 1966

	Total Central Business District commuters	*public transp.*	*private car*	*other means*	*public transp. rail*	*road*
			of which			
	000s	%	%	%	%	%
Birmingham	106	68	25	6	7	61
Liverpool	136	74	17	9	15	59
London	1192	84	11	5	66	18
Manchester	139	73	21	6	14	59
Newcastle	76	71	21	9	8	63

Source: Census 1966, calculated by Ray Thomas, *The Journey to Work*, P.E.P., London, 1968.

area, much less focused than other sorts of trip; though even they, expressed in terms of the density of attractions per acre, show some increase towards the centre. These correspond, of course, to fundamental physical and economic constraints, which any commuter well understands. The railway needs a large investment, which will not pay except where large traffic flows proceed along a restricted number of radial corridors; but when it does pay, it can move large numbers over comparatively long

TABLE II(a)

PERCENTAGE OF PASSENGERS ENTERING CENTRAL BUSINESS DISTRICT BY MASS
TRANSPORTATION ON WEEKDAYS, U.S.A., 1948-60*

Selected Cities	Percentage travel by Mass Transit	Date of Survey
Chicago, Ill. †	85	1960
New York, N.Y. †	85	1962
Newark, N.J.	80	1960
Philadelphia, Pa.	64	1953
Richmond, Va.	62	1955
Atlanta, Ga.	60	1953
Boston, Mass.	58	1954
San Antonio, Tex.	57	1955
Dayton, Ohio	56	‡
Cleveland, Ohio	56	1960
Youngstown, Ohio	54	1950
Pittsburgh, Pa.	52	1953
Detroit, Mich.	47	1952
New Orleans, La.	47	1953
San Francisco, Calif.	46	1959
Milwaukee, Wis.	45	1955
Minneapolis, Minn.	42	1955
Dallas, Tex.	38	‡
Providence, R.I.	37	1954
Wilmington, Del.	36	1947
Seattle, Wash.	35	1954
Los Angeles, Calif.	34	1960
Cincinnati, Ohio	33	1951
Washington, D.C.	32	1953
Spokane, Wash.	30	‡
Columbus, Ohio	30	1955
Kansas City, Mo.	28	1954
Louisville, Ky.	26	1953
Salt Lake City, Utah	25	‡
Springfield, Ill.	23	1948
Houston, Tex.	23	1963

* The central business district data do not reflect the fact that in outlying areas
and on weekends major dependence is on automobile.

† These figures are based on the total number of all transit passengers entering
the central business district and not exclusively mass transit.

‡ Not given.

Source: Wilfred Owen, *The Metropolitan Transportation Problem*, Brookings
Institute, Washington, D.C., 1966.

distances at higher terminal-to-terminal speeds than any other mode now
in general use. Thus it comes into its own in the biggest cities of the world.
The bus comes into its own in medium-sized cities, carrying rather lower
(but still substantial) flows along the radial corridors; in such cities, though
there are usually one or two important and well-patronised ring routes
through the inner residential and industrial zones, cross-commuting is less
efficiently catered for. Below a certain critical size of town, which is
difficult to establish with certainty in Britain today, the flow of traffic along
radial routes begins to fall below the level at which even the bus operates

TABLE II(b)

Means of Travel to and from Place of Work, Selected U.S. Cities, 1960*

City	Private Automobile or Car Pool†		Mass Transportation†	
	Central City	Suburb	Central City	Suburb
New York, N.Y.	20	63	65	23
Los Angeles-Long Beach, Calif.	75	86	13	4
Chicago, Ill.	45	70	43	16
Philadelphia, Pa.	42	70	44	13
Detroit, Mich.	68	86	23	5
San Francisco, Calif.	51	79	33	8
Boston, Mass.	38	67	43	18
Pittsburgh, Pa.	49	69	34	15
Wash. D.C.-Md.-Va.	43	77	42	12
Cleveland, Ohio	58	77	32	14
Baltimore, Md.	56	78	30	7
Newark, N.J.	46	68	42	20
Minneapolis-St. Paul, Minn.	64	83	21	5
Seattle, Wash.	68	85	19	3
Cincinnati, Ohio	63	76	24	12
San Diego, Calif.	64	73	8	2
Denver, Colo.	71	84	15	3
Tampa-St. Petersburg, Fla.	77	81	10	2
Phoenix, Ariz.	85	76	5	3
San Jose, Calif.	82	82	7	4
Fort Worth, Tex.	80	88	10	1
Akron, Ohio	76	86	13	4
Oklahoma City, Okla.	83	85	6	1
Sacramento, Calif.	75	87	11	2
Honolulu, Hawaii	71	58	16	2
Flint, Mich.	81	89	7	1
Fresno, Calif.	84	76	5	1
Wichita, Kans.	84	88	6	1
Standard Metropolitan Areas (Number of Population)				
Over 1,000,000	48	76	39	12
500,000 to 1,000,000	68	78	18	6
300,000 to 500,000	70	80	15	4
250,000 to 300,000	72	76	13	4
200,000 to 250,000	72	75	11	3
Under 100,000	76	64	6	3

* Survey conducted during census week, 1960.

† The balance other than private automobile, car pool, and public transportation represents 'walked to work, worked at home, and others'.

Source : Wilfred Owen, op. cit.

efficiently. At this point, particularly if origins and destinations are very diffused, the car comes into its own right, because congestion and parking problems are less serious in such a situation; on the other hand, the public transport system ceases to offer a viable alternative.

These relationships express physical factors, working through economic

TABLE III

EFFECT OF MODE OF TRANSPORT AND NUMBER OF WORKERS ON RADIUS OF CENTRAL AREA AND PERCENTAGE OF IT DEVOTED TO TRANSPORT

Mode of Travel in Town Centre	Radius of central area (Miles) Working population:			Percentage of Central Area for Carriageways Working population:			Percentage of Central Area for Parking Working population:		
	10,000	100,000	1,000,000	10,000	100,000	1,000,000	10,000	100,000	1,000,000
RAILWAY	0·11	0·34	0·08	0·2	0·6	2	—	—	—
BUS, wide streets	0·11	0·34	0·11	1	2	7	—	—	—
BUS, narrow streets	0·11	0·35	1·15	1	4	13	—	—	—
CAR, wide streets (multi-level parking)	0·12	0·37	1·48	5	16	16	11	11	7
CAR, narrow streets (multi-level parking)	0·12	0·42	1·79	9	26	60	11	8	5
CAR, wide streets (ground-level parking)	0·17	0·55	1·96	4	11	31	54	51	39
CAR, narrow streets (ground-level parking)	0·17	0·57	2·24	6	19	47	54	47	30

Source: R. J. Smeed, *Town Planning Review*, 33, 1962–1963.

constraints. To take the physical factors first: Professor R. J. Smeed has produced a valuable theoretical exercise for towns of different sizes, showing what the consequences for land use would be if all commuters to the central business district used the same means of transportation.[5] It is based on certain observed relationships between average speeds of vehicles, capacity and average occupance, giving an average land requirement per person carried for each mode of transportation. The calculation has been done for a town with 10,000 central workers (equivalent to a small market town), for one with 100,000 (equivalent to a major provincial city) and for one with 1,000,000 (equivalent to London). The results, which are set out in Table III, show clearly that as there is a shift to the private car, so the land requirement rises to prohibitively high levels. This can be mitigated somewhat if the city has wide streets (which is not usually the case in Britain), and more particularly if there are multi-storey parking structures. But these in turn are expensive to build, and unless subsidised their cost will be passed on to the car commuter.

The cost of parking is only one aspect of economic constraint. In most British cities, congestion today has reached a critical level at the peak hours: even slight disturbances, such as the failure of a single set of traffic lights or a minor accident, may, and do, cause occasional chaos. The system would not accept large increases in the numbers of car commuters without major road-building schemes. And partly because of the cost of the land and partly because of the cost of the engineering structures necessary, urban roadbuilding is very much more expensive than rural roadbuilding. British estimates, made some years ago by the economist Denys Munby[6] and set out in Table IV, indicate that an urban motorway may cost up to £12 million a mile on very expensive inner-urban land: forty times the average cost per mile of an inter-city motorway. Since then, the average cost per mile of rural motorway has risen somewhat, to about £700,000 per mile; the first stretch of real urban motorway in London, the Western Avenue extension, is costing almost exactly the £12 million per mile quoted as a high limit in the table.

These figures need to be compared with the cost of major construction in the public transport sector. The Victoria Line in London is costing a little over £5 million a mile for deep bored tunnel; the chief traffic officer of Leeds Corporation Transport, Arnold Stone, has estimated that a similar line in Manchester or Leeds would cost only £3·5 million per mile.[7] The Manchester Rapid Transit system, first stage, has been costed at £5 million per mile.[8] All these systems would be capable of very high capacities at the peak: up to 30,000 passengers per hour. In contrast, the urban motorway is capable at maximum of carrying only about 2000 cars per lane before serious congestion reduces its efficiency. With a dual three-lane motorway and an average occupancy of 1·5 per car (a figure observed in several studies of peak traffic in London) this gives a peak one-way capacity of only 9000 persons per hour at more than twice the cost per mile of the underground railway. Admittedly, this is not the end of the comparison; for the motorway will be used intensively at many hours of the day, when the under-

TABLE IV

COST OF MOTORWAYS, BRITAIN

	Miles	Cost (£m)	Cost per mile
London			
'A' ring road	11·1	130	11·7
'New Watling Street' radial from 'A' ring road to Aldenham			
(a) First four miles			3·75
(b) Rest of route			1·25
London County Council Development Plan Widening of roads to four–six traffic lanes (or new roads of same capacity)			
Inner area	27·5	70	2·5
Outer area	33	50	1·5
Total	60·5	120	2·0
British Road Federation ring road	25	(a) 83½	3·3
		(b) 62½	2·5
Alan Day's hexagonal network for London	170	500–600	2·9–3·5
Inter-City motorways			
London–Birmingham	75	21	0·3
Birmingham–Ross	50	15	0·3

Source: D. L. Munby in T. E. H. Williams, *Urban Survival and Traffic* (1962).

ground system is lying almost idle. But while the critical problem is that of the peak period, it does indicate why large centralised cities depend so greatly on public transport, and why the very largest of them—London, Paris, New York, Tokyo—depend so largely on their rail services.

To sum up the general model: bigger cities are more likely to have big, and dense, concentrations of activities. These produce heavy traffic concentrations which public transport is better geared to handle. The bigger the city regions and the more concentrated and large the concentrations of employment, the greater the continuing dependence on public transport. Because of the legacy of the past, the British conurbations and most of the major British free-standing towns remain fixed in this mould, and to a large degree, they are likely to remain so for a long time.

The difficulty is that this pattern no longer corresponds to the facts of social and economic change. Even in cities, people are buying more and more cars (though in general, they buy less of them than their suburban or rural neighbours);[9] the predictions indicate that in most parts of most urban areas, car ownership levels may rise to 70 or 80% of households by the early 1980's. The resulting conflicts are familiar to everyone. People with cars cannot use them freely. When they do, they suffer massive congestion. They may be inhibited from using the cars for work journeys, especially to the central area; but the vast growth of non-work trips, which car ownership makes possible, is mainly from suburb to suburb and is made predominantly by car. (Figures 1(a) and 1(b).) When engineers try to ameliorate this within the limits of their budgets, their interim traffic

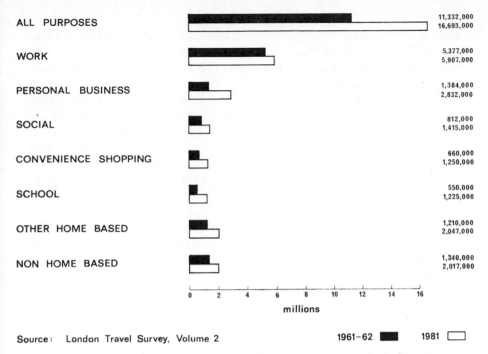

Source: London Travel Survey, Volume 2

1961-62 ◼︎   1981 ☐

FIG. 1a. Projected Internal Basic Trips by Trip Purpose: 1962-81, London.

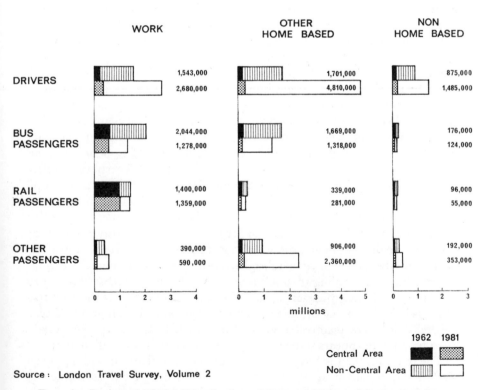

1962   1981

Central Area ◼︎ ▦

Non-Central Area ▥ ☐

Source: London Travel Survey, Volume 2

FIG. 1b. Projected Model Distribution of Internal Trips: 1962-81, London.

measures bring inconvenience and even suffering to many residents. Their longer-term investment plans, now being published for one British city after another, involve destruction of the urban physical fabric on a scale never before witnessed, with a rehousing problem of vast dimensions. The usual answer to the problem, which is laid down in the Buchanan report on *Traffic in Towns*, is to improve the quality of transportation planning, by integrating it within a framework of total physical planning. Yet even when this is done—and it was presumably done by Buchanan himself, in a plan like that for Cardiff—the result is still bitter controversy.[10]

There is, though, another possible approach to the problem. It is to look more closely at the critical relationship between activity patterns, traffic generation patterns and modal split. According to the criticism of Michael Beesley and John Kain, the central weakness of the Buchanan report on *Traffic in Towns* was its lack of realism on these relationships in its central predictions. In its work on Leeds, for instance, the report assumes that the city in 1990 will have the same pattern of activities as the city of 1960, though of course there will be a bigger total of such activities because of rises in population and production. In other words, because the activity in the city centre will increase *pro rata* with the general increase in activity, it will generate a traffic problem which will need large-scale investment to cure. But as Beesley and Kain point out, this assumption does not fit any of our knowledge about the general evolution of urban areas in advanced countries in the latter half of the 20th century. In North America, where this information has been most intensively analysed, it shows rapid decentralisation of activities out of cities—and above all out of their central business districts—into the suburbs.[11] It is arguable that in Kain's own contribution to the book *The Urban Transportation Problem*, he exaggerated the degree of this decentralisation.[12] A careful look at the statistical evidence, both in that book and in more specialised analyses like that of Berry and his colleagues for Chicago,[13] or that of Vance for San Francisco,[14] suggests two conclusions for North America. First, there is *absolute decentralisation of population*. The central cities are losing people, as the exodus of whites exceeds the influx of non-whites. The suburbs show large gains due both to natural increase among the child-bearing age groups who migrate into them, and to the migration process itself; most of the increases represent white people. Secondly, there is *relative decentralisation of activities*. Here the total amount of activity in the city is on average static; some cities gain marginally, some lose. But there is a very rapid re-sorting of city activities; the more generalised activities, like routine manufacturing, wholesaling and retailing of stock lines, move to the suburbs while more specialised activities ministering to the whole region or even the country, like specialised retailing or office functions, remain and even grow. These generalisations are mainly based on the statistical trends of the decade 1950-60. There appears to be no recent evidence that contradicts them.

The question then is how far American evidence does, or will, apply to English metropolitan areas. On this, the evidence so far assembled is contradictory; for it must be assumed that the process of evolution, if it is occurring, is less advanced in the English cities. The P.E.P. analysis of urban growth shows that in the 1950's British metropolitan areas were experiencing *relative decentralisation of populations* and that a few were experiencing absolute decentralisation; on the other hand, a very large number were experiencing *centralisation of activities*, generally of a relative sort. But in the early 1960's, there seems to have been a profound change. The decentralisation of population has become absolute; there is apparently a massive flight of population out of the bigger cities, a product probably of the slum clearance and redevelopment programmes of those years.[15] The analysis of employment patterns leads to the conclusion that here, too, a remarkable change has occurred. Greater London, for instance, is now suffering a very rapid loss of jobs, while the suburban zone outside is continuing to see large increases. Perhaps the great office building boom of the 1950's which generated so much controversy in central London, was, after all, the end of an era. The central business districts of the big cities are losing jobs rapidly (Table V).

TABLE V

CHANGES IN EMPLOYMENT IN FIVE CENTRAL BUSINESS DISTRICTS 1961 TO 1966

Central Business District	Decrease in employment 1961-66	
	(thousands)	(percentage)
London	89	6
Birmingham	11	8
Liverpool	16	10
Manchester	25	15
Newcastle upon Tyne	(change not significant)	

Source: Census, 1961 and 1966, calculated by Ray Thomas, *The Journey to Work*, P.E.P., 1968.

This analysis is of much more than academic interest, for all the evidence indicates that as both population and activities decentralise, the result is a major shift in transportation patterns. The movement from higher-density cities to lower-density suburbs encourages a higher proportion of families to own cars, which are both necessary and more desirable in suburbs, for the converse reason that they are less necessary and less desirable in cities. Additionally, average household incomes tend to be higher in suburbs than in most cities; and this too is directly related to car ownership. Car owners make many more social, or non-work trips, in the evenings and at weekends; the suburban family is therefore more mobile. All transportation studies show a very clear relationship between trip generation and the three inter-related factors of distance from centre, residential density and average household income; the relationships for London are shown in Figs. 2(a) to (c). If the suburban breadwinner is still a city worker, however, his freedom to use his car for work may still be restricted by congestion and parking problems at the City end. It is only when his work also is decentralised that the fundamental change occurs. At this point public transport is likely to become much less attractive, because the line between home and

work is unlikely to be a radial one, with the dense flows of traffic that maintain a good service. At the same time, the car is easier to use because the
journey is made over less heavily loaded cross-routes, with possibilities of
alternative routes to avoid congestion, and with much better car parking

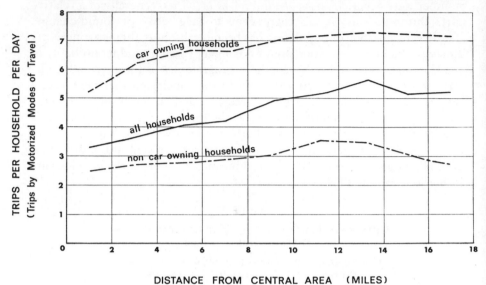

DISTANCE FROM CENTRAL AREA   (MILES)

Source: London Travel Survey, Volume 1

FIG. 2a. Effects of Distance from the Centre on Travel Generation: 1962 London

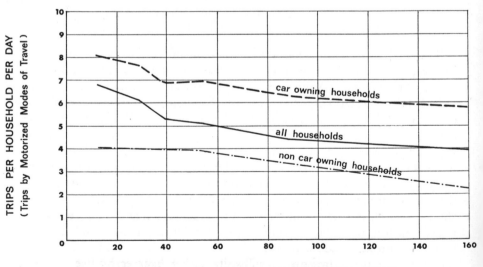

DENSITY   (PERSONS PER NET RESIDENTIAL ACRE)

Source: London Travel Survey, Volume 1

FIG. 2b. Effects of net Residential Density on Travel Generation: 1962 London

prospects at the work end. The result, in almost all suburban situations, is that the great majority of commuters rely on private transport to get to work; in this respect, English suburbs are very like American ones. The 1966 Census, which showed modal choice for the work journey for the first time, makes this clear. To caricature the situation by way of summary, the city is dominated by the radial public transport trip, the suburb by the criss-cross private transport trip.

Notice here that we are still using the word 'suburb' in a purely technical sense; it is the sense that the Americans use in defining their Standard Metropolitan Statistical Areas, where a suburb will be defined in terms of a certain range of population and employment densities and a certain predominant inward commuter flow towards the central city. The description says nothing about the physical form of the suburb. In England today, the suburb may take various forms. Around medium-sized cities like Leicester or Reading, there will usually be continuous additions to the existing town, outside its administrative boundaries. There will also be additions to quite separate settlements, perhaps small towns, perhaps villages, some distance from the central city; these will be separated from the city by a green belt, whether this is formally designated or not, and also separated from each other by open agricultural land. Around the larger conurbations, the continuous additions are likely to be much smaller; in the case of London they are insignificant. Here, virtually all the suburban growth will take place in the separate towns and villages beyond the Green Belt. This fact has profound implications for travel patterns, which have not yet been comprehensively analysed. In technical terms, it represents regional dis-

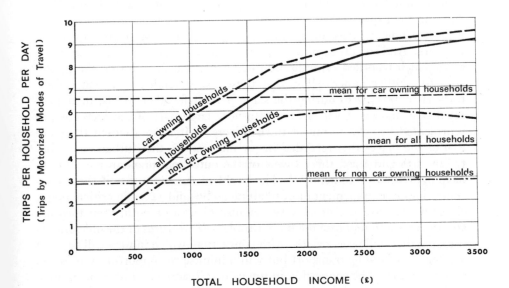

Source: London Travel Survey, Volume 1

FIG. 2c. Effects of Household Income on Travel Generation: 1962 London

persal coupled with local concentration, both of people and activities. Trips are similarly dispersed regionally (i.e. there are many cross-trips) but concentrated locally (i.e. trips are gathered on to a limited number of primary or secondary routes). In order to reach a given range of employment opportunities the worker has to travel farther in miles than if he lived in a suburb attached to a city or conurbation.

But the penalty in time terms is not as great as it seems, because travel speeds on the rural roads are normally rather higher than on urban or even suburban ones. Yet the very flows now generated on certain routes at peak hours may reduce this advantage. In the outer metropolitan area, where car ownership levels are among the highest in England and the dependence on car commuting is correspondingly high, it is observable that even rural main roads tend to assume urban characteristics at peak hours; they are full of traffic travelling at urban speeds, bumper to bumper. It is a moot point, in these circumstances, whether the advantages of regional dispersion are greater than the disadvantages. On the credit side are nearness of urban population to the countryside, the opportunity to many people to live in villages, the ease of use of the private car; on the debit side, the lack of effective public transport for those who need it and the progressive congealing of the main rural arteries.

This raises the critical problem of the location of the activity centres in the new suburban areas. While activity seems latterly to have been deconcentrating on a regional scale, it has been re-concentrating on a subregional or a local scale. This is most clearly seen in the outer metropolitan area, where many of the local suburban concentrations of activities are big enough, and dense enough, to rank as the centres of Standard Metropolitan Areas in their own right. It is clear that while the London Metropolitan Area is stagnant, these outer areas are among the fastest-growing in all England. And equally significantly, these include many of the metropolitan areas which recorded centralisation of people and jobs during the period 1951-61. Other indices show that these towns tended to enhance their rôles as central places during the same period: in other words, their total retail sales increased very fast, and a very large part of the increase was represented by sales to out-of-town buyers.[16] It is no accident therefore that of the places that recorded major increases in their urban status between 1938 and 1965, these towns of the outer metropolitan area should have figured so prominently.[17] The problem is simply that if these concentrations of employment or of retailing go beyond a certain critical point, either in absolute size or density per unit of area or both, then they are almost certain to replicate the more problematic features of the old concentrations; they will be associated with congestion, which in turn will support greater use of public transport but will minimise the opportunity to travel by private car. The congestion in towns like Reading or Luton or Slough, both at the peak weekday hours and during Saturday shopping hours, has already reached acute levels; although, of course, it is much more localised than in the major conurbations, and more susceptible to relief in the form of road works.

The P.E.P. study indicates that up to now, it is only in the outer London area that this process of secondary re-concentration is occurring. But that study is restricted to considering concentration at a certain minimum level of scale. Around Birmingham, for instance, the same process is almost certainly occurring, except that the concentrations of employment or of retail activity are smaller, and possibly less dense. Almost certainly, given existing planning policies and the existing administrative machinery of planning, the process will continue and extend. The conventional policies are dedicated to limiting the growth of large urban areas, but not the growth of smaller ones. The administrative division between the cities and the counties gives town councils every incentive to redevelop their central areas to accommodate more activities, particularly since high subsidies are available to cover most of some of the resulting costs, for instance the cost of ring road construction. At the same time the counties, who plan the suburban growth beyond the city boundaries, often have a basically preservationist attitude; they do not necessarily want big additions to activity in these areas. On both sides, therefore, the machinery manages to ensure that as population grows in the new suburbs, it will find much of its employment and its services in already existing urban centres, which if necessary will be redeveloped for this purpose.

Many planners will be found to justify this trend. They will argue that bigger existing centres provide a better range of jobs and services than new ones; that they are livelier and more interesting places to work in and to shop in; that such centres can support better public transport services for those who need them. But the disadvantages seem undeniable too. These centres are bound to suffer a higher level of traffic congestion, for any given level of car use, than new towns specifically designed for the car; this congestion can only be cured by heavy investment, involving destruction and displacement. The balance sheet will perhaps never be reduced to a unified statement. But at present, it does not seem that the choice is even apparent to many of those engaged in the planning process.

Yet this is the critical choice, given the present and foreseeable trends in urbanisation in Britain today. Within, say, the next forty years, it is inconceivable that the population growth will be housed, in any large measure, in the cities. It is inconceivable either that any large increase will be accommodated in totally new urban regions, well away from existing population centres. The bulk of the new investment will go into the sub-urban rings of the existing metropolitan areas, as I have defined them here. The question then concerns the future organisation of these areas. Is the population to be dispersed within them, or concentrated? Are the activities to be concentrated, and at what scale? Above all, are the areas of concentration to be mainly in existing centres, or in new ones? The answers to these questions will form the most important single set of factors controlling the patterns of transportation within city regions.

It should be possible to give precise expression to these relationships. Certain residential densities, certain sizes and densities of employment, coupled with certain information about occupational structures and incomes, and about the characteristics of the transportation network, should permit us eventually to predict traffic generation and modal split. This after all, in any individual metropolitan area, is the basis of the land use/ transportation study process. But at present we lack precise, comparable information on the variables for small areas in a wide range of metropolitan areas with different social and economic and physical characteristics. Suppose we ask a very generalised question, such as: How far is it possible to structure a very large metropolitan area, with several million people, on the basis of the great majority of people using the private car for all journeys? We know from statistics that this is very seldom possible. We know also that a metropolitan area like Los Angeles comes closer to it than any other very large metropolitan area. We recognise further that in Los Angeles this seems to be associated with an average residential density of the population —a density curiously close to that of an older city like Akron, Ohio, for instance[18]—but with an extreme dispersion of activities, giving no concentration of employment equalling the 2·3 million on 9 square miles of Manhattan Island. Furthermore, we notice that the metropolitan areas of western North America nearly all share the characteristic that a very high proportion of all journeys, even in the central cities, are made by car. We may suspect that this is related partly to low residential population densities, partly to socio-economic characteristics of the population, partly to extreme dispersal of employment and other activity, and partly to low land values which have permitted large-scale highway construction (and which in turn relate to low density and dispersion). But we lack the information that could give any precise form to these hypotheses, which is a major gap in our knowledge.

It might be argued that this is not very useful knowledge, because it assumes that our present transportation planning parameters will remain constant. But it can be argued that this is the only reasonable assumption we can make now. The technical parameters have remained fixed for an astonishingly long time: the basic means of transport available to us for moving about city regions were already all established by the first decade of this century, and have exhibited only detailed design improvements since. There are well-established relationships, established through international comparisons, between income and car ownership; they run the danger of being proved too conservative on the question of second car ownership, though modifications could be incorporated here without destroying the validity of the relationship. The economics of private car production, and of public transport operation, are unlikely to show any striking changes over the next three decades. The limited work so far done on modal choice does indicate that significant proportions of car commuters to a city centre may be shifted to public transport by pricing and other constraints. But such constraints are not likely to operate in large measure outside existing central business districts.[19]

The great majority of the suggested new technologies would have the effect, directly or indirectly, of making public transport more effective as a competitor, or making private transport less desirable in most urban situations. The most important suggestions concern not so much new propulsive systems or new rights of way, but rather new methods of controlling vehicles so as to give them more flexibility in meeting needs of passengers. Among the most important are:

i. a computer-controlled bus-taxi system, in which small buses (with between 18 and 20 seats) could be summoned to fixed stopping places by telephone, then running to a series of places in another part of the urban area;[20])

ii. a new, separate reserved track system, using a lightweight elevated right of way for the most part, which would accept both specially built small private cars (capable of running on and off the ordinary street system) and public transport vehicles. On the system all these would be automatically controlled and could achieve high system speeds;[21]

iii. a bus capable of running both on the ordinary street system and on a special reserved track, where it would be automatically controlled to achieve high speeds;

iv. a system capable of monitoring the progress of vehicles either on all conventional streets or on reserved access highways (for instance, urban motorways). This would serve the dual purpose of automating the flow of vehicles, allowing much greater flows at higher speeds than now, while the driver rode as a passenger; and of automatically charging for the use of the service at a rate which reflected congestion conditions, thus providing a built-in disincentive to drivers to use the road at busy peak times. Conceptually and technically these two features could be separated, one being introduced without the other; paradoxically, the first is likely to make the use of the car more attractive at peak hours, while the second may make it less attractive in many urban situations.

None of these more sophisticated systems of control is operationally feasible at present, though there seems to be no technical feature of any of them which presents overriding problems. The chief difficulty lies in the cost of the investments. All the systems involve highly sophisticated detection and control mechanisms, which represent a scale of investment quite out of line with what any British city is planning now. On the other hand, it could be argued that some of the proposals, especially in congested inner-city locations, represent an alternative to conventional highway construction, and should be so evaluated. In any event, the systems are not mutually exclusive, either with each other or with conventional highway construction programmes. The problem really reduces to a question of who is to pay the cost, and how.

This is complicated by the fact that there are different systems of paying for different sorts of intra-urban transportation. Until recently it was an axiom that public transport passengers as a whole paid the cost of their journeys, though passengers on some routes, at some or all times, would cross-subsidise other passengers on other routes or times. Now, it is officially accepted that public transport authorities may be subsidised by central government when they make major new investments which might include the improvements listed here. The rationale behind this is that there is an irreducible minimum of passengers—the young, the old, the infirm, and those simply unable or unwilling to drive—who must still depend on some form of public transport. This argument seems undeniable; it is being asserted with force even in the United States, where the decline of public transport has gone much further than in Europe. But this still leaves undecided the question of how much investment should be subsidised on behalf of the public transport operators, in order to make their services more efficient and more attractive for their users, in a situation where the elasticity of demand for public transport is probably very low.

Related to this is the problem of how the private motorist pays for his use of road space. At present it is asserted, and generally accepted, that the user of little-used rural road space pays too much for the privilege in licence and patrol taxes, while the user of urban road space at the peak hour certainly pays less than the social cost. The problem is what this true social cost is. Does it include what might be called the costs of amenity, or environment, inflicted by the motorist on residents in the areas through which he drives?[22] Can these be measured? (Despite doughty efforts, no one has had much success in doing so yet.) Even if the costs are restricted to the concept of congestion cost, and so can be regarded strictly as the costs imposed by road users on other road users—the approach used by the British Ministry of Transport in its report on *Road Track Costs*[23]—is it possible to measure congestion costs accurately? Does it matter if the system of charging only reflects the costs roughly, so long as the system is slightly more sensitive than the present one? These are the questions which are far more difficult than the development of the technology of control.

To sum up on the question of parametric change, then: though urban transportation technology has not seen a major change for seventy years, there is no reason why it should not see a change in the next thirty. A number of changes are technically feasible; they raise difficult economic problems of implementation. If they are realised, it is quite likely that they will improve the quality of transportation for a given group of travellers without any very profound effect on the total pattern of transportation. (And this is true now, for improvements within the present technical range; it is the almost certain effect, for instance, of the new Victoria tube in London.) Thus, the development of a dial-a-bus/taxi system might replace conventional buses, especially in suburban areas, and allow an adequate level of public transport to be maintained in those areas in face of the challenge of rising car ownership. It might have a limited effect in slowing down the growth of second- and third-car families, but would otherwise have no very profound effect on general patterns. Similarly, a dual-mode bus, capable of travelling both on streets and reserved tracks, would be most likely to be adopted in the older cities and conurbations where there was already a dense flow of conventional buses along a linear route. It is in fact a possibly cheaper rival to an underground railway, and its most likely effect is to give an improved quality of ride to those who already use public transport in these situations. The impact of new technologies, in other words, is still likely to be related to the basic facts of the urban situation and particularly the location of the basic activities that have to be connected up through the transportation networks. By manipulating these, we alter the nature and the scale of the problems that have to be met by new technologies.

It may be suggested that the transportation technologies I have mentioned here are not the relevant ones. Communications could be substituted for transportation: more effective electronic aids, such as the videophone, the personalised telephone, and the instantaneous transmission of documents, will greatly reduce the need for many personal journeys in city regions and for some goods journeys too. The difficulty about this view is that there is no historic evidence for it. Rather, the evidence is that electronic aids increase the incentive to make journeys, multiplying the possibility of preliminary contacts which lead to the need for personal meetings.[24] In any case, even if a certain amount of electronic contact is as efficient as the same amount of personal contact, the fact is that personal contact may be cheaper for the extended meeting. This is true even in the case of conventional telephone calls; with more elaborate systems, such as the videophone, the cost factor is likely to prove a major disincentive for most people and institutions.

The picture given here is a very conservative one, but it conforms to the available evidence. The existing city regions will continue to house the great majority of the population; they will continue to grow, and this growth will be channelled into their suburban areas. Transport technologies will remain largely as they are now, with some selective innovations here and there in the sphere of vehicle control and monitoring; and the most important choice for planning, because of its impact on the ways intra-urban journeys are made, is between different activity patterns in the suburban rings. If a research priority emerges from this above any other, it is to analyse the relationships between activity patterns and transportation patterns—above all, the modal split for the journey to work—in more detail. At its most basic level, this would be a straight statistical analysis of the relationships, considering as many metropolitan areas as possible for which data were available in Britain and in North America. By analysing the differences which would emerge between areas apparently similar in their physical patterns and economic levels, it might be possible to probe in more detail the forces that work to influence modal choice.

Inter-urban Transportation

The most important impact on the form of city regions is the impact of the intra-urban journeys, which begin and end within them. This must be so, because in large city regions a very high proportion of all journeys are the intra-urban journeys made by the population going to and from work, in the course of their work, and in pursuit of leisure and recreation. The impact of the longer-distance, inter-urban journeys is bound to be subsidiary. Just as with intra-urban journeys, the impact is two-way. Transportation at any point in time will affect subsequent urban growth.

But in turn the urban pattern affects the available choice of transportation.

Two particular kinds of inter-urban journey need looking at: inter-urban personal 'in work' journeys, and inter-urban goods journeys. Other types of inter-urban journeys, for instance journeys for recreation, may eventually have an impact on urban growth; but it is difficult to isolate this impact at present. All journeys arise because of activity patterns, and both the types of journeys we shall consider arise from economic activity patterns: that is, from the distribution of the places where people produce goods and services. We have already seen that there is a strong tendency for many of these activities to decentralise. Those that need most space per unit of product, and those that have least need of a complex network of subordinate contacts and services, will decentralise most readily, have in fact decentralised earliest in time, and are decentralising at the greater rate: they include most types of manufacturing (especially large-scale, assembly line manufacture) and wholesaling. Other activities, which need less space per unit of product or of profit, and which have a considerable benefit from external economies due to the presence of related activities, show the most reluctance to move out from the city centres; they include most offices (except those linked to productive functions) and specialised shops serving wide hinterlands.[25] However, there are now some signs that these activities are changing their locations. Up to now, even non-specialised retailing (food shops, for instance) has tended to concentrate in city centres, because the customers used radially-based public transport. The same applied to routine work in offices, because of the relative ease of commuting by public transport into the centre. But there is limited evidence that European city regions may now be following the trend set earlier by American city regions, where out-of-town shopping centres and campus office developments are now commonplace. This would be accompanied, as we have seen, by a great shift in the pattern of intra-urban journeys, which would become suburb-to-suburb and car-based, instead of suburb-to-centre and public transport-based. But there would be a considerable impact too on inter-urban journeys, which can be illustrated by a representative example.

Consider two functions, which can be interrelated for the purpose of simplicity: a central wholesale depot for a national chain of retail grocers, coupled with the central administrative offices of the firm.[26] For historic reasons, the complex is sited in a cramped position on the edge of the central business district of a major city. This site is close to the older part of the city's port, through which many of the materials are imported. But now the most important operational part of the port has moved down estuary. The site is cramped, and there is severe traffic congestion in the streets around. Goods have to be brought in from domestic factories and farms, or from the docks, through these streets, and out through them again to the retail outlets. The site is convenient for drawing in labour from the whole city, for it is near two main line stations and next to a busy road with a number of bus routes. An additional point is that the firm's hundred or so retail stores, like the national headquarters, are nearly all on congested High Street sites in city centres. The firm's senior personnel spend some time visiting these stores, and find it relatively easy to do so by train. If they have to visit farms or factories, they find it more difficult; they must arrange to have a car, or a taxi, meet them at the nearest station, and travel as much as thirty miles in this way.

Now consider the whole situation as it might well be at the end of the 1980's. The whole central complex has moved out of the city to a new town thirty miles away. It is in a landscaped parkland setting on the edge of an industrial estate, with direct access to a motorway interchange, which in turn gives access to the whole national motorway system. By that time the system is virtually complete, and serves almost every town in the country with a population of 150,000 or more. An orbital road bypasses the city, giving direct congestion-free contact between the new dock complex and the river mouth and the central depot. Equally, lorries passing out of the depot move on uncongested roads to the hundred or so retail outlets. Many of these outlets, too, have relocated themselves in suburban or out-of-town sites, close to motorway interchanges. The main motive was to tap wider hinterlands of shoppers who would come by car. But a subsidiary benefit was in the greater ease of getting goods into the stores. The central complex can draw on a wide hinterland for its labour needs, though nearly all come by car, causing severe localised congestion at the motorway interchange during short morning and evening peaks.

When directors and managers wish to visit stores, they find it more convenient to go by car, which takes them from door to door. If they used the train, they would waste time going back into the congested city, and when they got to their destination they would have to use a car or taxi to get out again. For longer journeys, they usually use the local airport. (At the present time, as shown by a study of European conditions, this critical breakpoint between rail and air is probably about 300 miles.)[27] This airport is ten miles away on the motorway and has bus-stop services which, with connections, serve most to the towns in the north of England, or Scotland, which the top personnel need to visit (Fig. 3).

This description may seem utopian. It is not intended to be. Already many firms have made this sort of move, with these sorts of consequences. The growth of the national motorway system seems assured, and so does the growth of local air services. If this is a realistic description, though, it does have some important consequences for inter-urban traffic patterns, which may be unexpected. The most serious are for the railways. At present, there is a comfortable assumption that the railways can hold their own and more: that traffic congestion on the roads, plus the arrival of a National Freight Corporation based on moving goods by the most efficient and economical means, will divert a modest but significant proportion of the growth in inter-urban traffic—both in goods and passengers—off the roads and on to the railways. But this appears to ignore the geographical changes which have just been described.

The questions for research, then, fall into two groups. One concerns the activity patterns. Which activities will disperse, and at what rate? With manufacturing and wholesaling, the answer seems in no doubt. With retailing, there is a bigger question mark: is there a point at which car ownership levels rise to such heights that there is a sudden development of out-of-town shopping? Is this something that is predictable from international experience, or do social customs and planning restrictions invalidate

The Situation Now

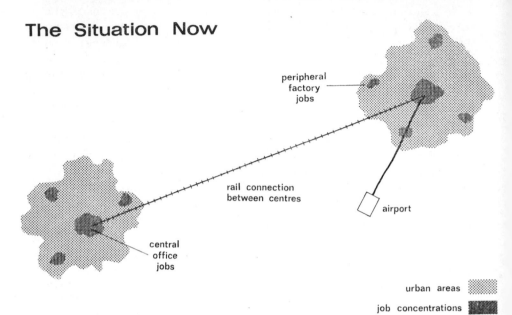

The Future Situation

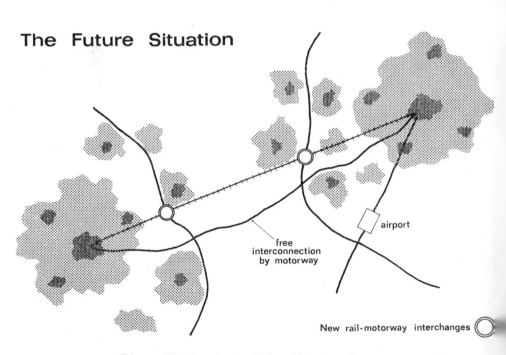

FIG. 3. The Developing Urban Transport Pattern.

such comparisons? Certainly, no European nation so far seems to demonstrate the same degree of decentralised retailing as the United States—
even Sweden, where car ownership levels are locally as high as in North
America. With offices, the evidence is even more contradictory: despite all
the controls and inducements, the demand for central London office space
seems to be almost inexhaustible.[28] Many other fast-growing activities
seem to follow no clear pattern. Higher education, one of the fastest-
growing of all, shows a bewildering variety: universities, and now poly-
technics, are located sometimes in city centres, sometimes in suburbs,
sometimes on green field sites. With the whole higher education industry
likely to be one of the major sectors of economic activity by the end of the
century, this is a question of far more than peripheral importance; it has
had little attention.

The other question concerns the impact of technology. There are first of
all the competing technologies of the different forms of transportation.
These are at various stages of development, and various degrees of certainty
can be attached to their introduction. The advanced passenger train, with
lightweight rolling stock and improved signalling controls, seems certain to
be operational by the mid-1970's, with initial speeds of 125 miles an hour
start to stop, and speeds of up to 200 m.p.h. by 1990.[29] This could cut
journey times between typical British cities (London-Manchester London-
Leeds) to as little as an hour—but with the proviso about the location of
activities, which has already been mentioned. On the roads, in contrast, the
prospect seems to be lower average speeds rather than higher ones. They
will be more certain and more sustained than now, because more of the
mileage will be on high-capacity motorways and improved trunk roads.
But it seems certain that the secular growth of traffic on the motorway
system will gradually force down permissible maximum speeds. We need
to look only at the example of the United States, where even 70 miles an
hour is an historic memory save in the deserts of Nevada. The whole
strategy of the railways, up to now, has been based on the inter-city
strategy: city-to-city, heart-to-heart, as the advertisements run. Therefore passenger services are improved between city centre termini, and
Freightliner terminals are built mainly in the older industrial areas only a
few miles from the city centres, often where there is severe local congestion
on the roads. These may prove to be just the wrong places in relation to the
likely patterns of economic activity in the 1990's.

The railways, if they are wise, will adapt their strategy accordingly.
They will develop new passenger interchanges in the outer suburbs and
even in green-field sites, where car parking is easy and where there is
immediate access to the national motorway network. These stations would
serve business travellers between suburban homes or offices and other
suburban destinations. They would also act as commuter stations for those
travelling into the nearby city, and wanting to leave their cars. British
Railways have made a start on these lines. On their reconstructed London-
Lancashire services, for instances, they stop many Liverpool trains at
Runcorn new town, and many Manchester trains stop at Wilmslow. But

the practice needs extending, and the sites need choosing carefully. Many expresses on the Western Region stop at Reading, and those on the London Midland Region stop at Watford Junction. But both these stations sit in the middle of acute local congestion. With the freight traffic, sites for new depots need even more careful choice in relation to the distribution of activities and the regional road network.

Even if the railways do their best to accommodate themselves to the new patterns, they will still face a built-in disadvantage. Essentially, both the inter-city passenger services and Freightliner services exploit the advantages of railways over other forms of transport, which Dr Beeching set out so well in his report: the ability to provide fast, reliable, high-capacity transport over a few main lines. But as economic activity disperses within city regions, this becomes less and less of an advantage; for it takes too long to travel to the terminal gathering and distributing points at either end of the fast line haul. The railways can seek to minimise this disadvantage, by careful resiting of these points in relation to the new accessibility patterns conferred by the motorways. But they can never hope to abolish it. Dispersed activity patterns associate naturally with dispersed transportation patterns, and they in turn with reliance on the motor vehicle. This is as true of inter-urban transportation patterns as of intra-urban ones. This situation will now alter unless and until automatic guidance and control systems can be introduced on a large scale on motorways. These systems, which could potentially run cars in electronically-coupled trains at up to 150 miles an hour, are being actively developed in the United States. At present they would be prohibitively expensive to instal. But this is above all the area where extremely rapid technological breakthrough is accompanied by extremely rapid falls in cost. Developments in computers and in micro-electronics (such as integrated circuits) could make it possible by the 1980's to fit all cars with control systems which would now be astronomically expensive, but which by then could be little more than the cost of a cheap transistor radio. The train, then, may have a short period of relative advantage, followed by a period when all the existing tidy notions about public and private transport have to be discarded.

With air travel, the directions of technological advance are difficult to see beyond 1985. VTOL (Vertical Take off and Landing) is subject to very large problems of noise and investment costs; in any case, if activities will disperse from city centres, the main *raison d'être* may be lacking. More important, probably, will be developments in STOL (Short Take off and Landing) which is showing very rapid growth in the United States. STOL would not normally be used, save in very special circumstances, in or near city centres. But it could have important applications in suburbs. It could lead to a great multiplication of the numbers of small airports, giving very rapid access for virtually the whole population to air travel. Large and even medium-sized factories, offices and universities would have their own airports. Because STOL would virtually eliminate the problem of ground access to airports, it could lead to an unknown increase on the numbers of relatively short air journeys between one suburban location and another.

Journeys of between 50 and 100 miles might be made most quickly by air. This could have profound implications for the future pattern of inter-urban passenger travel in Britain, but only if it were accompanied by improved methods of air traffic control.

In addition, there is the possibility that other forms of communication will increasingly be substituted for the movement of goods or people. The argument here is essentially the same as for intra-urban transportation. All the evidence is that as people use more and more electronic communication, they also use more and more personal transportation. Indeed, if a researcher were to make an international historic comparison extending over the last hundred years, he would probably find that the two curves march very closely together, and appear to be related to the general level of economic development. The psychology of person-to-person communication is exceedingly complex, and it is probably safest to conclude that as advanced western economies become more spohisticated, they simply multiply the opportunities for rapid and economic inter-communication of all sorts. If, therefore, there were an unprecedentedly rapid development of electronic communication during the period up to 2000, it would almost certainly lead to no reduction in the number of personal journeys at all. By multiplying incentives to travel, it might indeed lead to an increase.

Conclusion : Urban Transportation and Urban Form

The distinction between intra-urban transportation and inter-urban transportation has proved a useful one here. But increasingly, it is an artificial one. Metropolitan areas, defined in terms of commuting fields, become steadily bigger. More commuting journeys are made from one metropolitan area to another. For journeys over a certain distance, whether or not they cross a metropolitan area boundary, the questions are similar. There is a problem of leaving an origin, running as fast as possible on a line, and then arriving at a destination. It is possible for these three jobs to be done in the same vehicle, but also possible to use three separate vehicles. This may increase efficiency (in terms of speed or carrying capacity) for one stage of the journey, but only at the cost of introducing an interchange problem. Thus the suburban car owner, whether he is going to work ten miles away or to a business meeting a hundred miles away, may well leave his house by car, because there is no efficient alternative. The question for him then is whether to leave the car and take some form of public transport, or to drive all the way. The answer may be affected to some extent by comfort and to some extent by cost—though the motorist's own valuation of car costs, based usually on the cost of petrol alone, would not satisfy an economist or an accountant. But to a very large degree it will hinge on time and convenience. To overcome the resistance to changing from one form of transportation to another, either the main-line journey will have to be especially fast, or there will have to be some positive disincentive to taking the car all the way. Into the first category would come some longer inter-city journeys; into the second, journeys into congested city centres where congestion is great and parking difficult.

The point about this analysis is that it applies to all sorts of journeys, intra- and inter-city, passenger and goods. There is a very powerful incentive to using the single mode from origin to destination; it is convenient and, unless interchange is very efficient, it will often be quicker. In situations where origins and destinations are dispersed, then normally the start and end of every journey will be made by the private mode: the individual car or the individual goods van. Therefore, the incentive will be to use this form of transportation for the whole journey, whether it be ten miles or a hundred miles long. The only limitations to this principle will be longer inter-city journeys, which will be made by suburb to suburb passenger express train, or freightliner train, or bus stop (probably STOL) plane; and any journey, whether inter- or intra-city, where there is localised concentration of activities at one or both ends of the journey. This brings us back to the critical question. As city regions disperse on the regional scale, are they to reconcentrate on a local scale? How far should localised high density nodes of activity, linked to high density public transport but with inevitable congestion limiting private transport, be permitted and even encouraged in the growing outer peripheries of our great metropolitan regions? This, above all, is the central question for urban organisation in Britain, and in Europe, for the years up to 2000.

REFERENCES

[1] *Cf.* Kingsley Davis, *The World's Metropolitan Areas*. Berkeley and Los Angeles: California University Press, 1959, pp. 10-11, 17-20: T. W. Freeman, *The Conurbations of England and Wales*. Manchester, University Press, 1966, Ch. 1 passim.

[2] Evidence to be published in the author's section of *Megalopolis England*. London: Political and Economic Planning, to be published 1971.

[3] J. R. Meyer, J. F. Kain, M. Wohl, *The Urban Transportation Problem*, Cambridge, Mass.: MIT Press, 1965, p. 366.

[4] Manchester Rapid Transit Study, Vol. 3, *The First Priority*. Manchester: The Corporation, 1968, p. 105.

[5] R. J. Smeed, 'The Road Space required for Traffic in Towns', *Town Planning Review*, 33, London, 1962-3, pp. 279-92.

[6] D. L. Munby, 'The Economics of City Traffic', in T. E. H. Williams (ed.), *Urban Survival and Traffic*, London: Spon, 1962, Table 6, p. 228.

[7] A. Stone, 'The Future of Road Transport in our Cities', *Journal of the Institute of Transport*, 31 1965-6, p. 272.

[8] *Manchester Rapid Transit Study, op. cit.*, Table 5.3.2. and Table 6.1.

[9] See for instance the evidence in *London Travel Survey*, Vol. 2, London: Greater London Council, 1966, para. 12-17 and Diagram 12-2 (reproduced here as Fig. 2 (b)). Since publication of this report, car ownership rates in Central London have risen even less rapidly than was forecast.

[10] John Barr, 'Cardiff's Hook Road', *New Society*, 8 May 1969.

[11] M. E. Beesley and J. F. Kain, 'Urban Form, Car Ownership and Public Policy: An Appraisal of Traffic in Towns', *Urban Studies*, 1, 1964, pp. 184-5.

[12] Meyer *et al.*, *op. cit.*, Chapter 3 passim. This is criticised in Peter Hall, 'The Urban Culture and the Suburban Culture', in Richard Eels and Clarence Walton (ed.) *Man in the City of the Future*, New York: Macmillan 1969, 125.

[13] B. J. L. Berry *et al.*, *Commercial Structure and Commercial Blight*, University of Chicago Research Paper 85, Chicago: The University, 1963, p. 29.

[14] J. E. Vance, 'Emerging Patterns of Commercial Structure in American Cities', in *Proceedings of the IGU Symposium on Urban Geography*, Lund, ed. Knut Norborg, *Land Studies in Geography*, Series B, 24, 1962, pp. 517.

[15] Evidence to be published in Megalopolis England, *op. cit.*

[16] 'Report of the Socio-Geographic Enquiry', in *Local Government in South East England*, Research Report No. 1, *Royal Commission on Local Government in England*, London: H.M.S.O., 1968, para. 3.43.

[17] R. D. P. Smith, 'The changing Urban Hierarchy', *Regional Studies*, 2, 1968, pp. 1-19.

[18] Robert B. Riley, 'Urban Myths and the new cities of the Southwest', *Landscape*, 17/1, Autumn 1967, pp. 21-2. A city like Phoenix (Ariz.), which is much newer than Los Angeles, has about half its average density.

[19] D. A. Quarmby, 'Travel Mode for Journey to Work', *Journal of Transport Economics and Policy*, 1, 1967, pp. 297-300.

[20] Department of Housing and Urban Development, *Tomorrow's Transportation*, Washington DC, Government Printing Office, 1968, pp. 58-60.

[21] *Ibid.*, 60-68.

[22] As argued, for instance, by E. J. Mishan in *The Costs of Economic Growth*, London: Staples, 1967, pp. 97-8.

[23] Ministry of Transport, *Road Track Costs*, London: H.M.S.O., 1968, para. 17.

[24] *Cf.* Peter Hall, *The World Cities*, London, etc.: World University Library, 1966, 241, and the paper by Peter Cowan on 'Communications' in this issue.

[25] Folke Kristensson, *People, Firms and Regions : A Structural Economic Approach*, Stockholm: School of Economics, mimeo. 1967, passim. To be published; already published as *Människor Företag och Regioner*, Stockholm: Almqvist and Wiksell, 1967.

[26] At least one well-known firm corresponds to the description. But the illustration is purely hypothetical.

[27] Albert S. Chapman, 'Trans-Europe Express: Overall Travel Time in Competition for Passengers', *Economic Geography*, 44, 1968, pp. 288-95.

[28] There is evidence that the growth in central London employment may have ceased—at least temporarily. Cf., the commuting figures to central London for 1962-67 in London Transport, *London Transport in 1968*, London: H.M.S.O., 1969, p. 39.

[29] 'Railays of Tomorrow', supplement to *The Times*, 9 July 1969.

COMMUNICATIONS

PETER COWAN

Introduction

Forecasts about communications vary between two extremes. On one hand are the optimists. They suggest that, in years to come, society will function better, and that people will be happier because of improvements in communications. Such forecasts have much in common with nineteenth-century optimism and belief in progress through the advance of science. On the other hand there are gloomy forecasts. These stress the social problems created by the technology of communications. Invasion of privacy and the terrors of thought control loom large in such predictions, which have something in common with Carlyle and other Cassandras of the Victorian era.

It is my task to bring together some of these modes of thought and to trace out their possible effect upon the pattern of urbanisation in Britain. I shall begin with some general observations about the future of communications until the year 2000. I shall then present some speculations about the cultural effects of changes in communications, followed by a few ideas of the peculiarly urban problems which may face us in the future. Finally, I shall attempt a review of major policy issues created by changes in communications, and will suggest areas in which further study is needed.

The Future for Communications

Demand for communications will grow during the next thirty years. We expect the population of Britain to increase from its present 55 million to some 70 million people by the end of the century. This, in itself, will mean an extra 15 million people for whom communications facilities must be provided. But the load will increase more than this. In any situation the number of links between points increases faster than the number of points themselves. While it would be ridiculous to suggest that every single individual in Britain should be linked to everyone else, simple calculation shows that, even if cultural, economic, and technical factors are held constant there will be a massive increase in the demand for communications facilities during the next few decades. And of course cultural, economic and technological factors will not remain constant, they will change and create more demand for communications.

The G.P.O. estimates that there has been an increase in telephone installations from 7,360,000 or 0·14 per head of population, in 1958 to 11,390,000 or 0·21 per head of population by 1967. Current estimates suggest there will be 16,800,000 telephones in Britain by 1971. There will probably be a 'phone for every family by 2000. The demand for postal services seems to be growing more rapidly than population increase would suggest. The number of letters delivered rose from 9,700 million or 194·0 per head of population in 1956 to 11,300 million or 210·6 per head of population in 1966. There have been some curious changes in the demand for telegram services. While the number of inland telegrams delivered fell from 49,253,000 in 1937 to 9,338,000 in 1966, the number of overseas telegrams increased from 9,238,000 to 21,628,000 over the same period. Presumably the decline in inland figures reflects the increase in telephone calls, while the increase in overseas telegrams goes some way to confirming the views of some observers concerning a developing 'world-wide community'.

So far as the mass media are concerned the major event has been the growing ascendancy of television over other modes of communication, with the exception of newspapers. The following table shows the patterns of change over the past decade or so.

TABLE I

NUMBER OF RADIO AND TV LICENCES ISSUED YEAR BY YEAR, 1956-1966
('000's).

Year	1956	1957	1958	1959	1960	1961	1962	1963	1964	1965	1966
Radio Licences	8,522	7,559	6,556	5,481	4,535	3,909	3,538	3,256	2,999	2,974	2,611
TV Licences	5,740	6,966	8,090	9,255	10,470	11,263	11,834	12,443	12,485	13,253	13,567

Source: G.P.O.

Of course the figures for television licences will also include radios, but the figures do reveal the sharp decline in 'radio only' households. We should be wary of extrapolating these figures far into the future, for it is unlikely that radio will disappear altogether. We can be sure that television will penetrate most homes in the next few years and that by the end of the century there will be increasing demands for more choice, more channels, and more outlets in each home.

Investment in communications will undoubtedly grow during the next few decades. Once again we must qualify our guesses by stressing the dangers of straight extrapolation. However, the changes are so striking that they make the future very clear. Consumer expenditure on postal, telephone and telegraph services rose from £122 million, or £2·4 per head of population in 1956, to £187 million or £3·4 per head of population in 1966. At constant prices this may in fact represent a *decrease* in expenditure; but such a surprising result *may* be attributed to the cheaper cost of communication to the consumer. In the public sector, figures from the G.P.O. confirm that massive increases in investment have been taking place for some time. The table below shows how the total investment in postal and telecommunications services has changed since 1964, and suggests how such changes may continue into the early seventies.

TABLE II

CURRENT AND PROJECTED EXPENDITURE ON POSTAL AND TELECOMMUNICATIONS SERVICES

£ Million (1964 Prices)	1963-64	1964-65	1965-66	1966-67	1967-68	1968-69	1969-70	1970-1
	176·0	192·5	233·1	264·3	301·7	326·6	337·3	346·0

Source : G.P.O.

Figures for the private sector of the communications industry are more difficult to find, but some indication is given by the development of the electronics industry. The growth rate of electronics as a whole has been phenomenal over the last decade. Growth has occurred in all areas, from transistors to electronic capital goods such as radar installations. There are some problems in trying to identify the growth rates of particular areas and bits of areas. In an industry producing a wide range of items, each changing very rapidly, it is very difficult to gather proper statistics. In spite of these difficulties it is still worth indicating the rapid growth and change, that has taken place in the industry.

The table below gives the output of the British electronic computer industry between 1959 and 1966.

TABLE III

OUTPUT OF ELECTRONIC COMPUTER INDUSTRY IN BRITAIN 1960-1966

Value £ Thousands	1960	1961	1962	1963	1964	1965	1966
	8,196	10,903	13,440	24,752	44,164	34,567	74,764

Source : C.S.O. Annual Abstract of Statistics.

These few statistics indicate that the computer industry will become 'an industry with a multi-billion dollar future' and therefore powerful outside its actual product area as a political lobbyist, employer and cultural standard maker.

Integration between systems of communication transmission and communication storage, retrieval, sorting, and so on will distinguish the future use of computers from their now relatively separate functioning. This will make possible the fourth generation of computers, distinguished by 'compatibility'. This compatability enables the same programme to be used with different scale machines, within the same range.

The fourth generation of computers will evolve gradually from existing hard and software. Within the next few years, as companies become more able to use computer services they will demand higher levels of operation. Full-time availability will present demands for computers tailored to the particular requirements of individual industries.

Companies agree that the challenge of the next few years will be to get whole organisations 'on line', to a computer. Any on-line facility must be able to absorb continuous streams of information, instructions and requests fed in by direct line from widely dispersed terminals—the data net.

The rudiments of such data nets are already in operation, but it will be some time before they become commercially attractive for the average business organisation.

Software and memory store systems must be greatly improved and better methods introduced to keep the programming work entailed in setting up large data banks within reasonable cost limits.

The development of large-scale integration is one of the results of the computer producers' intensive efforts to solve the 'memory problem'. At present information is usually given an address, indicating its location within the machine. New developments are leading towards an 'associative memory', which will enable data to be called from a common memory pool.

Assuming such problems are overcome, the production and installation of a data net similar to that being designed at the National Physical Laboratory could come into operation. In this system the user feeds his message in at a terminal and it is transmitted straight to an 'interface' computer, which links local lines to the national network. The 'interface' machine puts the message into a standard form and stores it ready to be forwarded as soon as an opportunity arises. It will only take a hundredth of a second to transmit a message from one end of the country to another.

A data net will behave in a completely different way from the telephone system. In practice both systems would share many facilities. Local telephone lines could be taken over for the data net by connecting them directly to the 'interface' computer.

The Post Office National Data Processing Service hopes to sell on-line computer time to anyone in the country with a terminal. On-line facilities can be provided easily and will be cheap. This could open up an enormous market outside the existing computer market of large companies, corporations and the nationalised industries.

Computers and data nets are only one striking example of the future of communications. There are many others. For example the present means of transmitting financial information is costing enormous sums of money, not only to the financial institutions, but also to account holders. In 1967 the U.S. banks handled 20 billion cheques which cost all those concerned $3·7 billion.

In response to this enormous volume of work (and money), computer designers employed by banks and other financial institutions have suggested many ways of eliminating all or most of the paper work involved. One method would be to link terminals directly to the central computers of the banks. The location of the terminals could be in the home, the office, or in shops, in fact anywhere an ordinary financial transaction takes place.

Integral with any electronic system that replaces cheques is the credit system. The credit card as a link in the communication chain raises difficult social and political problems.

To operate an adequate credit card system on a wide scale, considerable information about a person's credit worthiness is required. It is important to guard against the fraudulent use of cards, which raises many issues concerning how the establishment identification is made. In the end, it needs to be both foolproof and automatic. Once again the pessimists are confronted by the optimists for the future of credit cards.

All that I have said above has concerned one aspect of communications in future society—that of the transmissions of ideas. The movement of people and goods will be covered in more detail in Peter Hall's paper on transportation.

To sum up, the combined effect of all the increasing demand for communications services during the next few decades will make everyone and everything within easy reach. Demand will rise rapidly and technical and social innovation will respond, investment will go on rising and so on. Indeed, the communications industry, like the space race or the learning industry, could be one of those necessary fly-wheels to absorb the vastly increased opportunities to spend, which may face the western world during the closing decades of this century.

Communications, Urban Culture and Politics

The cultural impact of communications and future urban society have been considered by many authors, and increased technical capacity for communications forms a central part of most forecasts of future societies. That communications are bound up closely with major changes in society, and especially with urbanisation and automation is well put by Servan-Schreiber in *Le Defi American*[1] when he says 'Urbanisation, automation, and communication have obviously separate effects, but much of their impact interacts. We may consider them as convergent forces which will forge a new society, which is the accomplishment of the second industrial revolution.' Clearly we must accept this view, for it is reinforced again and again in the literature, and perhaps more important, it seems most sensible and probable.

However, the effects of such changes seem to form a dividing point for discussion. Here we come up once more against the optimists and the pessimists. The optimistic view is that growth in communications will bring with it increasing education and choice, growing sophistication, and a development of questioning attitudes among wider and wider segments of the population. Thus the population will not be so easily led, and will be able to make up its own mind on many issues which at present confound it. Such changes will put a brake upon the powers of politicians and planners, and will enable democratic choices to be made on a sound basis. People will be better informed and will spend more time choosing among all sorts of interesting alternatives on a variety of personal, social, economic, and political issues. Everyone will be happier as his range of choices is widened and constraints fall away.

Pessimistic forecasts take a different view. They suggest that changes in information-handling mean invasion of privacy, thought control and all sorts of other evils. They point out that technical improvements call for social inventions which are usually directed towards the centralisation of information, which makes the individual vulnerable to spying. We have seen that the growth of credit card systems is a favourite target for this kind of gloomy forecast.

Whether we take an optimistic or a pessimistic view of the impact of communications innovations upon urban culture we must recognise its over-riding importance. Certainly the effect will be to spread ideas even more rapidly, and to contribute to the blurring of distinctions between 'urban' and 'non-urban' ways of life. Already most people in Britain are able to know, hear and see the latest news and current events very soon after they happen. The networks of radio and television, and the rapid distribution of national newspapers mean that, despite regional differences, most people in Britain share a common background of information which assists in the formation of a common culture.

There are those who regret the passing of urban and rural cultural differences, and for whom the resurgence of regional and national senti- ments represent a last hope for retaining a richness and variety of life styles which would be sadly missed. Others say that the advantages in terms of equalising opportunities, and perhaps reducing the dominance of particular groups through wider diffusion of information, far outweigh the disadvantages.

My own view is that *both* effects will operate, and that this will form the major area for friction at many levels. It seems sensible to suggest that improved or more communication opportunities provide means for both greater collaboration and greater conflict. The more we get to know about other people, other regions, or other institutions, the more we may grow to like and understand them. On the other hand distance does sometimes lend enchantment to certain views, and understanding someone else may not always make it easier to forgive. I suggest that 'communication or conflict' may be the major social issue raised by the ever-increasing flow of informa- tion in our culture.

Communications and Inter-Urban Patterns

In a strict sense the development of mass communications means that traditional distinctions between 'urban' and 'non-urban' places and patterns no longer exist. In Mel Webber's[2] sense, all Britain is urbanised. As I noted in the previous section, most people in the developed part of the Western world share a common culture, which is highly urban. Neverthe- less, in this country, some people live in cities and some outside, despite the fact that more and more of the population is migrating towards the major urban areas. The paper on the physical framework by Emrys Jones[3] suggests that this situation, in which it is possible to distinguish urban from non-urban spatial patterns, will be with us for several decades to come. It is therefore legitimate to ask what the effect of communications on this pattern will be.

Many major inventions and innovations will have little effect on the overall pattern of settlements in Britain. For example, telephones, tele- vision, radio, video-phones and many other technical advances are unlikely to affect very greatly the disposition of major urban areas across the face of the country. These are all essentially 'blanket type' inventions. There is no evidence to show that the telephone, by itself, has had any major influence upon the overall settlement pattern of Britain, and yet it has been in use since the late nineteenth century. On the other hand, the telephone and telegraph assisted greatly in the exploitation of other aspects of the late industrial revolution. Seen in this light, the development of new means of communications may have a marginal but significant effect upon the growth rates of settlements in different locations. But such innovations will have a much greater effect upon the intra-urban pattern, which I shall discuss in the next section. For the present we can simply suggest that the effect on these innovations upon the overall pattern of urbanisation in Britain will be small.

Other forms of communications may have considerable effect upon settlement patterns in Britain. They are concerned primarily with the movement of goods or of people. Strictly speaking such innovations must come under the heading of transportation and are dealt with by Peter Hall,[4] so I will only touch on them very briefly.

Most changes will speed up movement *between* places, and it is unlikely to be worth stopping on any route, except at a major centre. On a wider scale these changes in transport communications may have considerable international effects, especially in the tertiary sectors. In those industries where communication and face-to-face meetings become ever more important, changes in communication and transportation technologies may have a striking effect upon the location of meeting places, and this in turn will be affected by political changes in the years to come.

As the affairs of the world become ever more inter-linked, the location of these meeting places may change. The importance of some cities will decline while others will move up the scale. With the development of South America or Japan, Africa and South-East Asia their capital cities may become primary nodes in the world network of transactions. Such global changes may be complemented by the growth of new city centres at airports, hoverports or other communications' interchanges. It is at this level that the major effects of communications upon patterns of urbanisation will be felt.

Communications at the Intra-Urban Level

The effects of future changes in communication patterns at the intra-urban level will be considerable. Nearly all the forecast changes in communications have to do with patterns of work, and since cities are closely bound up with work patterns their form must be affected by these new innovations. Changes and innovations which are most affected by intra-urban patterns are just those which do not affect the scale of inter-urban distribution. The telephone and its associated inventions and other inventions such as automation and computers will have a major impact on urban form, because of their association with particular kinds of jobs which will become increasingly important in the urban sociaty of the future.

If we consider the particular impact of automation and computers on the future of cities we must first of all expect it to be felt in manufacturing industries. These inventions will then begin to affect service industries. The impact of computers on office growth is growing and will continue to grow. This is most important, because it is the office sector which seems likely to be the major focus of urban work in the future.

All these inventions will speed up messages *between* activities. *Within* activities, messages are, at present, slowed down and processed by hand. The telephone, telegraph and videophone enable contacts to be established quickly and orders and messages can be flashed from one office to another with great speed. But once they arrive in a particular organisation, messages and orders are dealt with one at a time by manual labour. The object of the office automation movement is to speed up some of these hand-processing phases. The movement seems likely to gain ground, although there may be a time when the retention of manual work in offices may be necessary, to occupy a certain amount of surplus labour. But, of course, the final decisions which are the key part of most offices must be taken by hand, and it is this particular decision function which may govern the future pattern of urbanisation under the impact of communication inventions. These changes are so important for the inter-urban pattern of the future that it is worth dwelling upon them. The office is perhaps one of the keys to the future. We have seen that the office function is closely linked to the patterns of communication in society, and that we should expect any changes in such patterns to have a profound effect upon the office.

A report by the Department of Economic Affairs[5] lays stress upon the importance of communications in determining office location, and considers in detail various modes of communication and their availability in different regions. The general conclusion is that London holds a dominant position for most kinds of office work, although certain routine activity might be moved out. A policy to achieve such decentralisation must include financial assistance to communications functions, and a tax on floor space in central areas. This study confirms the importance of communications as an element in deciding office locations, and points to the forces which are affecting two distinct sections of the office functions—centralised decision making and dispersing routine data processing. The same two things seem to be occurring in the United States. First, the decision makers, the leaders of industry, finance, communications and so on—what has been called the 'élite group'—are finding it more and more necessary to locate in the centre of the city. These people are those whose business and indeed survival, depend upon rapid communication—they flourish upon the newest ideas, and must react instantly in order to maintain their place in the system. These people, the élite, also need to be near, or have immediate access to their own information which is contained in the more routine parts of the office organisation. The second trend is for those more routine parts of the office function to become more footloose; able to locate in the suburbs, near to the female labour force, and away from the high rents and access difficulties of the centre.

Lichtenberg[6] points to this process at work in the New York Region, 'Like producers of unstandardised products, the central office executives "produce" answers to "unstandardised" problems, problems that change frequently, radically, and unpredictably. . . . These problems are solved quickly only by consultation with a succession of experts. But, like stockbrokers or high-style dress manufacturers, most central offices would find it inefficient if not impossible, to staff themselves internally with all of the specialised personnel and services that they must call upon from time to time to solve their problems. Nor is it convenient to transport the experts to their plants or maintain effective contact by telephone or letter. The importance of speed blunts the effectiveness of the fastest means of transportation and the complex and subtle nature of the problem often precludes the use of the telephone. All of these considerations dictate a concentration of offices in a tight cluster near each other and near their "suppliers".'

The office function splits, and the two elements have different location and space needs. Once again the importance of communications becomes clear. Élite groups locate in the centre where they can have immediate face-to-face contact with a wide variety of people. Routine functions may be suburbanised at the end of an airline, a telephone wire, or a television circuit—the finer nuances of communication are not necessary for the kind of messages which flow between executive and routine office plant.

For the next few decades this pattern is by far the most probable but are there any longer-term prophecies we might make? Or are there details of this general picture which we might refine?

The answers to such questions will depend upon how far we think electronic communications can become an effective substitute for face-to-face meetings in the future metropolis. There is a considerable divergence of views on this issue. At one end of the scale are those who believe that a total substitution is possible, and that in the future we shall all live entirely physically separate lives, although bound together by electronic links of all kinds. Such views are common in science fiction—E. M. Forster's *The Machine Stops*[7] is an early example of the genre. On the other hand there are those who think that very little advance can be made upon our present systems of communication, and that the investment in existing cities is so great that they cannot be changed much, even over a very long period. Most observers fall somewhere between these two positions. Developments in communications technology are selective in their effects. Although some more routine types of transaction, for instance the instructions necessary to pass orders from an executive to his staff, or from an office to the factory floor may be carried out by remote control, others, especially those requiring a sensitive awareness of a multitude of surrounding circumstances, will still require direct contact between individuals.

This seems a probable pattern for the office function in the city for some time to come. But it may well be that the *number* of the *élite* decision-makers decreases as improvements in communications enables each individual to deal with a greater number of problems in the course of a day. Therefore, the actual concentration in the centre of the city may grow smaller, there may no longer be a need for large office buildings, and businesses may be run from social-gathering places such as restaurants or private houses or apartments in the city centre—a return to the coffee houses of the Baroque city.

In addition to these changes within existing patterns, changes in communications may call into being entirely new facilities and requirements. In another part of the work of our group Cedric Price has called attention to the need for new facilities in each home as it becomes a centre of learning, and has pointed to the possibility of communication exchanges, located at strategic points in large cities, where a mass of information in various media would be immediately available. The location of such new kinds of facility presents problems, but it is certain that they could play a vital rôle in shaping the central city, if this were thought to be an appropriate location.

Conclusion

The question which overhangs all this is: Will our urban areas continue to spread? The short answer is yes they will, but not simply because of changes in the pattern of communications. Many other social, political and economic factors will shape our urban areas, and we must beware of assuming that changes in communications are of over-riding importance in making over the shape of society or the pattern of society, but it is also a mirror of changing social attitudes. The way new developments in communications will be used is as important as the inventions themselves.

Nevertheless, new developments in communications and the changing volume of transactions over the next three decades will present a number of policy issues. Should the creation of a National Data Network be a public or private responsibility? How far can we use the almost infinite development capacity of the communications industry as an economic regulator? What is to be the relationship between the private sector of the communications industry and the G.P.O. in its new commercially-orientated rôle? What kind of safeguards should be built into the development of credit-card systems? How can we plan for the growing demand for more and more communication facilities in each home? How and where should we locate major communication exchanges? Finally, how should we deal with increasing public demand for active participation in all kinds of planning processes?

These policy issues raise a number of topics for research, but one stands out above all others. What is the substitutability of communication technology in face-to-face communications? A number of writers have commented upon this problem but none has so far come up with a satisfactory proposal. Clearly some transactions can be carried out in face-to-face contact but the fist fight and the embrace are likely to elude the videophone for at least another three decades!

There are a number of other research topics. How has the pattern of investment in communications changed in relation to other aspects of urban development and how should we expect the ratio to change in the future? Can we predict the diffusion rate of innovations from past models? How many contacts does an individual make during the day, and how is this affected by age, sex, socio-economic class and so on? Is it possible to conduct controlled experiments concerning the effect of social and/or technological innovations, such as meetings by videophone, limited cheque card systems and so on? These are just a few of the topics which need investigation before we can define the impact of communications upon the future of urbanisation.

REFERENCES

[1] J. J. Servan-Schreiber, *Le Defi American*, Denoel, Paris 1967.
[2] M. M. Webber, 'The Urban Place and the Non-Place Urban Realm' in Webber *et al.*, *Explorations in Urban Structure*, University of Pennsylvania Press, 1964.
[3] E. Jones, 'Resources and Environmental Constraints, *Urban Studies*, Vol. 6, No. 3, pp. 335-346.
[4] P. Hall, 'Transportation', *Urban Studies*, Vol. 6, No. 3, pp. 408, 435.
[5] Department of Economic Affairs, 'Office Decentralisation', mimeo. London 1965.
[6] R. Lichtenberg, *One Tenth of a Nation*, Harvard U.P., Cambridge Mass., 1960.
[7] E. M. Forster, *The Machine Stops*.

FORECASTING AND TECHNOLOGY

DAVID BAYLISS

*My interest is in the future, because I'm
going to spend the rest of my life there*
CHARLES F. KETTERING

Introduction

It is doubtful if mankind will ever be able to establish with any confidence
to what extent the development of civilisation, the onset of urbanisation and
its subsequent progressive absorption of the human race, was brought
about by technological advancement or vice versa. What is apparent is that
the two phenomena are inextricably linked and in so far as it is possible to
anticipate changes in the future of some areas of technology it is possible
to foresee changes in the character of towns and cities.

There is little doubt that man's basically gregarious nature is the motive
force behind the formation of communities of all kinds. Before the dawning
of civilisation, as we know it, the existence of tribes and tribal settlements
showed man's propensity to share his problems and resources with his
neighbour. Why then were the first urban communities formed a mere
5,000 or so years ago? This question is explored at length by Mumford[1]
and the principal reason emerges as the establishment of rural hinterlands
able to serve the needs of relatively large communities. The production
capacities of these hinterlands were limited by their size, as defined by the
need for daily access by workers from the city, and the rate of food yield. As
agronomy developed, food yield increased to a point, in certain good river
valley locations, where cities of several thousand people could be supported.
Subsequent advances in agriculture, storage and transportation, along with
the disappearance of the need to retreat to the walled city for safety each
night, have allowed a continuing expansion in the scale of urbanisation to a
point where quite different constraints control growth. Since these early
days a number of notable surges in its scale, interspaced with periods of
more gradual change, the agricultural revolution, the industrial revolution,
the late industrial transportation revolution, have characterised its progress. As time has gone on the variety and pace of the changes in technology,
promoting (or permitting) the changes in cities has increased until today
they can scarcely be properly regarded as ambient trends but must be considered, perhaps quizzically at first, as subject for serious speculation in
considering how our present urban systems might mutate.

---

*David Bayliss, formerly with the Centre of Environmental Studies, is now a senior
planner with the Greater London Council.*

Forecasting Dilemmas

Forecasting is not a new activity for man, indeed if it is regarded as deriving guidance from past and present circumstances for future actions, it might be taken to be more than a small part of that which distinguishes man from his fellow primates. It does, however, pose certain dilemmas, which twentieth-century man may be more aware of than his biblical forebears, but is little nearer resolving.

Probably the most difficult of these dilemmas is that of casual anticipation and negation ('self fulfilling and cancelling prophecies'). For example if an outcome of an election is advertised widely to the electorate it is indeed more probable that the specified outcome will be achieved, as any good campaign manager knows. On the other hand the prediction to a community that something it treasures may be lost will, quite probably, secure its preservation. In the field of town planning the situation is slightly different and forecasts likely to be even more directive of the future. Where a forecast is made about the future state of a settlement or region a complex array of investment and legislative devices becomes geared towards the fulfilment of that forecast. In such a situation how is it possible to establish whether the forecast was a good one or whether it was realised simply because all alternatives were precluded once it was made?

A sensible awareness of this problem is probably the most effective way of reducing its importance. This awareness is contained in the formal division of forecasts into two major groups; *normative* and *exploratory*. Exploratory (trend following) methods involve detached observation of the development of phenomena in a temporal context or some other context which will eventually be related to time. The validity of exploratory forecasting rests on the assumption that the observed phenomena are occurring 'naturally'; i.e. in an environment which will exert constant effects during the forecasting period. This is sometimes modified by introducing constraints on future developments but beyond these constraints the system is held to be open. Exploratory techniques are therefore only valid where the operating context of the subject system is largely invariant. Normative (goal selecting) techniques are specifically geared toward the achievement of certain ends deemed to be desirable; the possibility of alternative futures appropriate to different measures of desirability are not necessarily explored. Each of these styles has a body of forecasting technology associated with it, and in assessing the worth of these one must decide at the outset whether the exercise in hand is designed to glimpse into the future or to try and shape one of its aspects.

Another major dilemma in forecasting is that of needs versus opportunity. Many aspects of the future are inherently predictable as no change is expected, or because the rhythm of change is so smooth and credible that it can be projected with facility and confidence. Take the position of the planets and their moons in the solar system as an example. The patterns of movement are sufficiently well understood for us to be able to predict the location of planets as far into the future as we could wish as to be able to launch a satellite from the earth to take pictures of particular sections of the moon's surface using programmes devised months in advance with negligible 'in flight' intervention. The opportunity to predict the positions of heavenly bodies in the future is enormous; the need as yet, is quite slight. Scientific and technological advance stand diametrically opposed to this, the novelty and spontaneity of scientific and technological invention suggests that it is inherently unpredictable, the methodological style used to deal with this difficulty is described by Jantsch.[2] If the opportunity is slight the need is correspondingly great. Of late our expectations of what will exert momentous effects on the future have changed and a new attitude is developing toward the selection of subjects on which to speculate as well as changes in style of speculation. Galbraith[3] has warned us of the dangers of massive government and business organisations (the technostructure) moulding the future to suit their own ends. This has been put more passionately by Jungck[4]:

> The fact that technological forecasting is not hardware, neither a machine, nor a weapon, has made it appear as something interesting but rather innocuous. It is high time that we began to use it as a potent intellectual instrument with possibly and probably decisive impact on events to come. For if we spoil the future as we have spoiled our (present) environment through avidity, narrow-mindedness and neglect of possible consequences we are in for an era of despotism and desperation, of tyranny and revolt.

In urban planning in this country the dangers are potentially great with its tradition of very strong government participation and control, and widespread acceptance of interference with the processes of individual choice. These difficulties have been stated succinctly by Mackenzie[5] in stating the circumstances under which a political system is suitable for expression of choice:

a) Where the number of issues to be settled at any one time is limited.
b) When major issues arise at relatively infrequent intervals.
c) If the issues are presented simply and the choices clear cut.
d) Where the decisions are subsequently reversible without unreasonable cost.

None of these circumstances prevail in urban planning; to what extent then should the planner predetermine the future through the political machine? Should not forecasting, in a situation like this be opportunistic rather than prescriptive?

The Emergence of Technological Forecasting

The degree of participation of the forecaster in trying to fulfil his predictions affects the breadth of view that he takes of the subject. Thus the pure technologist typically confines himself to a specific technology whilst someone concerned with a more general future will take account of wider social issues. This is shown clearly in Peter Hall's paper on transportation where consumer choice is taken to be a major factor directing the development of urban transportation hardware. Thus it is difficult to differentiate between social and technological issues and these are sometimes brought together under the heading of social-technology.[6]

Whatever the appropriate term is, the ability of man to regulate his environment and its resources for his own purpose, and the consequences of extensions of this ability for the species internal social economic and political equilibrium, is a subject with a substantial and respectable history. Although earlier examples can be found this sort of speculation, as a serious and continuing activity, can be seen to have grown out of the one with which some intellectuals regarded the dramatic expansion of our technological capability wrought by the industrial revolution. This was heightened by the gradual transition from the basic technologies of the early nineteenth century to the more refined 'consumer technologies' of the late nineteenth century. The individual and dramatic possibilities of these new-found capabilities were sampled with remarkable accuracy by such well known writers as H. G. Wells,[7] who described an 'atomic bomb' thirty-two years before its detailed technology was invented, and Jules Verne,[8] who described a trip by missile to the moon some ninety, or so, years before it took place. Other writers were more concerned with the effects of these developments on the codes and organisational structure of society. Aldous Huxley[9] and Sigmund Freud[10] introduced a series of perceptive and alarming warnings of the directions in which society might be impelled if science and technology were not properly managed. This theme was developed by George Orwell,[11] and such fables are now quite common.

As the world's economy adjusted after the second world war the effects of the previous fifty or so years of scientific discovery started to make themselves felt in the industrial and commercial spheres; development programmes became larger and more complex, discovery and innovation became increasingly commonplace and potentially very profitable.

On the other hand failure to keep up with the field in the major technologies could be financially disastrous. This situation prompted a few big business organisations to undertake long range planning and technological forecasting. The success of these initiators was such that such activities are now becoming, within a period of ten years or so after their first introduction, standard practice in many business and government organisations. What has happened in the business world has taken place to an even greater extent in defence technology and a lesser extent in social and political science. In a survey carried out three years ago by Jantsch[9] it was found that at least 600 firms in the United States spent $25m-$30m annually on technological forecasting. There are no similar figures available for defence and socio-political forecasting, but it is likely that jointly these are at least of a similar order. Today, more than ever before in history, technological achievements are forming the milestones of progress and setting out the path into the future. Today, more than ever, the nature of these milestones and the direction of this path must be at least anticipated and to some degree predetermined.

Some Baselines for the Future

This collection of essays amounts to a lightly disciplined exercise in intuitive thinking, hopefully the next phase will introduce greater rigour and sharper purpose. The prototype of such a formalisation has been created by Kahn and Wiener[13] and demands a set of baselines to structure the arguments and evidence advanced. Deutsch[14] selects five such baselines as appropriate to speculation on a national future:

a) Technological change.
b) Psychological and sociological changes.
c) Political problems.
d) Economic and demographic factors.
e) The international aid question.

With the possible exception of (e) these baselines afford a useful set of themes for investigating the future of urbanisation. These are explored in some detail in the accompanying papers but it is useful to set out possible changes in these aspects of our life very crudely as a basis for looking at the impact of technological change on our cities.

Economy, Demography

The population of the United Kingdom is likely to rise to about 70 million by the end of the century.[12] The work force will rise much more slowly with a greater proportion of our lives spent being educated and in 'retirement'. A slightly larger proportion of the population will be urban in the sense that they have adopted urban life styles but it is possible that a lower proportion of the population will be living in urban areas as defined by our present criteria. (See Figure 1.)

By the year 2000 the G.N.P. of the United Kingdom is expected to rise from its present figure of £35,000m to at least £70,000m and possibly

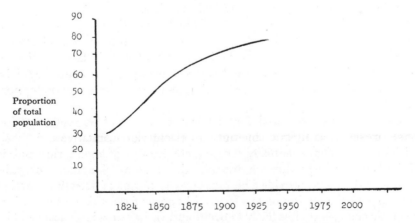

FIG. 1. Urban population of England and Wales

£100,000m. Assuming a constant standard of living, population increase would require a G.N.P. of about £50,000m; add to this a further £15,000m for the relief of poverty and squalor and there remains possibly £25,000m to £35,000m which appears discretionary. This is probably an over-estimate as the machinery of the national economy is not that adaptable.[15] But if £15,000m of this could be set aside for selected purposes, this is equivalent to £200 per head of population (at present-day values) and would allow us to completely reconstruct a major conurbation such as Manchester or the West Midlands each year, around the turn of the century if we wished, or alternatively to construct a new motorway network for every urban area each year. Important choices which must be made in relation to this extra wealth are how it will be distributed between public and private purses and between different groups of the population. The answer to these questions is of major importance to the future form of urban areas as 'he who pays the piper calls the tune'—to a degree which I suspect would make many planners surprised.

Political Problems

To look at our political future as being essentially problematic is probably excessively pessimistic although there are many who would argue that the political establishment is heavily committed to the status quo and as such changes are made as a result of breakdown or potential breakdown in the present situation rather than by opportunities in future situations. Apart from changes in the mood, character and aspirations of the community, political changes will involve alterations in the basis, form and scale of representation and the issues involved. How the issues of political debate will change is hard to visualise, but in general it seems reasonable that rising wealth, if distributed effectively, will lessen the need for public welfare programmes of certain kinds. Housing, non-basic education and other services, which are not intrinsically public could be provided increasingly in the market place. On the other hand the activities of big business combines, foreign aid, defence, and technological progress could become increasingly the concern of the political machine.

The basis of representation has altered little since the enfranchisement of women and is extremely simple at the moment. This base could change to one of need, power or merit and will probably change in the direction of the latter. If anything this would suggest that political control will be more acceptable and liberal and planning less restrictive and more opportunistic.

The arguments presented for richer forms of public representation beyond those presently available through electoral, consultative and quasi-judicial means must eventually take effect. Modes of monitoring public opinion continuously through time, and across a wide range of sub-electoral scales could provide a highly sensitive means of detecting reaction to changes in the environment. It would appear from this that grandiose autocratic changes are less likely to occur and variety on a large scale will be replaced by variety at a lesser scale.

On the other hand strategic issues are more likely to be handled more comprehensively at a strategic scale; the expanding scale of the environment is already predicting a movement from the folk scale of government[16] and there is little to suggest that this trend will not continue. Indeed past experience of the pace of government reform does not lead to optimism in considering how it may keep pace with developing needs. This shift in scale will strengthen government effectiveness at the strategic scale; thus the role of government in the development of the environment should be increasingly development of overall spatial and economic frameworks within which a greater degree of local choice will be permitted.

Psychological and Sociological changes

From the conventional town planning view point probably the most important factor of social change will be that of the continuing change in the activity structure of the working population. A crude attempt to show how this might develop is made in Figure 2. Despite the arrival of increasingly sophisticated machinery (computers, control systems etc.) human activities will involve less and less physical effort and more and more mental effort. It seems to be in the nature of the technological beast that it is best suited to producing brawn* rather than brain. This is illustrated very nicely by the way in which technology has been employed to carry out laborious physical tasks; except where a process is so straightforward that it is entirely mechanical no substitute for human skill has yet been devised. The best general purpose navvy that modern technology affords is a powerful hydraulic skeletal structure which a human operator straps on to become a superman; the only control the mechanical structure has over itself is a device to stop it 'rupturing' its 'muscles'. The massive reduction in need

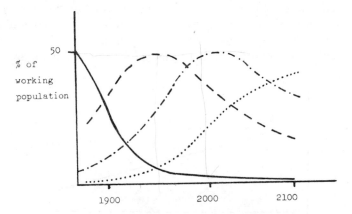

FIG. 2. Trends in activity structure (diagramatic)

(1) Extractive   (3) Distributive
(2) Manufacturing   (4) Informative

* Intellectual and physical.

for human physical effort may not be matched by a similar rise in the satis-fiable need for mental effort. As such, if the population is not to become much less active (which is a serious possibility) new means of consuming mental and physical effort will have to be devised. Leisure activities will surely expand and we may even see the arrival of 'pseudo-work'. (It has probably already arrived, e.g. Kuwait, where about half the indigenous working population are civil servants.) This trend toward a shorter working life is already clearly observable (see Figure 3).

An important factor in dealing with this situation will be the pattern of incidence of non-work activities; thus a halving of our lifetime work period could occur as a four-hour day, a four-day weekend, a six-month annual holiday, a twenty-five year normal working life (education till thirty or long mid-career breaks or retirement in one's early forties or even dual careers for the talented) or some combination of these. The exact mix is highly relevant to urbanisation patterns, as at the one extreme facilities for local leisure would be needed whilst at the other, leisure cities, regions or con-tinents might be more appropriate.

Changes in the work activity of social groups is not necessarily, at least in the short term, matched by changes in non-work activity. This may just be a lag effect or perhaps intrinsic variety within the community which, in the face of long term occupational convergence, may manifest itself in *increas-ingly* diverse non-work activities. A possible intervention in what ever natural processes are taking place is offered by bio-engineering. The ad-justment of community balance has been going on for sometime through medicine, public health improvement and effective legal systems. Today the weak, the insane and other disadvantaged groups are protected from the natural forces of destruction and allowed to play a part in a controlled community life. This could lead to a general mellowing in human attitudes.

A third major factor which could have considerable effects on the charac-ter of society in the future is that of change in the human sensory system; new taboos, new ideas are likely to emerge and reshape behaviour, possibly dramatically. Kahn[17] suggests that society is likely to become less pre-occupied with supernatural and etherial values and become more material-

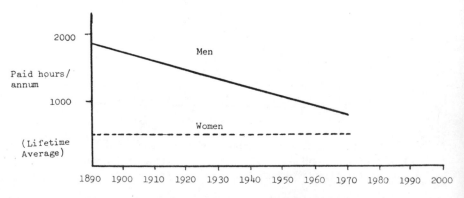

FIG. 3. Trends in working time—Source: Jantsch

istic and humanistic. This tendency would be reinforced by man's realisation that, apparently at least, he is increasingly becoming master of his own fate. As the physical environment and its development is a powerful symptom of materialism it is likely that it will be regarded as a more important component of 'total life' in the future. Thus one would expect both individual and comparative interests to pursue its improvement more actively.

Developments in Technology

Of the four baselines appropriate to urbanisation that of technological change is of central interest to this paper. Some of the crucial aspects of this are dealt with specifically in other papers in the series; where these are referred to in this paper my concern will be with presenting possible alternative views rather than reinforcing those already stated. For convenience possible developments will be discussed under a series of specific headings; these are merely starting points and in no way exclusive or comprehensive.

Transportation

The ubiquity of urban transportation networks, their structural robustness through time and the massive investment they represent means dramatic changes are unlikely in overall *system* configuration, except in completely newly constructed environments. By and large changes will be incremental and will probably include:

a) Widespread availability of car-type vehicles from the present level of 16m to 40m or more by A.D. 2000.
b) Almost complete elimination of the various forms of environmental intrusion by all forms of urban transport.
c) The emergence of ground effect vehicles for special purpose transportation (e.g. heavy loads).
d) A limited spread of the urban traffic problem into the airspace above cities.
e) New motive systems for cars and buses.
f) An increased use of tunnels for transport routes in busy urban areas[18] (see Figure 4).
g) The arrival of extensive central direction systems over individual vehicles possibly allowing compulsory control of errant vehicles.
h) Automated control of rapid transit.
i) Limited introduction of new modes of transport (see Figure 5).

The analysis carried out by Bouladon[19] and illustrated in Figure 5 shows a sector of the urban transportation spectrum where available technologies are obsolescent and as yet no new system appears suitable. As innovation proceeds and wealth rises it is quite conceivable that a new mode or new modes will emerge to fill it. The exact form is not easy to predict but some types of continuous integrator or personalised system of public transport seem most promising.

Materials and Structures

Perhaps less than any other man-made product the bulk of the built environment will be affected by changes in material technology. Typically the materials used in bulk construction are won from the ground, processed simply and cheaply nearby, transported directly to the theatre of operations where they may undergo secondary processing and then put in

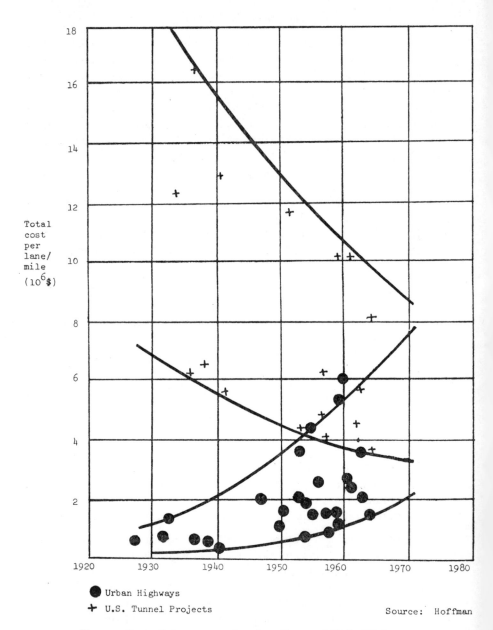

FIG. 4. Cost of aboveground and undergound U.S. Highways.

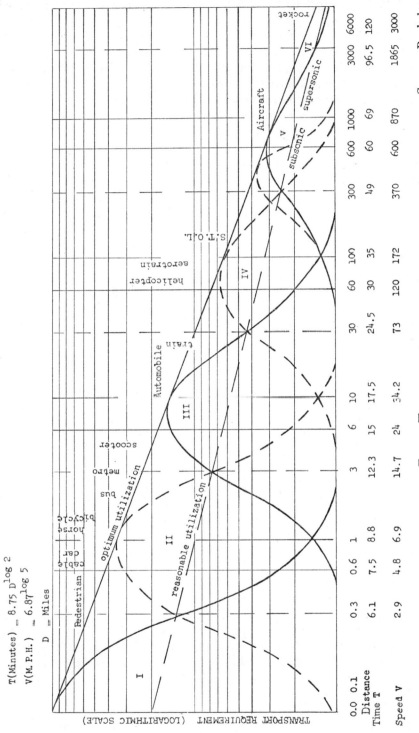

$$T(\text{Minutes}) = 8.75 \ D^{\log 2}$$
$$V(\text{M.P.H.}) = 6.87^{\log 5}$$
$$D = \text{Miles}$$

FIG. 5. Transport systems concepts.

Source: Bouladon

Distance	0.0	0.1	0.3	0.6	1	3	6	10	30	60	100	300	600	1000	3000	6000
Time T			7.5	8.8		12.3	15	17.5	24.5	30	35	49	60	69	96.5	120
			6.1													
Speed V			4.8	6.9		14.7	24	34.2	73	120	172	370	600	870	1865	3000
			2.9													

TRANSPORT REQUIREMENT (LOGARITHMIC SCALE)

position. There appears to be opportunity for little other than marginal improvements in the physical properties of these types of materials.

Where changes are likely to occur is in the possibilities of producing multiple material units, affording purpose-built combinations at low cost. Thus structurally strong, light, weatherproof well insulated, low cost composite building materials could allow building space standards to rise without cost increases even in the face of rising labour costs.

Probably more important than developments in the form of building materials 'per se' will be the continued refinement of industrial processes for the formation and production of building elements. The present shortcomings of building systems should be solved in the next decade so allowing widespread use in residential, commercial and industrial buildings. In addition to the bulk materials of construction there are those required for special uses; furnishing equipment and structural purposes. It is here that there will be extensive innovation of new materials and diffusion of recently introduced users. Metals, plastics and hybrid materials will be produced with mixtures of properties not presently available. This will allow new economical structural forms, reduced maintenance, brighter and more durable finishes and a general increase in comfort levels of the internal environment. The plastics industry is planning to increase the use of plastics in housing from its present level of 1-2 cwt. per house to 1-2 tons per house by the year 2000[20].

We are already at a stage when our abilities to build structures of many kinds exceeds our desire (measured in one way or another) to have them built. Major changes will occur in the relative economy of different structure types along with a continuing expansion in the art of structural engineering. Very high buildings will be increasingly feasible; whether or not they are likely to be generally desirable is another matter. The enclosure of large areas will be quite easy by the end of the century allowing many more activities to be insulated from climate influences. Reductions in tunnelling costs will allow transportation and other activities to take place to a greater extent beneath the earth's surface. This will be specially useful in relieving congestion in areas of concentrated activity. Earth-moving will become easier with the construction of large and more efficient earth-moving plant; the topography of towns and cities will be much more a matter of choice, and it is conceivable that the day is not too distant where at least a hill, if not the mountain, can be brought to 'Allah'. The relaxation of material constraints on building design will allow new forms of construction which in their turn permit structural complexes highly adaptive to changes in use both through cyclical and historic time. To what extent these possibilities will be realised will almost certainly depend very largely on how progressive and flexible the organisational frameworks within which the urban environment is developed and managed.

Public Utilities and Services

There are marked and credible trends in the ease of providing the principal public utilities. General technological advance and particular advances in nuclear power generation will reduce the real cost of electricity.[21] (See Figure 6.) Subterranean natural gas sources will allow continuing reductions in gas costs. These two trends in cheap power will make large environmental control an economic possibility; whole city centres, recreational areas etc. could be covered, air conditioned, heated and cooled, moisture controlled and efficiently illuminated. Possibilities such as this suggest ways of providing the intensive leisure capacity—likely to be needed if outside leisure space is not to be overloaded.

New utilities are likely to become feasible in new high density areas (piped heat, communication channels etc.) and for industrial purposes (encapsulation multi-commodity pipeway systems) allow bulk carriage by wheeled transportation to be reduced in congested transportation corridors. The widespread use of these (with the notable exception of communications channels) will probably be deterred by the widespread availability of cheap power.

Water costs are not likely to fall significantly between now and the end of the century. In the South-East for example the £100m additional supply programme will barely keep up with the increase in demand between now and 1980. Beyond 1980 technological developments, probably in the form of reprocessing and desalination, will be required to meet the extra demand which is expected to amount to 1,100 million gallons per day.[12] Neither of these methods is likely to be very cheap and as such the possibility of extensive hydro-engineering as a device for changing the urban environment is remote.

Whereas much of the land take for water supply is outside the urban area and service reservoirs, pumping stations and the like can readily be put underground where they have to be constructed inside the urban areas, allowing the space above to be used for low-density activities. Sewage disposal is rather different. Clearly water supply and effluent processing are

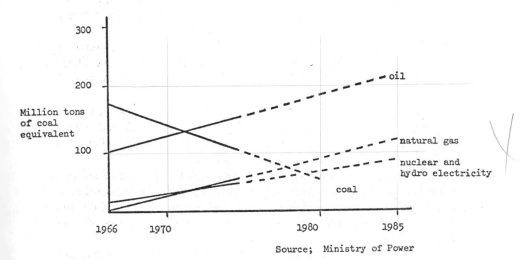

Source; Ministry of Power

FIG. 6. Trends in Fuel Consumption

highly correlated and significant increases in the capacity of sewage treatment plant will be needed during the next thirty years. Competition for urban land, sewerage costs and technological progress will probably mean that in future processing plants will be larger capacity units with large sections situated underground. The re-use of processing wastes for industrial and agricultural purpose is likely to compensate for the higher capital costs of these plants. The disposal of dry municipal refuse is likely to present problems of increasing magnitude and will again result in the widespread use of industrial as opposed to natural disposal methods. The potential re-use of dry waste for fuel and, mixed with other processed effluents, for agricultural purpose should allow costs to be kept down for this form of disposal.

It would seem therefore that although the 'sharing' function of the city, which demanded its initial compact form, is increasing in many ways, its compactness is decreasing. The principal reason must be the relaxation of the physical proximity constraint with the rise in our abilities to share at a distance. This 'speed-up' of communication and transportation would seem to indicate a continuing reduction of urban densities. An important issue here is at what point do the benefits of lower densities start to be overtaken by the restriction of variety and choice through increased homogeneity? The likely spread of airline and landline communications is discussed at some length in Peter Cowan's paper; this aspect or urbanisation is crucial as it introduces a new dimension of freedom in the organisation of the city, allowing compactness or sprawl heterogeneity or homogeneity according to which ever suits the purposes of the city of the twenty-first century.

Beyond the urban horizon

Outside the urban area some technological developments will impinge on the functions and pressures within it. To try and list these comprehensively would be an almost impossible task; a few are set out for illustrative purposes.

Local satellites present an opportunity for new types of regional information and communication services. These could include surveillance of various kinds (including aerial photography), broadcasting, weather forecasting at a local scale etc.

Accurate medium-term weather forecasting and perhaps even limited weather control could present considerable problems for urban dwellers. It will be possible to plan one's leisure effectively if the problems of congestion associated with this predictability can be solved.

Continuing improvements in agronomy and the advent of submarine farming and cheap synthetic food production reduce the rural/urban conflict for lowland allowing urban sprawl[22] and increased use of the countryside for non agricultural purposes. (See Figure 7 as illustrative of trend to lower densities.)

High speed, relatively cheap inter-urban/intra-megalopolitan transportation weakens the 'regionalism' movement and allows an increasing number

of important functions and events to be staged at one of the several principal foci.

A crisis of intrusion of the public environment (centred around atmos-
pheric pollution and noise of various kinds) brings about a considerable
increase in resources and technological effort into solving these problems
so initiating a period of environmental reclamation toward the end of the
century.

The use of the off-shore sites for accommodating some less-acceptable
activities (power stations, intrusive industry etc.) will further relieve the
demand for urban land and generally improve the urban environment.
(The ideas of constructing floating cities in the sea at our latitudes is barely
credible; other noxious activities are much more likely contenders.)

The availability of automatic birth control requiring a specific decision
for conception and the ability to choose the sex of unborn children will
make the demographic structure highly sensitive to fashion and cultural
cycles.

From these few possible changes in the potential and application of
technology it can be seen that quite general developments, not directly
related to the way in which our towns and cities are built and operated can
have considerable consequences for urbanisation. Presented another way,
it is difficult to pick out any major advancement in science or technology
that does not have either consequences for, or produces 'spin-offs' relevant
in some way to, the urban environment.

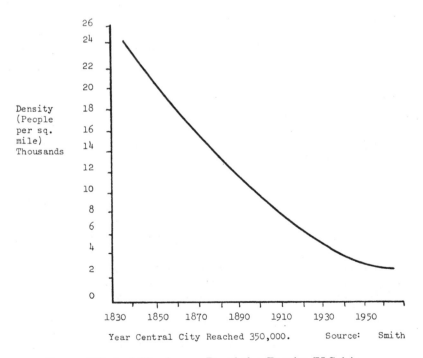

FIG. 7. Effect of City Age on Population Density (U.S.A.)

Issues

The principal issue of the future of technology in general is that of the extent to which it is accidental, spontaneous, unplanned and to what degree conscious effects are made to control and direct it. If man has any interest in the future and how it may turn out he must attempt to anticipate its progress where he can take account of this in his present actions. Glib remarks such as this do not help very much in planning technology much of which is neutral and can be put to good or evil purposes. No, there is little case for deterring the development of any area of technology as such, provided society has the strength of mind to use it for its own good. Where planning is required is in the identification of the most needed lines of advance in technology and the conscious pursuit of these.

Given an acceptance of the need to intervene in the future how are the appropriate actions to be identified? Technology is merely instrumental, a means to another set of ends; before technological change can be planned therefore the ends must be identified and the relationship between these and alternative states of technology established. If these ends are human and social in character, as they almost certainly are, we are brought back to the subject of social technology. The derivation of goals is relevant across the planning board and is discussed at greater length in Alan Wilson's paper. What does emerge from this discussion is the need to expand our understanding of the relationships of technological and social change.

The specific relationships between science and technology and the large scale built environment have received scarcely any attention from planners at large, presumably because the slow pace of change in our towns and cities has made such speculation seem to be largely fantasy. This is changing, still rather slowly, but the built environment has a long life and we are now at a stage where innovation and discovery are commonplace and nothing is insulated from technological escalation.

Beyond developments in urban technology, work in other fields of activity is having noticeable consequences for our ways of life. Could we have anticipated the effect of quick freezing on shopping habits? Probably any intelligent person could if he had thought about such a possibility.

However, changes, perhaps even more significant, are taking place today and technological speculation and forecasting is still regarded as being barely reputable in urban planning. We have already paid dearly for this lesson; we should now be taking advantage of it.

REFERENCES

[1] L. Mumford, *The City in History*. Secker and Warburg, 1961.
[2] E. Jantsch, *Technological Forecasting in Perspective*. O.E.C.D., 1967.
[3] J. K. Galbraith, *The New Industrial State*. Boston, 1967.
[4] R. Junck, 'Technological Forecasting as a Total of Social Strategy', *Proceedings of the European Conference on Technological Forecasting 1968* (to be published).
[5] W. Mackenzie, in report on the Conference 'The Future of the City Region' by M. Chisholm, Centre for Environmental Studies IP 5, 1969.
[6] O. Helmer, *Social Technology*. Basic Books, 1966.

[7] H. G. Wells, *The Shape of Things to Come*. Hutchinson and Co., 1933.

[8] J. Verne, *Journey Round the Moon*. Sampson Low and Co., 1876.

[9] A. Huxley, *Brave New World*. Chatto and Windus, 1932.

[10] S. C. Freud, *Civilisation and its Discontents*. Vienna, 1930.

[11] G. Orwell, *Nineteen Eighty Four*. Secker and Warburg, 1949.

[12] H. Kahn, and A. J. Wiener, *The Year 2000. A framework for speculation on the next thirty years*. Macmillan, 1967.

[13] K. Deutsch, 'Toward the Year 2000–work in progress', *Dacdulus*, Summer 1967.

[14] Registrar General, recent unpublished forecast.

[15] For an interesting discussion of the adaptability of capitalist economies, see Report from Iron Mountain, Avon. Macmillan, 1968.

[16] See evidence submitted to the Maude Commission.

[17] H. Kahn, and A. J. Wiener, op. cit. *The Year 2000. A framework for speculation on the next thirty years*.

[18] G. A. Hoffman, *Urban Underground Highways and Parking Facilities*. Rand, Santa Monica, California, 1963.

[19] G. Bouladon, 'The Transport Gaps', *Science Journal*, April 1967.

[20] W. F. Watson, 'Technological Forecasting for Materials–Polymers', Seminar Manual, National Conference on Technological Forecasting, University of Bradford, 1968.

[21] Ministry of Power, *Fuel Policy*, Cmnd. 3438. H.M.S.O., 1967.

[22] W. Smith, *Transportation and Parking for Tomorrows Cities*. Automobile Manufacturers Association, Detroit, 1967.

LEARNING

CEDRIC PRICE

Present Situation—Potential for Learning Service

Present educational patterning in U.K. is related largely to two major age groups—those between the ages of 5 and 15 and those between 16 and 25. A major difference is that the former group are educated compulsorily, the latter through choice.

Thus while members of the first group can be equated to both population projections and current legislation the second group is not directly influenced by either and indeed may be far more influenced by conditions and pressures entirely unrelated to the present educational structure.

At present the first group are entirely 'full-time' participants in the present definition of the term, while the latter are part-time to full-time in the proportion 5 to 2.

In 1964 a total of nearly $7\frac{3}{4}$ million children aged 15 or less were receiving compulsory education while a further $3\frac{1}{2}$ million people over that age were involved in full or part-time education.[1] Thus, approximately one person in five was subject to a system of education based largely on pre-conceived standards of attainment to such a degree that the Robbins report can refer to 'the annual contribution made by different sectors of higher education to the Country's stock of *qualified manpower*' discounting 'all those who begin courses but do not successfully complete them'.

In both cases, whether at advanced education level or at school, the nature of the present education patterning is such that it allows the educators an opportunity for assessment at a particular time or stage of work of those being educated. The abolition of, say, streaming in comprehensive schools does not in itself change this, nor does the increasing flexibility in both curricula and teaching methods. The various likely alterations in family patterning in the near future, whether they reach the proportions suggested by Edmund Leach[2] or merely echo the movement to middle class affluence investigated by Peter Willmott,[3] will not necessarily cause major changes in the present stratified nature of formal education since these already echo a middle-class pattern of advancement through dilligence.

The primary and secondary school time-tables with elevenses and afternoon 'tea' breaks echo those of the middle-class household, while curricula are still largely aimed at producing educated adults not intelligent children in fixed periods of time. There is increasing pressure for all children and

---

Cedric Price is an architect

students, good or bad, to pass through school and college at the same speed.
The pipeline cannot afford to be blocked.

Thus, varying degrees of 'qualified manpower' are continually produced
for forty years productive activity. At present, when the end products fall
short of their pre-supposed performance, society provides an increasing
range of tuning-up facilities such as evening classes, mid-career courses and
Government retraining schemes. Still a stratified form—particularly in the
time scale—is maintained and phrases such as 'knowledge of a lifetime' are
not recognised as ridiculous. What is likely to cause the real change is the
increasing variety and rate of learning available to all in forms,[4] and at times
and places, unrelated to the present educational structure. Thus advances
in technologies not necessarily linked with education are likely to have an
increasing effect on its usefulness and in general to encourage the particular-
isation of rigid educational patterning not so much in content as in form
and mode of exchange. Schools will become more places where you meet
teachers than where you learn on your own. Already in universities and
colleges of advanced education student discontent is increasingly related to
lack of involvement in the academic administration of the institution
rather than the content of any particular course. In effect the desire is for
participatory learning. It is doubtful whether universities as today constituted can alone ever provide ideal conditions for this multi-disciplined
self-pace learning.

With the increase of quaternary activities based on communications,
present methods of education, together with other means of communication, will become major forms of employment in their own right. The
growth of the information storage, transference and retrieval industry ex-
emplifies this. In such a situation the individual will undoubtedly be
involved in a learning process throughout his life in which continued up-
dating of his understanding of society will be accompanied by repeated
opportunities and pressures to change his job.

In considering the effect that increased opportunities for learning may
have on developing patterns of urbanisation it is assumed that the existing
stock of school, university and college buildings will alter in direct relation
to the priorities given to a national education policy. Thus, while it is important to note the likely effect on existing urban areas that such educational
complexes as the Potteries Thinkbelt can cause,* the main concern of this
paper is to discuss the effect on urbanisation of the individual and non-
academic learning 'industry'. While it has been suggested that the existing
stock of education buildings will alter primarily as a result of national
educational policy, their individual value, relevance and short-comings are
already being tested in day-to-day use. In the case of schools, particularly
secondary schools, there is developing a marked difference in the actual
operative use to which the buildings are put dependent on whether they are
centre-city or suburban schools. The centre-city schools tend to become a
sub-culture grouping in which the problems and pressures of city life tend
to take precedent over concern with new pedagogical techniques. It seems

* Ref. Case Study No. 1 (below).

likely that this difference between schools due to their location is likely to increase.

Increasing suburbanisation and individual mobility will accelerate this difference and the social obsolescence of the city school is likely to occur before its suburban or regional counter part. Thus, efforts to renew and refurnish old school structures must be viewed not merely in relation to the potential of the existing structure but also in relation to the socially valid life of the watershed area. It may, in the very near future, make better sense to maintain the village schoolhouse rather than re-wire the city guild school.

Post-war schools have been designed to accommodate an increasingly wide range of both activities and groupings of pupils as if in an attempt to compensate for the activital poverty of the homes of their occupants. So little attention has been paid by architects and educationalists to increasing affluence and range of choice open to the child (often greater than that of his parents), that the position is rapidly being reached where the school, however well equipped, cannot match for excitement, immediacy, interest and thus learning value, the artifactual environment open to the child for the remainder of the day—his self-pace free-will conscious period.

The high-school in Cumbernauld with it's multi-thousand-pound language laboratory laid out as a Dickensian school room including the master's high desk compares strangely with the likely appetites of a new town child in 1968. (The Manchester school boys who rioted because their school trained them 'too much for the obsolete University System' gave a good example.) The same sort of comparison can be made between the self-conscious neo-medievalism of the new Cambridge colleges and the student working through the *Telegraph* or *International Times* for a suitable job. Town halls, museums, art galleries, civic centres and public parks unfortunately display with increasing obviousness a total lack of awareness of the global village within which all in the U.K. already live. Admittedly the extent of our involvement in the global condition is uneven but the uneveness is becoming more and more a question of choice rather than economics. Particularly in relation to individual interest the methods by which one can learn without any formal framework are too frequent and omnibivalent to be avoided. Radio, television, cinema, the press, the telephone, transport systems, tax and relief structure, banking, insurance and credit modes are avoided by few.

In addition most of these learning tools require no particular physical recognition in order to function. Indeed some can function in conditions previously considered educationally detrimental—the T.V. in the ill-lit classroom. The activities resulting from such learning conditions therefore become increasingly important when planning and designing for learning in the future.

The secondary and not the primary patterning becomes the key function for which to design and since such patterning is continuously varying the major physical static requirement is likely to be for *well serviced anonymous space* related to the secondary patterning rather than the primary patterning.

Sportsfields adjacent to school rooms will soon be seen as much a left-over of social impoverishment as pit-head baths. While existing educational buildings are likely to become less critical to a healthy community, the capacity of the invisible ideas and energy networks will become more critical. The number of channels that E.T.V. controls in an area will matter more than the individual terminal condition. Gadgets, simple in themselves, such as small battery operated television sets, are revolutionising not only the speed of communication but also the attitude that the receiver has to the content. People no longer feel that a classroom, concert hall or street corner is the necessary physical locational pre-requisite for being educated. (The architects and professional educators are of course likely to be the last to realise this.)

This availability of learning for all, young or old, does not mean that there will be an eventual common knowledge or indeed tolerant understanding between age groups. Indeed it is likely that there will be increasing despair on the part of the young with their elders who will, in many respects, be no longer their betters. Equally, parents will be given abundant evidence that they are unlikely to know 'what is good for their children'.

Whether the resultant reduction in family coherence and aims produces Leach or Willmott conditions the demands made on domestic space, location and services are likely to be similar.

Primarily, this will involve more space for varied activities particularly individual activities, combined with the equivalent increase in storage space and improvement in the capacity to isolate activities environmentally. These new demands on existing housing may well result in a change in total numbers of occupants relative to today, a re-use of rooms, additions and alterations and an increasing rate of obsolescence due to unsatisfactory space standard.

It should be noted that a great deal of effort has been spent by official architects since the war in space economy. It is not at all certain that the eldest section of present housing stock will become the first social slums of the near future.

Again Willmott has referred to increased use of the family house and this combined with increased mobility of labour may well lead to a reversal of the present situation regarding the second home. The small house in the centre-city area following employment and frequently changing, may become the second home to the suburban or rural family base.

While opinions differ on the frequency and individual periods of leisure, or more accurately, free-will periods that will be available to the majority of the population it seems probable that such an increase in free-will time will take place and the possibilities for varied use of such time will increase. With such an increase the phasing of any centralised educational servicing, whether electronic or not, will have to take into account the possibility of self-chosen shift work in learning. Thus, for example, educational T.V. may well have to be available 24 hours a day while courses will have to take increasingly more cognisance of 'free time' cycles than 'work' cycles. (Difficulty is already being experienced in U.K. by secondary schools who wish to operate a 7 working day week in using national educational T.V. which has a 5 day programme cycle.)

Before commenting on any likely development of new forms of learning as a constituent part of the individual's free-will activital patterning, it is essential to note and record the increased availability of information in relation to existing and in some cases, extremely rigid pre-packaged forms of entertainment.

Some free-will activities pre-assume a certain level of education of three R's type. Reading any book is an example of this while the visual acuity essential for total enjoyment of a film has in the past been considered a natural faculty not requiring further training.

Detailed knowledge of the rules and risks of particular sports such as football or motor racing can be gained first-hand by the spectator or as is increasingly common in a way one or two steps removed from that actually watched. Motor racing as a spectator sport has flourished largely due to increased family car ownership.

Relative cheap methods of audio and visual recording by the individual has, I suggest, increased the range of interests of the individual and such an increase is impossible to separate from learning even if such learning is limited to the digital dexterity required to operate an Instamatic.

Additional methods of explanation already available in industry, commerce and government can, in their application to leisure activities, provide a learning condition of an intensity and immediacy which would be impossible in a school room. An example would be the provision of instantaneous translation facilities in the theatre.

Many of the means of communications listed by Peter Cowan[5] in themselves provide operational techniques automatically to their users. While the introduction of the National Giro and other similar schemes make the ability to write one's name less important, a basic understanding of the system is a prerequisite to confident participation.

The change to metric is a superb example of a national learning programme that will inevitably involve everyone although the degree of involvement and resultant learning required will vary enormously and reasonably painlessly. ('diversity within unity', P. Willmott).

An increasingly large part of everyone's life will consist of a continuous learning process, only part of which will be subject to the sort of restraints an individual can adopt if he personally opposes change.

Just as in the home the basic instruction equipment (a T.V. screen or telephone) is likely to occupy less space than the resultant secondary gear and activities initiated through the initial education feed, so also it is probable that the capacity any activity has to instruct or educate will have a major effect on the resultant space and location required for such activities.

Thus, the sports arena can become a major centre for instruction ranging from personal hygiene and first aid to crowd psychology; the town hall, the classroom for citizenship and civil law. However, in all such cases the usefulness of an existing institution as a teaching machine will be dependent on the amenability and convenience of its location combined with its capacity to provide a greater degree of immediacy and involvement than that obtained at the end of a 19″ cathode tube.

This, in effect, is the calculation that will have to be made increasingly to determine firstly the viability of an existing built complex and secondly in judging the validity of any new proposed multi-faceted social activity concentration—whether a building or a stretch of beach.

Thus, one effect on urban patterning of an increase in the conscious and unconscious demand for learning facilities, will be a measurable fluctuation in the public usage of different facilities and buildings. The un-used museum and theatre have long been a civic headache. Lord Goodman has suggested that no unsubsidised theatre can exist outside the three or four major cities in this country. The town hall is peeling and the war memorial collecting weeds while the new comprehensive school has to beg the mother's union to use it in the evening.

No town centre is now planned without a commercial component—'to introduce vitality and sparkle' they say. (But already the Oxford Street traders are worried, Knightsbridge stores stand empty, while the mail order is still the fastest retail sales growth.) The whole concept of town centre as a finite entity is already questionable in rather conventional civic design terms while its inadequacies in communication terms have been exposed by P. Cowan. As a conglomerate capable of increasing the citizen's capacity for self-pace learning it is a non-starter since its very concentration—far from allowing one to search and rote information—contributes to the operator's misconception that since all information facilities are together there is no need to increase their availability to the casual user at varied times and places. In fact, too often the attitude that 'if it's good for you it should be difficult to get' would seem to underly many authorities' attitudes to information which they hold. In many cases this is probably due to nothing more than the inflexibility of existing structures to enable random public access and occupancy.

There would appear to be little incentive or reason for widespread reorganisation or conversion of such civic conglomerates particularly since for many other reasons they no longer have any relevance in their location. Local government reform, even prior to the Maud Commission, had rendered many town halls, police stations and libraries redundant. Assuming that major and minor alterations will be made continuously to local government structuring, in fact if not in statutes, it will become less and less valid to establish a fixed network of education/learning outlets since such a network, if too rigid, might well become one of the major restraints on population movement and employment change.

It is extremely worrying that at a time when it is asserted that schools are understaffed and the school building programme is so insufficient, the school, particularly the primary school, should be fast becoming a reason for the immobility of the family. This is not to condemn those who do not wish to move but to question the validity of those institutions, however insufficient, which can restrain people against their will.

While learning is increasingly possible without educational buildings it is likely that the capacity for learning will become a more frequent factor in the selection of job, house, or area in which to settle. This in itself is a pattern-making factor in future urbanisation.

Case Studies

The following projects, through their initiation and/or the extent of co-operation offered during their preparation, are indications of the increasing range of institutions, statutory bodies, local and public authorities, private industry and commerce, and minority groups who are prepared to consider and assist the establishment of learning/information servicing outside the normal educational framework.

In all cases no rigid limit has been set on the maximum numbers of users, it is assumed that as the user becomes increasingly familiar with the facilities then he will spend a proportionately shorter time on one task.

All the schemes could start immediately and are seen to have a maximum life in their present form of 15-20 years. In all cases, the physical proximity of existing forms of advanced education has had little or no effect on the design of the new structure whereas the possible or agreed 'invisible' links with such institutions have a direct effect on the contents.

In the project for a private concern the local authorities and public educational bodies agreed both to co-operate with and to contribute towards the complex.

In the two projects for public and national concerns, private industry and commerce promised co-operation and funding.

In no case are the selected sites at present scheduled for any educational use.

CASE STUDY 1

Potteries Thinkbelt

Ref: Architectural Design, Oct. 66
      New Society 2-6-66
      New Directions in British Architecture—Landau—Studio Vista 1968

- A 100 square mile 20,000 student advanced educational network over the Potteries.
- Emphasis on industrial and technological training.
- Planned as a major new industry to tune up the area.
- Largely mobile short-life flexible structures, shelters and vehicles utilising existing rail and road networks.
- Housing, provided and controlled by the Local Authority, forms an integral part of the educational servicing.
- Utilisation of wide range of industries and skills in its initial construction.

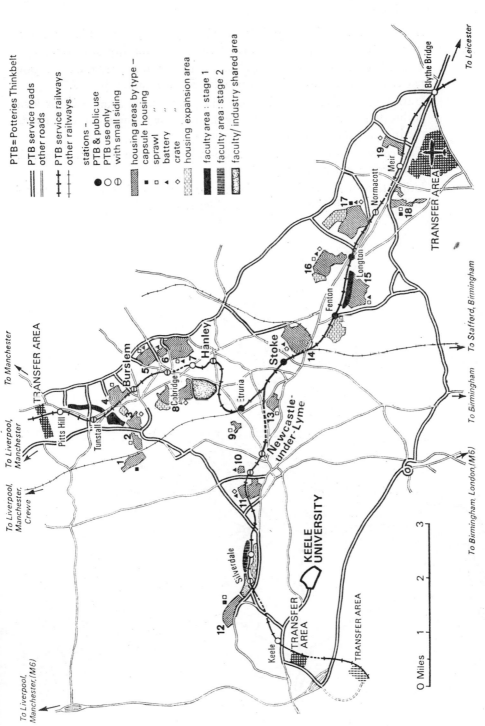

FIG. 1. Plan of the Potteries Thinkbelt,

Peculiarities

- Adaptation of existing public service systems, timetables, vehicles rolling stock and equipment to accommodate learning facilities.
- Utilisation of existing road and rail networks for a programmed flow pattern based on educational servicing at termination points.
- Introduction of entirely new servicing and spatial standards for local authority housing to accommodate increased learning facilities for both the individual and family.
- The construction of large short life industrial-type structures capable of experimental variation.
- Utilisation of industrial waste land for both housing and educational buildings—such land hitherto considered unusable.

FIG. 2. Diagram of primary road net of Potteries Thinkbelt, with desire lines of linkage between housing, faculty and transfer areas.

Case Study 2

Oakland County—Greater Detroit
New Forms of Learning

Ref: OCC Annual Report 1966-67
OCC An investigation into New Forms of Learning—Price

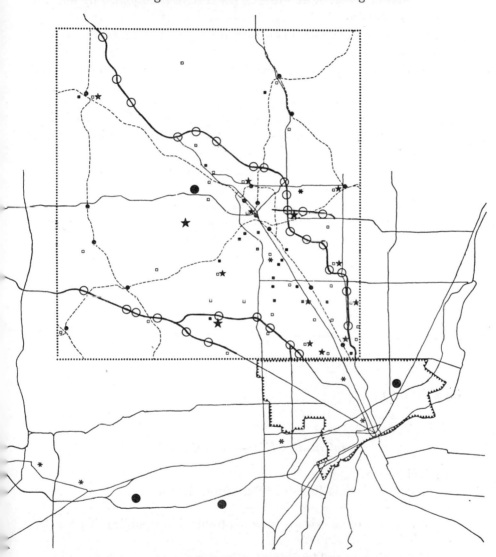

Fig. 3. Plan of Oakland County, as existing 1968, in relation to
Detroit and S.E. Michigan.

———	Freeway	○	road traffic interchange
———	major road	●	airport
-------	railway	•	railway station
▫	public high school		
▪	non-public high school		
★	OCC Campus		
★	OCC extension centre	▲▲▲▲▲▲	boundary of Detroit
*	University	········	boundary of Oakland County

[*Scale :* Oakland County measures 30 miles by 30 miles]

- An additional regional educational servicing agreed as essential to involve large minorities—underprivileged either by colour, poverty, age and boredom.
- Initially a 900 square mile Think Grid.
- A high degree of industrial involvement is promised.
- Consortia of Public Authorities as client have been joined by militant minority groups.
- A possible prototype for a new form of fragmented community college system.
- Essential first stage is the establishment of four pilot projects all of fixed duration.

Peculiarities
- A large dependence on mobile teaching and learning facilities requiring rapid resiting.
- A resultant land use plan related more to activities and rate of change than to physical location and areas.
- The introduction of sophisticated machinery, systems and shelters into depressed areas to improve immediate conditions while avoiding permanent re-inforcement to the social validity of the areas.

CASE STUDY 3

Information Hive—Central London

Ref: Architectural Design May 1968
    New directions in British Architecture—Landau

- A conversion of an existing building to provide a public self-pace skill and information centre.
- Eating, drinking and lounging facilities.
- Computer link.
- Facilities for electronically assisted conference activities.
- Private company client with promised co-operation from local authorities and central Government.
- The London Hive was seen as a producer and controller of small

information agencies in other properties throughout the country particularly the Midlands.

– Maximum 20-year life.

Peculiarities

– Large-scale electronic (invisible) linkages to Central and Local Government Agencies providing random 24-hour access to information for the general public.

– Programmed instruction in various skills and techniques (e.g. languages, driving) for the public available at random times, i.e. regular attendance is not required.

– Introduction into an established shopping area of retail guidance in easily assimilable forms.

– New use large complex structure.

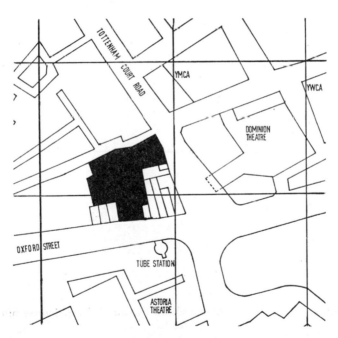

FIG. 4. O.C.H. (Oxford Street Corner House) Site —
Centre City, London

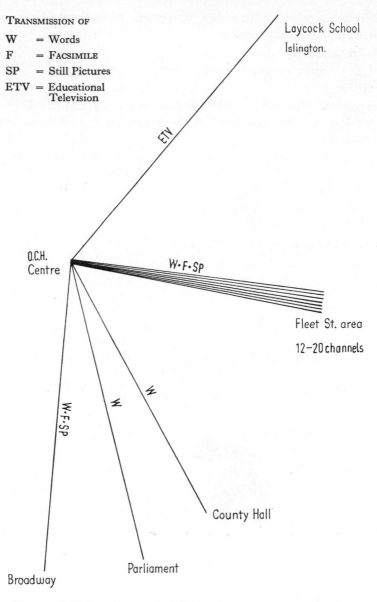

Transmission of
W = Words
F = Facsimile
SP = Still Pictures
ETV = Educational Television

Laycock School Islington.

ETV

O.C.H. Centre

W·F·SP

Fleet St. area

12–20 channels

W·F·SP

W

W

County Hall

Parliament

Broadway

Fig. 5. O.C.H. — Extent of invisible two-way information/learning feeds.

Case Study 4

Birmingham and Midland Institute—New H.Q.

Design—started late 1968

- A centre city development providing a new headquarters for an old-established educational, scientific and cultural organisation.
- Extensive user surveys and other relevant social data prepared over a period of years by the 'client'.
- The production of an extended range of activities and facilities for public and members.
- In addition, such a design must increase the availability of the BMI's services throughout this, at present, extremely compartmented city.
- The content provides facilities for both audience-orientated and individual/involvement activities. These include a theatre, film, concert and recital areas, lecture rooms, music, film and T.V. studios and work-shops, planetarium and science laboratory.

Peculiarities

- Large involvement of other public, governmental, industrial and educational bodies in a new situation and relationship.
- Investigation of extended city links increasing the availability of the BMI's facilities requires the design determination of the proportion of fixed serviced facilities to mobile or 'invisibly serviced' facilities.
- The physical design of structure, its components and servicing is aimed at producing a large social machine sensitive to the appetites and interests of its users and capable of heavy 24-hour use on and off site.
- Local and national radio and T.V. and information linkages are integral with the internal servicing of the centre's activities.

Summary

Over and above any servicing offered by existing educational patterns there is a likelihood of an increasing public demand for a learning/information content in many of the existing organised activities and organisations in which they are required to participate.

The emergence of a probably unplanned but extremely coherent national network of recreational/learning routes and locations is likely to accelerate the acceptance by Authority of such facilities as an essential constituent of physical planning (cf. Public Health Acts).

It is likely that there will be increasing delight by the consumer/public in superficial regionalism enabled by an increasingly rich 'invisible' socio/information service grid throughout the U.K.

With rapid acceleration in the necessity for the new literacy (response to machine dominated control systems, visual acuity, capacity to accept un-even and unrelated rates of change) it seems probable that a continuous socio/educational servicing available to all—particularly the over-30's—will have to be made available as an easily digestible additive to every day life. (It is considered unlikely that such services as are envisaged in the

Open University or as exist at present though local and central Government will be of sufficient social intensity to meet this need.)

An increase in the availability of learning conditions enabling self-pace participation over and above that which exists at present could well put demands on more formal educational modes which in their present form they would find hard to meet (e.g. a large influx of married middle-aged students into university; heavy demands for specialist technological re-training to be made available at part-time institutes).

The phrase 'knowledge of a lifetime' will become ludicrous.

The learning servicing that will be required must be more than merely useful to the immediate situation.

The following questions should be continually re-answered:

What degree of public support is needed?

What amount of private promotion can be expected?

What restraints, if any, should be put on private information/learning systems and network?

What social cost-benefit method can be used to equate the availability of adequate shelter or food with adequate learning facilities?

What degree of collective self-programming is possible at a national scale?

Should a disaster kit be available nationally for areas of persistent ignorance?

REFERENCES

[1] *Statistics of Education 1964*, H.M.S.O. 1965. Also *Higher Education* (Robbins Report), H.M.S.O. 1963, chapter III para. 52.
[2] Edmund Leach, *A Runaway World?* Reith Lectures, 1967. B.B.C. Publications, 1967.
[3] Peter Willmott, 'Some Social Trends' (supra).
[4] Emrys Jones, 'Resources and Environmental Constraints' (supra).
[5] Peter Cowan, 'Communications' (supra).

CONCLUSIONS

PETER COWAN and DEREK DIAMOND

Introduction

Our purpose is to focus some of the topics which have been raised by the Working Group on Developing Patterns of Urbanisation. We shall try to review the work of the group so far, as represented in the papers, and shall also consider the possible futures which are open. This second objective is important, for it has become obvious in the work of the group and in discussions so far, that there may be a gap in our thinking. This gap concerns the nature of the 'patterns of urbanisation' themselves, which is our major theme. Thus although the group has considered the facts of urbanisation from a variety of standpoints, for example in terms of social development, resource availibility, the existing physical framework, transportation and so on, no clear idea has emerged of the kind of Urban Britain we shall be living in thirty years from now. We need, therefore, an integrating statement of the end results of what we have been describing.

Our conclusions are divided into two parts. First we deal with some of the major themes which have come out of our work so far. There are a number of common features between the papers, but also some differences. We try to identify these factors and to comment upon them. Secondly we try to identify the patterns of urbanisation which may arise during the next 30 years. We use material from the various papers to speculate about the possibilities which lie before us. Some of these we can control and plan for, others are beyond our gasp.

What are the Issues?

As we have mentioned, a number of broad themes have arisen from our work. Common to all approaches has been the assumption that there will be a continuing growth of urbanisation due to population growth. In addition, three major topics have dominated our writing and discussion— social and physical mobility, the constraints of the past, and the planners and the planned. These topics are not presented in any special order of priority.

Social and Physical Mobility

Several of the papers have, as one of their major themes, the notion that

---

Mr Diamond is Reader in Regional Planning, London School of Economics and Political Science

future society in Britain, as in other developed nations, will be more mobile, both socially and geographically.

Peter Willmott identifies two trends and suggests that there is, in Britain, a movement towards home-centredness and, at the same time, a growing geographical dispersal of social networks. Although these two trends may seem at first glance to be contradictory they may complement each other. Peter Willmott has also noted the filtering downwards of certain middle-class life styles, according to de Tocqueville's principles, but it does not seem likely that such filtering processes will occur continually or universally.

Peter Cowan, in his paper on Communications, suggests that developments in communication technology will aid social mobility, and that the diffusion of urban and middle-class life styles will be affected to a great extent by improvements in communications.

Peter Hall points to the effects of changes in transportation patterns upon physical mobility and shows how such changes are related to the growth of outer suburban areas. Clearly such changes in physical mobility will be of great significance in physical patterns of urbanisation although, as Peter Hall suggests, urban growth seems most likely to occur in the outer fringes of existing metropolitan areas. Brian Rodgers shows how social and physical mobility combine to place a burden on a limited set of resources for leisure and recreation. He also confirms the views of Peter Willmott about the need for more space for home-centred pursuits, but adds a whole new range of demands for resources away from home. These demands will grow largely as a result of changes in social and physical mobility.

These papers seem to give a fairly consistent view of one aspect of the future pattern of urbanisation in Britain. They suggest a very strong tendency to spread, both geographically and socially. The continuing and continual raising of standards must be a major factor in calculations of future demands for urban services. There will undoubtedly be large increases in demands for space, both inside the home and away from home, for leisure and for learning which are likely to occupy more and more of each family's time. Finally, some patterns of physical mobility will be affected by the substitution of communication for movement although the extent of this substitution is at present severely limited.

Constraints

The above trends could lead to a very diffuse pattern of urban settlement in Britain. However, there are certain major constraints which will give a quite definite form to the pattern. As we have already mentioned, Brian Rodgers has identified major constraints on resources for recreation which vary from region to region. At a more local level he has raised a policy question concerning the rationing of scarce recreational facilities in and near major metropolitan centres; such questions have many consequences.

Two other papers concentrate on constraints. Emrys Jones considers in great detail the constraints on land and other resources. He considers the supplies of land, water resources and so on and finds such resources to be fairly abundant in the Britain of the future. His paper suggests that the main constraint on future patterns is what we have already built. We have in Britain a massive investment in pre-existing structures, and because of this we can make only marginal changes and additions to the stock. What is more, most changes can only occur to the extent that the past can be destroyed, so that there is unlikely to be much physical change in patterns of urbanisation in Britain during the next thirty years. However, Emrys Jones goes on to say that quite massive social and functional changes can occur within the existing framework. From his paper perhaps emerges the view that the future is a question first of all for the social scientist rather than the geographers.

Peter Stone considers the economic constraints upon the future and takes up the same point as Emrys Jones about existing frameworks. His study shows that we do not have sufficient financial resources to remake everything, and he suggests that a preferable policy might be to concentrate on upgrading the existing environment rather than devoting too many resources to new construction.

The Planners and the Planned

The interaction between changes in mobility and constraints raises many policy issues, which are dealt with in each paper. However, over and above these individual issues is one major problem which is specified or implied in three of the papers. This issue concerns the relationship between the planners and the planned.

Alan Wilson describes the new kind of planning activities which will evolve under the impact of computers, data banks and mathematical analysis. This kind of planning will be different in kind from today's, and in particular the whole process is likely to be speeded up many times. Such changes will make planning processes at once more accessible and more removed from the understanding of the people as a whole. It could give rise to major strains and stresses in our planning system.

Peter Cowan describes how improvements in communications may add to the problem by making the population more immediately aware of what is being done by the planners. He suggests that this issue could become a major political theme in the very near future.

Nick Deakin describes the problem of a particular minority group who are already caught up in this debate between the planners and the planned. He describes how the problem has been made worse by contradictions in the planners' behaviour which are plain for everyone to see. Signs of an explosive political situation are contained in the concept of the planners and the planned, and the racial minorities focus such problems very clearly.

General

These major themes are complimented by a number of other issues, which are taken up individually in various papers. Both Peter Stone and

Emrys Jones have touched upon the problems of planning for contraction. How can we deal with towns which are shrinking rather than growing? Planners are used to dealing with expansion, but the post-industrial age in Britain may bring about changes in the location of jobs, which in turn will lead to the decay of old industrial areas. We have not so far developed means of dealing with these new problems. There are all sorts of other issues which must yet be woven together before we can compose a coherent picture of the future. For example, in another part of our work, David Bayliss* has traced the likely influence on the built environment of major innovations which may dramatically improve productivity in the construction industry and Cedric Price* has pointed to the major upheavals in social mobility which may follow the participation in higher learning of a greater and greater proportion of the population. These, and other issues, must be evaluated before we have even a rough framework on which to build our speculations of the future.

Future Patterns

No-one seems to doubt that urbanisation in Britain will increase in the next thirty years, in the sense that there will be a further spread of the diverse physical structures, roads, houses, telephone exchanges etc., which are associated with today's urban life. However, as the papers in this volume demonstrate, although there is agreement on the general trend, there is little certitude as to the exact spatial pattern that will emerge.

There are several reasons why our ability to foretell the spatial pattern of urbanisation in Britain at the end of the century remains rather limited. It is not just a question of insufficient understanding of the present situation, though this is certainly an important reason, but it is also a consequence of the nature of the social changes that are expected to occur. Many of these, as several of the papers reveal, are conflicting and will therefore involve people in making difficult choices. For example, what type of residential location will be chosen by a family wanting to obtain a good choice of employment for all the working members of the family, convenient access to the required standard and quality of educational facilities, a density of residential development that enables a high degree of car-usage and proximity to recreational open space in the countryside? However, even if it were possible to assess with confidence the weights likely to be attached to the various aspirations of the population there is still a further difficulty to resolve. This stems from the nature of the relationship between form and function in the urban context. It has been pointed out by several of the contributors how urban forms and structures have adapted to a change in their function and how this process must always be present in urban areas as a result of the different rates of physical and social change.

It is this adaptability of the existing pattern of urbanisation, together

* Please see *Developing Patterns of Urbanisation*, edited by P. Cowan, Oliver and Boyd, 1970.

with the powerful constraint of the limitation of resources that leads most of the contributors (particularly E. Jones and P. Stone) to expect that to a very considerable extent, the broad pattern of urbanisation in 2000 A.D. will look surprisingly similar to that of today. This may seem a rather tame and unimaginative conclusion but it is perhaps worth noting how similar the spatial pattern of urbanisation is today with that of thirty years ago. Significantly, the population increase since the publication of the Barlow Report in 1939 has been a gain of 7·5 millions, which is considerably less than the forecast of growth to the end of the century. Nevertheless, the 'distinctive features of British urbanisation', as Barlow called them are still very visible today; the high proportion of the population living in the conurbations; the very large size of the London conurbation, the above-average rate of population growth in the Midlands and South-East, and the rapidly expanding suburban peripheries of the conurbations and other major cities.

This picture, of an increasing concentration of the population on the national and regional scales, coupled with a deconcentration of population on a metropolitan scale, which is as good a description of 1967 as of 1937, illustrates another difficulty in attempting to describe future patterns of urbanisation; the problem of terminology. The pattern of urbanisation is the outcome of function, but as the preceding papers have pointed out a change in function does not always create an altered pattern, nor are different patterns necessarily an index of different functions (Hall). Much of the confusion which exists arises because such terms as city-region, megalopolis, and suburb are used by some authors as functional terms and by others as descriptions of particular forms. In an attempt to reduce the confusion to a minimum it may be helpful to view the future pattern of urbanisation at these varying spatial scales.

Perhaps the most widely recognised feature of modern urbanisation is the city region or metropolitan area, where until very recently both the form and function approaches described a single entitity. P. G. Hall describes their historical development, pointing out that some are more complex than others but all can be defined functionally as having a maximum of interaction (trips) within it and a minimum of interaction across its boundaries. Journey-to-work is the traditional criterion of delimitation. It is the persistence of this residence-workplace relationship that causes several of the contributors to suggest that metropolitan areas, albeit more extensive and in a modified shape, are likely to retain their basic identity.

Physical expansion to accommodate growth coupled with a growing decentralisation of many activities provides an opportunity to re-shape the metropolitan area, and adjust its urban form. Thus the city centre becomes increasingly the purveyor of cultural goods. Nevertheless, the outcome is still expected to be a nodal region of mixed land-uses in which the vast majority of trips occur over small distances and occupy a very limited duration. Several recent British transportation studies (excluding London) record that 80 per cent of male work journeys extend to less than five miles and occupy less than 25 minutes. Even if average journey speed were to double and the acceptable journey time to double, most people would live within 20 miles of their work. This remains a sufficiently restricted distance to continue to give some spatial identity to expanded city regions. The problem of providing very accessible open space in the countryside for these expanded city regions may further help to delimit individual city regions by providing zones of lower densities of movement.

The spread of the city region and its accompanying decentralisation, not only of work places but also of service provision, will be hastened by the trend to lower-density residential development and its related trend to increasing home-centredness (P. Willmott). That the average suburban plot in New York (in their equivalent of Harrow or Orpington) increased from one-fifth to almost one half-acre between 1950 and 1960, and is continuing to increase, gives some indication of the strength of this trend.

The expansion of city regions is thought most likely to take the form of radial or corridor extensions of development, along which a variety of urban centres are strung out at varying distances along lines of high-speed communication. In fact, examples of such corridors are already being implemented in Britain under current planning proposals as for example Glasgow—Cumbernauld, Grangemouth/Falkirk—Livingston—Edinburgh, or London—Hemel Hempstead—Luton—Milton Keynes—Northampton. Since there will be substantial journey-to-work flows between the several centres of the corridors it is necessary to regard them as an evolution of the city region, as yet un-named, rather than as self-contained city regions acting as counter-magnets.

As physical expansion continues and improved transport and communications are provided, several of these extended, tentacular metropolitan areas will join up. This will occur at the same time as an increase in the interaction between the centres of these extended city regions occurs. It is only when both increased intra-city region and inter-city region interaction arises that one will be justified in talking about megalopolitan Britain.

All the contributors appear to agree that there is sufficient land suitable for building on and that such land is available adjacent to or within easy access of major existing urban concentrations. In this process (more properly called metropolitanisation than urbanisation), the dominance of London and the associated belt of almost contiguous urban development that stretches to Leeds and Liverpool will increase, and the infant megalopolitan heart of Britain will come to manhood. Perhaps its most outstanding characteristic will be the intensity and diversity of its transport and communication channels. The currently projected motorway network which will become its High Street will be paralleled by other networks, such as those referred to by Cowan and Wilson.

Beyond this megalopolitan core there will be only two urban concentrations of more than a million people; central Scotland and Tyne-Tees, together with a limited number of smaller (about a quarter of a million) free-standing cities such as Plymouth, Norwich, Carlisle and Aberdeen.

The projected estuarial cities of the Severn, Solent, and Humber will then be among the fastest-growing parts of the periphery of Megalopolis. Although it can be expected to retain its poly-nuclear structure, inherited from the past, the flows of people, goods, ideas and information between these internal nodes is expected to increase greatly. The high level of internal interaction will be matched by the presence of new and improved facilities for contact with the megalopolis of North-West Europe, and North-East United States.

If the city regions which have emerged from the conurbations do integrate to create megalopolis, then we have to ask if there is still a discernible intermediate or regional scale of human activity. Inter-city region activity we have already defined as megalopolitan, intra-city region activity we may define as metropolitan, thereby excluding a provincial or regional level. This is perhaps best illustrated by the anticipated rôle of the non-metropolitan areas located on the periphery of megalopolis; the south-west peninsula, north and central Wales, the Lake District, Pennines, Yorkshire Moors, Southern Uplands and Highlands.

These are the areas widely suggested (and indeed currently utilised) as providers of major outdoor recreation space. It is the exception rather than the rule to find these areas, in terms of week-end or holiday recreation, readily accessible to only one of the metropolitan cores of megalopolis; most will be used by the residents from several. Day trips to the countryside will also occur in limited parts of these areas and in this case the selected localities will usually be dominated by the residents from a single city region. This will not be true of much of the recreational open space within megalopolis where the demands of neighbouring city region (i.e. metropolitan) areas will compete with each other. The solution to this problem is as clearly metropolitan in nature as the solution to the provision of major recreational open space requires a national view.

The pattern of future urbanisation which emerges from this review is complex because its functional basis is diverse. The pattern must encompass a larger population with a very much larger proportion of families made up of young parents and young children with their marked preference for suburban living as well as meeting the need for a small but increasing number of people, engaged mainly in information processing (decision-taking), to move rapidly between the nodes of the extended metropolitan areas, both within Britain and between Britain and the rest of the world. Increasing outdoor recreation, increasing home-centredness, and increasing physical mobility are all forecast. A future pattern of urbanisation that will satisfy as many as possible of these diverse requirements is needed. A. G. Wilson argues that planning this environment will be technically possible, and the other contributors outline the emerging social, economic and technical structure which is the fundamental first step towards intelligent management of the developing patterns of urbanisation.

INDEX

Page numbers in italics refer to papers in this volume

209